KINGSMILL PLANTATIONS, 1619–1800

Archaeology of Country Life in Colonial Virginia

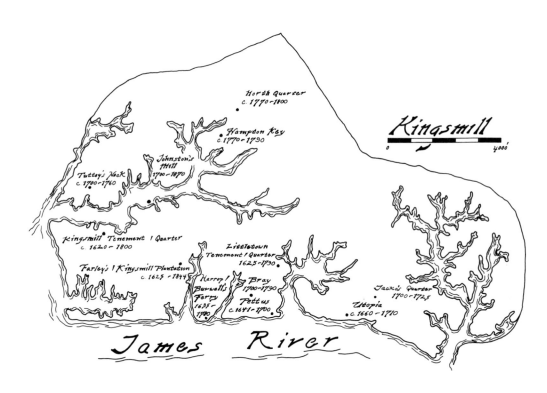

Archaeological sites at Kingsmill, Virginia

KINGSMILL PLANTATIONS, 1619–1800

Archaeology of Country Life in Colonial Virginia

William M. Kelso

ACADEMIC PRESS, INC.
Harcourt Brace Jovanovich, Publishers
San Diego New York Berkeley Boston
London Sydney Tokyo Toronto

Figures 8 and 59 are reprinted from *The Mansions of Virginia, 1706–1776* by Thomas Tileston Waterman. Copyright 1944 The University of North Carolina Press. Used with permission of the publisher.

Figures 9 and 11 are reprinted with permission from *Winterthur Portfolio* 16, (2/3). Published by the University of Chicago Press. © The Henry Francis du Pont Winterthur Museum.

ACADEMIC PRESS, INC.
1250 Sixth Avenue, San Diego, California 92101

United Kingdom Edition published by
ACADEMIC PRESS, INC. (LONDON) LTD.
24/28 Oval Road, London NW1 7DX

Library of Congress Cataloging in Publication Data

Kelso, William M.
    Kingsmill plantations, 1620-1800.

    (Studies in historical archaeology)
    Includes index.
    1. Kingsmill Plantations Site (Va.) I. Title.
II. Series: Studies in historical archaeology (New York,
N.Y.)
F234.K56K45   1984   975.5'425   84-6337
ISBN 0-12-403480-2 (alk. paper)

PRINTED IN THE UNITED STATES OF AMERICA

88 89   9 8 7 6 5 4 3 2

Studies in
HISTORICAL ARCHAEOLOGY

EDITOR

Stanley South

Institute of Archeology and Anthropology
University of South Carolina
Columbia, South Carolina

ADVISORS

Charles E. Cleland
John L. Idol, Jr.
Mark P. Leone
Kenneth E. Lewis
Cynthia R. Price
Sarah Peabody Turnbaugh
John White

To JCH and INH

CONTENTS

LIST OF FIGURES

PREFACE

It will undoubtedly come as no mild surprise that one primarily trained as a social historian should contribute to a series in archaeology. No wonder: There are few practicing historical archaeologists in the field today who are other than card-carrying anthropologists. On the other hand, it should be obvious to even the most casual student that *historical* archaeology necessarily requires both historical and anthropological thinking—the ability to see and interpret significant particulars in light of historical documents, as well as to recognize and interpret patterned human behavior. Yet no single university program has produced an individual with doctorate-level accomplishment in both fields. Consequently, some of the many anthropologists studying historical sites have trained themselves to find documents and interpret what the written word can tell them about the buried past, and a few archaeological historians have listened to and read enough anthropology to apply some of its methods and theory to their in-depth understanding of the historical context of archaeological sites. And, fortunately, some of the resulting literature, as scarce as it is, has proven useful for students of American material culture.

Most of what has been produced in this series has been principally anthropological, with the historical particulars kept in the background. This book is an attempt to reverse that emphasis, providing a more complete historical context for archaeological and anthropological conclusions. Although its subject matter is the archaeology of seven plantation sites at Kingsmill, near Williamsburg, Virginia, it is something more than a string of site reports and local history. It is rather an attempt to reconstruct a typical setting within which all strata of Virginia's rural society developed and changed over two centuries. For that reason, considerable effort has been made to place Kingsmill in the greater context of Virginia's colonial history and material culture, and to summarize the written documentation of the settlement and development of Kingsmill's homesteads and estates, while providing names and personalities for the sites that are discussed in detail.

This book is written for historians who have hoped that historical archaeology could offer them a new source of data with which to study Virginia's colonial period, for architectural historians who are interested in vernacular architecture and historical landscapes and to whom historical archaeology can offer at least the skeletal remains of long-lost buildings and gardens, for historical archaeologists who are interested in quantified data relevant to similar work elsewhere, and for the interested lay public who may be curious about how one of America's first rural neighborhoods grew and developed.

ACKNOWLEDGMENTS

There is no way to express adequately my gratitude to the scores of people who contributed their talent to the Kingsmill project over the 11 years since it began. With so many involved for so long, it is inevitable that I will overlook someone. In any case, a most sincere effort is made herein to cite all who contributed, and if that list should prove incomplete I can only hope that those overlooked can recognize and forgive an unintentional error.

Perhaps the proper place to begin expressing appreciation would be to the institutions and officials who, through their funding efforts and policy decisions, made the Kingsmill project possible in the first place. First, sincere thanks should go to the Anheuser–Busch and its subsidiary, Busch Properties, Inc., for their unprecedented cooperation during the 1972–1976 fieldwork and for their contribution of over one-quarter million dollars for the work. I would especially like to thank Walter Diggs, Jr., past president of Busch Properties, Inc., whose interest in antiquities made initial contacts between the state and Anheuser–Busch easier and who recognized the significance of the archaeological and historical resources of the property. Other Busch Properties officials responsible for making the fieldwork a pleasure include James B. Shea, Jr., Dennis Long, Richard G. Knight, and Harry Knight.

I would also like to express my deepest appreciation to the Virginia Historic Landmarks Commission and staff, especially past executive director, James W. Moody, Jr., who gave me a green light in spite of his recent experience in archaeology, and past directors Junius R. Fishburne, Jr., who was a constant encouragement for the development of the state's archaeological resources, and Tucker Hill and H. Bryan Mitchell, who helped find funding sources for analysis. Appreciation also goes to the United States Department of the Interior, National Park Service, for matching some of the Busch funding, and for the help of Mark R. Barnes, NPS staff archaeologist.

I also appreciate the help and encouragement of the Governor's Advisory Committee to the Virginia Historic Landmarks Commission, especially William W. Abbot, Mary Douthat Higgins, and Elizabeth Egleston.

Of course, many of the staff members of the Virginia Historic Landmarks Commission's Research Center for Archaeology, under whose umbrella the fieldwork was done, had much to contribute to the Kingsmill project for which I am appreciative, especially for the fieldwork of David K. Hazzard and his remarkable sense of discovery, Frazer Neiman for his field efforts both physical and mental, Keith Egloff for his field supervision, Carter Hudgins for his contribution of brain and brawn, and Merry Abbitt Outlaw for her untold hours of artifact processing and research. Beverly Bogley assisted with the artifact processing and research, and Martha McCartney initially processed artifacts, and then, years later, put in many unselfish hours of historical research. I would also like to thank the photographers, Kemble Bauman, David Restuccia, and Catherine Fauerbach, who produced many of the Virginia Historic Landmarks Commission photographs, and the conservators, Marc Friedhaber, Richard Martin, and Mark Witkowski. I especially thank Nicholas Luccketti for his supervision of the North Quarter excavation and his interim report of that work, and I am grateful for the efforts of Beverly Bogley both in field supervision and in artifact processing during and after that same excavation. I also sincerely thank Suzie Peters, of the Virginia Historic Landmarks staff, and Peter Pudner for their historical research, and Camille Wells and James McClure for their master's theses, which were particularly helpful in understanding the Bray and Burwell plantations.

Special thanks also go to Colonial Williamsburg's research department, particularly to past director, Edward Riley, to Harold Gill, and to director Cary Carson for his help in our attempt to decipher the seventeenth-century building sites. I am also grateful for the help of architectural historians Paul Buchanan, Edward Chappell, Jack Finglass, and Del Upton, and archaeologist Gary Wheeler Stone. I. Noel Hume, resident archaeologist for the Colonial Williamsburg Foundation, read and commented on some of the field reports, and Audrey Noel Hume was always willing to help identify the artifacts. I am most grateful for their assistance.

I also appreciate the detailed analysis and reports of the faunal remains offered by Henry Miller, Laboratory Director, St. Maries Citty, Maryland, and for Michael Barber's study of the faunal remains from the Bray well.

Jon Kukla, Assistant Editor for Publication, Virginia State Library, most graciously volunteered to read and comment on the "Context" section, as did William W. Abbot, William W. Pettus IV, a descendant of Colonel Thomas Pettus, and Lewis Burwell, a descendant of the Lewis Burwells of Kingsmill, all of whom saved me from many needless factual errors. Special thanks also go to Stanley South and the editorial board of *Studies in Historical Archaeology* for their encouraging revision of this manuscript.

Anna Gruber, current laboratory supervisor at Monticello, completed many of the illustrations throughout this volume, and Sondy Sanford, past Monticello laboratory supervisor, labored to produce the locational maps. Douglas Sanford produced the North Quarter SYMAP, for which I am most appreciative.

My deepest appreciation is also expressed to my wife, Ellen, for the years of tolerating both the overenthusiasm of discovery and the guilt of nonpublication.

1

INTRODUCTION

You might say that rescue archaeology at Kingsmill (Figure 1 and Frontispiece) began with a rumor. I was directing exploratory excavations at nearby Carter's Grove for the Colonial Williamsburg Foundation in 1970–1971 when I overheard the gardener say that the night watchman was a strange "fella"—he never went to bed. That might not seem too unusual for a nightwatchman, but further inquiry revealed that he actually never did go to bed, night or day. Having been raised with the notion that the human body at some point requires sleep, I resolved to find this bionic watchman and learn his secret. A stocky, weathered man that I guessed to be in his late sixties greeted me at the door of the watchman's house. With a stuttering voice he invited me in. While getting on with a rather awkward introduction, I let my eyes quickly search the one-room building, but sure enough, no bed. Catching my searching glances, Mr. Carroll Brizendine explained his secret of perpetual consciousness. A heart condition, he said, kept him constantly upright, and when he had to sleep he did so in the enormous leather easy chair in the corner. My curiosity satisfied, I prepared to leave. Not a chance. Although Mr. Brizendine's speech impediment made conversation difficult, he was not about to let me get away without hearing his life story. But, fortunately the subsequent 2-hour dissertation turned out to be a gold mine of folk tales about the place where he had grown up, Kingsmill Plantation.

As the narrator reached the end of his Kingsmill memoirs, which begin with his arrival there in 1916, he said, "uh, by the way, yesterday while fishin' on the river off the place, I saw somethin' I know that you diggers would like to see. Someday I'll uh take you over there." I could not resist. The next day I boarded Mr. Brizendine's pickup truck and set out for Kingsmill, on what quickly became a fascinating trip back in time. Our first stop took us to the riverbank and, after fording a marsh, my tour director stopped below a steep, eroded cliff. "There she is," he said, "uh, it must be right old don't ye think?"

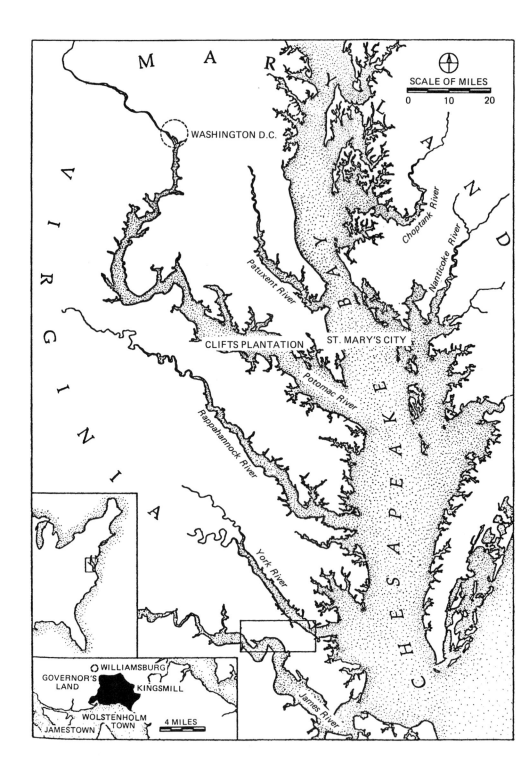

MARYLAND

VIRGINIA

WASHINGTON D.C.

SCALE OF MILES
0   10   20

Choptank River

Nanticoke River

Patuxent River

CLIFTS PLANTATION

ST. MARY'S CITY

Potomac River

CHESAPEAKE BAY

Rappahannock River

York River

GOVERNOR'S LAND

WILLIAMSBURG

KINGSMILL

WOLSTENHOLM TOWN

JAMESTOWN

4 MILES

James River

A colonial brick well-shaft exposed by river erosion projected from the face of the cliff before us and it was indeed "right old" (Figure 2). To most people, the scene might not have seemed particularly exciting, but to me, a historical archaeologist, the sight of the well had a thrill not unlike the discovery of some ancient tomb. To be sure, old well shafts are usually not gold-filled burial chambers, but often they are time capsules all the same. Once they stopped providing water, abandoned wells often became convenient trash disposals, and the rubbish of the past, even a past as recent as Virginia's colonial period, can sometimes offer a unique and candid view of early American life (Figures 3 and 4). All this flashed through my mind as Mr. Brizendine and I first stood gazing at the cliff.

From there, he led me into the jungle of honeysuckle behind the cliff where the undergrowth hid the remains of an earthen fort. In fact, one bank of the fort covered the top of the well shaft, indicating that the well dated before the construction of the earthwork. I was also aware, having read the documents, that American fortifications were attacked and captured by the British at Kingsmill in 1781, and it is little wonder that my imagination rushed on to embrace the possibility that the well contained arms and equipment hidden there to prevent them from falling into British hands.

As we trudged along the beach back to Mr. Bryzandine's pickup truck he said, "Now let me show ya the mansion house, ahh Mister Kelso. Some right old buildins' up there, yessiree." The dirt road led up a rise from the shore. Out of the gray morning mist appeared two identical old brick buildings, parallel to each other and aligned with the landscape in such a way that they seemed to bracket something between them. Brizendine said, "These here are the outhouses from Kingsmill, and I'm told the mansion house stood over that buried foundation. The hill's terraced below. Look, you can still see the steps of it."

Although overgrown with weeds and teeming with wood ticks, the mansion site was as inspiring to me as the well. I already knew that Colonel Lewis Burwell had built the place before 1736 and the exposed part of the foundations carried the patina of its 250 years with particular grace. Other wells, walkways, outbuildings, trash pits, and gardens were surely buried about. The prospect of uncovering and seeing more of these things again fired my imagination.

That was in October 1971. Later in the month I learned that Anheuser–Busch, Inc., the new owners of Kingsmill, planned to build a residential housing development on the land. The master plan, published in the local newspaper, proposed houses, golf courses, other recreational facilities, and a conference center. Since good building sites for conference centers, golf clubhouses, and houses have always been good building sites, the Anheuser–Busch planners had selected some of the same high, well-drained land near water that had appealed to colonial settlers.

The proposed construction clearly spelled doom for the archaeological re-

---

Figure 1 Location of Kingsmill, Virginia. (After a drawing by Shearon Vaughn and Cary Carson.)

Figure 2 Excavation (1972) of a brick-lined well first exposed by river erosion, probably the sole remnant of Harrop Plantation.

mains at the historic sites. Modern earth-moving required by building codes would remove the shallow colonial artifacts without a trace. Rereading Kingsmill historical maps, in particular the remarkable accurate French reconnaissance series of Revolutionary War vintage (1781), I saw that, if something were not done soon, by 1975 most of the major eighteenth-century remains would be scraped away. For instance, if the river erosion did not get it first, Mr. Brizendine's well was scheduled

Figure 3 Pewter porringer recovered from the Harrop well (ca. 1740).

Figure 4 Some of the two dozen iron hoe blades recovered from the Harrop well. These are probably "lost" counterweights for the well bucket.

to be covered by the seventeenth green on the golf course. Inevitably, most of what previous occupants had left buried at Kingsmill would disappear. But a great deal of money was needed if the extensive archaeological record at Kingsmill was to be properly recorded. Anheuser–Busch, Inc., was not in the historic preservation business, and federal environmental laws did not protect the sites from private development or fund any salvage. It occurred to me, however, that Mr. Brizendine's well, of interest in itself, might prove to be the key, somehow. Anheuser–Busch personnel and Walter Diggs, Jr., the president of its new development subsidiary, Busch Properties, Inc., fortunately had some sympathy for the idea of preserving Kingsmill's past. Mr. Diggs was aware that the purchase agreement with the previous owners of the property, the Colonial Williamsburg Foundation, explicitly stated that the historic sites (probably only referring to the Kingsmill Plantation building site) would be preserved. In addition, Diggs had a personal interest in antiques and enough imagination to see that history in that area could become as much a property asset as its natural beauty. But before he would agree to fund any excavation, he needed to be shown something tangible.

After I made preliminary contact with Mr. Diggs in January 1972, Diggs, his wife, and I hiked down to the James River shore to look at Mr. Brizendine's well site and the nearby plantation outbuildings. The well was sufficiently tangible to impress my tour group, and after our trip he secured the funds to support at least the well excavation. Since part of the mission of my employer, the Virginia Historic Landmarks Commission, an agency of the Commonwealth of Virginia, was small-scale rescue archaeology, the work on the well became a state project.

Although it was not filled with Revolutionary War artifacts, the well fortunately contained sufficiently interesting colonial objects to interest Anheuser–Busch in funding a long-range archaeological excavation of sites threatened by construction. The research was designed to compare the sites on the property so that a model of a cross-section of Virginia colonial tidewater rural society could be constructed. Ironically, as late as 1972 when excavations began, archaeologists had paid little attention to rural colonial Virginia. After John D. Rockefeller became interested in restoring the town of Williamsburg in the 1920s, those involved in its restoration recognized the importance of uncovering the buried remains of the colonial capitol's buildings, and pioneering work in historical archaeology focused on the urban side of eighteenth century colonial Virginia society. When the National Park Service approached the two hundred fiftieth anniversary of the founding of the first permanent English settlement in America, archaeologists took a look at seventeenth-century colonial town life at Jamestown. But aside from the Park Service's work at Governor Berkeley's Greenspring Plantation near Jamestown and a preliminary survey at Williamsburg's Carter's Grove, the archaeology of rural life was ignored. The study at Kingsmill, where numerous plantation sites represented the entire social and economic range of plantation life in colonial Virginia from her earliest years, promised to reveal for the first time substantial archaeological information about country life.

I had no difficulty deciding where to dig first. Anheuser–Busch's master plan for developing the Kingsmill tract laid out the construction schedule for the first 5 years of its projected 20-year undertaking. These projections in turn dictated our archaeological schedule. Clearly we first had to test those sites in the path of the immediate construction, determine to what extent each was significant, then work before any important sites were disturbed by the builders. The first scheduled construction project was a conference center complex on one of the commanding views of the James River property. As one might guess, that commanding view had also once appealed to a colonial planter as a place to build his home. Further construction dictated the sequence of excavations: a proposed marina would totally destroy what turned out to be the seventeenth-century location of the Colonel Thomas Pettus plantation known as Littletown; a tennis center would erase a seventeenth-century site on the eastern end of the property; residential housing would lay a path over several seventeenth- and eighteenth- century domestic sites; the golf course would seriously disturb a commercial shiplanding and the Revolutionary War site on the river; and, finally, additional residential housing and a second golf course would surround both the main plantation and the slave quarters of Colonel Lewis Burwell's plantation, Kingsmill, on the western section of the property. The pages that follow narrate the story of the archaeological discoveries there, and consider their significance for the historical archaeology of rural colonial Virginia.

2

ABOVE GROUND

CONTEXT

The first serious attempt by the English to settle the Mid-Atlantic Region of North America accomplished little more than giving Virginia a name. Sir Walter Raleigh's settlement in the land he named after the Virgin Queen, Elizabeth (now Roanoke Island, North Carolina), began in 1584, only to be "lost" in mystery 4 years later. When supply ships finally arrived after a 2-year delay, all that could be found of the ill-fated colony was an Indian name carved on a tree. Dreams of any serious English influence in the New World had to wait.

It was not until the *Susan Constant,* the *Godspeed,* and the *Discovery* unloaded 105 passengers at Jamestown Island, some 50 miles up the James River from the Chesapeake Bay, that England succeeded in getting any lasting hold on American soil. But that first grasp in 1607 was, all the same, a feeble one, and why Jamestown did not dissolve into the wilderness like Roanoke is a wonder. The original group of hopefuls was composed of the types of people least likely to make a successful life in the wild. Many were classified either as "gentlemen" whose station in life had always been not to work, or as specialized craftsmen whose particular talents were not really necessary for survival. The rest, many from the swelling ranks of England's idle poor, had neither the will nor the skill to work. Little wonder then that 70% of the population of the colony died from disease, starvation, or Indian raids during the first 7 months. Only the timely arrival of supply ships from England in January and April 1608, and a compulsory work program of the take-charge leader, Captain John Smith, kept the sputtering village from folding altogether. Few settlers seemed to learn soon enough that their survival depended on homegrown food and that there was no one to grow it but themselves.

Another hard winter with no provisions, the starving time of 1609–1610, added hundreds of fresh graves to the island and it was again only the timely arrival of English ships that saved the colony. Although the bad times were not by any means over, things began to improve thereafter. Reforms by the colony's sponsor, the Virginia Company, led to a decade of relative growth and some stability, during which time it became increasingly clear that if the colony were ever going to make a go of it at all, it would have to rely on producing the staple crop, tobacco. To encourage production, the company formalized by its Great Charter of 1618, a way for individual planters to own land. Now those who paid their own way to Virginia or the transportation of others qualified for a headright, 50 acres of land for every new immigrant. Consequently, it was not long before the new land-owners, their tenants, and their indentured servants began to fill the arable empty land all along the James River banks as far as the fall line, where white water and rocks prevented further navigation (Figure 5).

But all was not as secure as it seemed. At home, company mismanagement soon led to financial disaster. To make matters worse, a devastating Indian mas-sacre struck in 1622, catching the planters spread too thin. Over 340 were killed during the carnage. Both the company's dismal finances and the inability of the colony to defend itself proved too much for King Charles I. In 1624 the Crown made Virginia a royal colony.

By the time Virginia did come under royal control, its population had swelled to 1300 souls, settled on plantations from Eastern Shore on the Chesapeake to the site of modern Richmond, 75 miles inland. The area was politically divided into the corporations of (from east to west) Eastern Shore, Elizabeth City, James City, Charles City, and Henrico. By 1619 Virginia had already begun to produce a reasonably steady supply of tobacco for the European market. Soon the high profits took care of any incentive problems of the "idle." The 1620s became a particularly prosperous decade for the colony, leading to a "boom town" lifestyle:[1]

> All our riches for the present doe consiste in Tobacco, wherein one man by his own labor hath in one year raised to himselfe to the value of 2001 sterling, and another by the meanes of six servants hath cleared at one crop a thousand pound English. . . . we are not the veriest beggars in the worlde, our cowkeeper here of James Citty on Sundays goes accowtered all to freshe flaming silke; and a wife of a collier. . . weares her rough bever hatt with a faire perle hatband, and a silken suite thereto correspondent.[2]

There is no doubt that some cashed in on the good times, especially the landowners and tenants, but servants whose efforts were so essential for the success of the labor-intensive tobacco culture were left with few shares of the pie:

> since I came out of the ship, I never at[e] anie thing but pease, and loblollies (that is water gruell) [we] must Worke hard both earelie, and late for a messe of water gruell. . . people crie out dau, and night, Oh that thry were in England without their lymbes. . . I have nothing at all, no not a shirt on my backe.[3]

Probably in reality life during the boom period was not all that grim or glamorous, but there can be no doubt that Virginia's new-found prosperity salvaged its bad reputation back home. Even with a shockingly high death rate, the colonial popula-

Figure 5 Artist's conception of the early seventeenth-century settlement at Martin's Hundred near Kingsmill, circa 1622. (© Richard Schlecht, National Geographic Society.)

tion managed to double by 1629. Immigration undoubtedly accounted for most of the increase; without the steady numbers of newcomers during the second decade of settlement, Virginia's predominantly male population would have steadily declined. In any event, for those that did survive beyond a "seasoning time" (their stifling first tidewater summer), there existed the very real opportunity to amass considerable land holdings and a secure income from the growing tobacco trade. Prosperous, too, were the few women among the early populace. They began to accumulate landholdings by marrying, outliving, and inheriting the property of a succession of husbands. There were also a few hardy men who played that game the other way around, compounding their own good fortune with the estates of rich widows.

The same Virginia Company Great Charter that permitted the liberal granting of land also gave some of the colonists a start at self-government. The first legislature, a General Assembly of 22 burgesses elected by the inhabitants of each of the major plantations, met at Jamestown in August 1619, the first representative assembly in America. By 1634 the plantations instituted another traditional English political entity, the county system, forming the shires of James City, Henrico, Charles City, Elizabeth City, Warwick River, Warrosquyoake, Charles River, and Accawmack. County lieutenants were appointed, and the burgesses and sheriffs were elected by the voters at large. Soon many of those who could survive long enough to get in a few bumper tobacco crops found themselves not only relatively wealthy but at the head of small political dynasties at the county level. Virginians were beginning to learn early the pleasures of landholding and home rule.[4]

But planting and not politics was the main business of a Virginian. Tobacco, the only agricultural commodity grown for serious profit, occupied a man 9 months of the year. Sowing, transplanting, weeding, topping, worming, stricking, and curing were time-consuming, hand-labor operations. And so were the off-season chores of clearing land, building fences, and making casks for shipping. Even the adoption of Indian methods of cultivation—that is, "clear a field by girdling trees, plant it in tobacco for three or four years, to corn (or wheat) for a few more, and then clear another stretch and let the first recover its fertility by reverting to forest"[5]—failed to cut corners. Consequently, field labor became particularly dear to the Virginia economy; using hands for anything else like building houses of any substance became inordinately expensive.

But despite the high cost of labor and fluctuating prices after about 1630, a single man could raise 1500 pounds of tobacco yearly and come out ahead. Consequently, the days when Englishmen would rather cut off "lymbes" than come to Virginia had passed. Life in Virginia became a reliable alternative for some of the landless of rural England or some of the beggars of London. Even Virginia's servants eventually became free and, although they could not count on owning their own land, as tenants they were entitled to keep half of what they could produce. During the boom years, their half was considerable, and even the poorer returns they received between the good times were better than the nothing they would have gotten back home. The governing council could no longer lament, as they had in 1626, that most planters saw Virginia as a temporary residence, good for only the "present corpp and their hastie retourne [to England]."[6]

That is not to say that Virginia did not perpetuate a rigid English economic, social, and political structure. The few, through a political buddy system, came to dominate the many. The resident Governor, appointed by the King and his council of 12 to 16, all in the best English tradition, grabbed the lion's share of the best land. In the 1620s an elite of hardy, self-made men, whose wealth came primarily from the boom tobacco years, consolidated their control of the council and the militia. By 1640, however, a tamer and more promising Virginia began to appeal to the younger sons of the more affluent English landlords and merchants, who in

Figure 6   Sir William Berkeley.

any case were not in direct line for family inheritance back home. It was not long before the well-born newcomers, quite familiar with running things, acquired seats on the council, considerable landholdings and ultimately the reigns of provincial power.[7]

The new elite rallied around Governor Sir William Berkeley (Figure 6), who started his more than three decades of Virginia leadership in 1642. And well they should; Berkeley's first reign as governor gave Virginia a surge of economic growth. By virtually eliminating the Indians as a serious threat to the security of eastern Virginia after another massacre (1644), Berkeley opened the door to the rapid settlement of five new counties. By advocating a liberal trade policy, he encouraged the Dutch to exchange their "wares and merchandizes" for tobacco at favorable rates. Berkeley also managed to give Virginia more political clout by resisting England's parliamentary rule during the Commonwealth Period, and although he lost the governorship for a time he did win autonomous rights for the general assembly.

But things did not go all that smoothly for the colony after the Stuart Restoration of 1660. The relative prosperity of the preceding decades was shattered by the Crown's decision to strengthen and enforce the Navigation Acts of 1650, which by the 1670s had legislated the Dutch and any other foreign country completely out of the English colonial import and export trade. The English–Dutch wars of 1664 and 1672 had serious impact on Virginia's economy as well. Dutch raids on the tobacco fleets and the plantations took their toll. To make matters worse, the Great Gust of 1667, a hurricane, leveled much of Virginia's tobacco crops and apparently most of her buildings, and at the same time disease ran through the colonial cattle herds, killing an estimated 50,000 head.[8]

The economic woes, of course, had the least effect on Berkeley's friends, who owned most of the land best suited for planting. Hardest hit were the poorer farmers and the growing ranks of immigrant indentured servants who had earned their freedon. Consequently, the bad times and the scarcity of worthwhile property created a mob of poor, disappointed, or unemployed "would-be" farmers forced to seek a hand-to-mouth existence on poor soil at the fringes of settlement. Indian incidents there were inevitable. In 1676, led by Nathaniel Bacon, the frontier planters and the landless struck back at the natives in an escalating conflict that became known as Bacon's Rebellion. Although Bacon was one of Berkeley's councillors, the governor took a dim view of the unauthorized action and eventually declared Bacon and his followers outlaws. When the rebels began plundering the plantations of Berkeley's councillors and friends, the dispute erupted into open civil war.

After several months of violence, Bacon died suddenly, leaving his troops without a strong leader. The revolt soon folded. Berkeley quickly captured the remaining forces and 23 rebels went to the gallows. In the meantime, all the civil unrest and its vindictive aftermath proved to be too much for the Crown. Berkeley was recalled to England. His landlord friends, however, were left in their positions of wealth and power.

Meanwhile, despite the devastation caused by the rebellion and earlier by the Dutch wars, desease, and violent weather, tobacco cultivation went on. The problem of a labor shortage remained, but after about 1660 Negro slavery became more and more appealing to the planters. Because of the warfare on the seas and an improvement in the social and economic conditions at home, fewer white servants came to Virginia. As life expectancy rose, servants-for-life became a better buy for the planters. During the last quarter of the seventeenth century the black population of Virginia rose from 1000–3000 in 1674 to 6000–10,000 by 1699. By the middle of the eighteenth century the numbers had increased to 100,000, almost accounting for one half the entire population of the colony.[9]

So it was that close to a century of tobacco culture transformed Tidewater Virginia from a state of nature into a biracial pastoral patriarchy, with the lion's share of the landownership, social standing, wealth, and political power in the hands of the white, slave-holding few. Symbolically, it was almost precisely at the end of the seventeenth century that Jamestown was abandoned as the seat of the Virginia colonial government in favor of a new and planned community at Williamsburg. There, in elegant brick palace, capitol, and parish church, the well-born would gather for the next three-quarters of a century to decide the fate of lesser planters, yeoman farmers, and black slaves—that is, until the British defeat at nearby Yorktown would finally give some of the common folks a piece of the action.

But that is getting ahead of the story. The first half-century saw the transformation of the landholding immigrants of the 1600s into Virginia's native-born Georgian Plantation aristocracy. Perhaps most symbolic of the new century was Robert Carter, appropriately nicknamed King by his contemporaries, who combined inheritance from his seventeenth-century immigrant father with his own business prowess to create indeed a small kingdom of no less than 350,000 acres, principally on Virginia's northern neck (Figure 7). Carter ruled his home plantation "Corotoman" and his various "quarter" farms and hundreds of slaves with particular skill and, perhaps to prove his station in life and to improve his chances in the hereafter, built what was reputed to be the grandest mansion and finest parish church of the day.[10] It was also at this time that Carter's peers were establishing their own country seats wherever they could find a prominent place along a major waterway that was assured to be in full view of the colonial populace. Few seemed to be aware that their conspicuous consumption only existed at the good graces of their London agents who advanced far more credit than hogsheads could ever pay for. Nonetheless, the Virginia landscape (Figure 8) took on a remarkable appearance:

> I went by ship up the [York] River which has pleasant seats on the bank which show like little villages. . . most of these have pleasant gardens and the Prospect of the River render them very pleasant.[11]

This scene was duplicated on all the river banks as far as the Blue Ridge Mountains by the end of the century.

Beyond the Blue Ridge, the fabric of settlement was similar to the East, but the threads were considerably different. After about 1715, a flood of German and Scots Irish immigrants filled the Shenandoah Valley, bringing different folk tradi-

Figure 7 Robert "King" Carter of Corotoman. (National Portrait Gallery, Smithsonian Institution, Washington, D.C.)

tions to the land. All the same, the region soon mirrored the East in that it became rural and agricultural in nature, although the landholdings, in most cases slave holdings, and architecture were on a smaller scale.

But soon the recurring problem of the availability of the best land began to plague that area as much as it had in the East, which led to pressure for yet further western settlement. This time, however, the problems became more international in scope in that the west was not only where Indians lived, but the territory was also rather firmly in the hands of their allies, the French. From 1745 to 1763, the

Figure 8   Conjectural view of Rosewell Plantation on the banks of the York River, Gloucester County, Virginia. (Waterman, 1946, p. 106.)

Virginia frontier became a battleground with skirmishes between the English, Scots Irish, or German farmers, on the one hand, and the Indians on the other. As the war spread into a global conflict, England found France a formidable foe, requiring many British and American lives and considerable expense to subdue.

The ultimate British victory led to the acquisition of vast western land, assuring for some time enough space for westward expansion of population. But a huge postwar debt and the need to protect the newly won territory with a standing army strained the coffers of the Crown so much so that it seemed a good idea to tax the American colonists and to raise funds by reenforcing the heretofore disregarded Navigation Acts. So began King George III's ill-fated Colonial Policy, which included, among many other things, the Stamp Act. Enthusiastic colonial orators such as Patrick Henry began to draw attentive audiences. By the mid-1770s the lines had been drawn. When Governor Dunmore declared martial law and began raising a loyalist army, the American Revolution had come to Virginia.

The revolution in Virginia was a result of an era of social and economic transformation. Despite its Anglo appearance, the Virginia of Patrick Henry had grown very different from the Old Dominion of Robert Carter. Although tobacco continued to be the eighteenth-century cash crop, as the years passed the growing demand for corn and flour in New England, Southern Europe, and the Caribbean changed the nature of commercial agriculture. At first many Chesapeake planters grew wheat and corn as a marketable complement to tobacco, then a number of farmers stopped growing the "weed" altogether in favor of the more stable and less labor-intensive grains. As a result, many of Virginia's planters drifted away from their dependence on British merchants in favor of strong commercial ties with the growing business community at Philadelphia.[12] At the same time, however, many of those who continued the traditional tobacco trade with England and the extravagent Georgian country-house lifestyle found themselves seriously overextended.

As the British merchants and government officials began losing their grip on the pocketbooks and affairs of the future patriots, so too colonial souls began to slip from the grasp of the Episcopal clergy. The great following during the second half of the eighteenth century of the evangelistic religions, particularly the Baptists and the Methodists, forcefully questioned the authority of the Church of England in America, effectively casting aside yet another strong tie with the mother country. In short, many hearts, minds, and wallets had left the nest long before anyone could fire the first shot of rebellion.

George III, of course, was not about to let his American upstarts go without a struggle, regardless of how far the two had drifted out of any natural colonial relationship. But 5 years and many thousands of lives later, England's colonial experiment in Virginia abruptly ended. The surrender of the British Army at Yorktown signaled the birth of an independent national experience for America and a well-deserved celebration in Virginia. But when the fireworks faded on that last battleground and as the century drew to a close, the Tidewater area of Virginia fell on hard times.

As late as 1795 the French traveler Liancourt described the lingering impact of the war on Yorktown and the countryside generally:

> General Nelson's house, the most considerable ediface in the whole town [Yorktown]. . . is pierced in every direction with cannon shot and bomb shells. . . . That house since his death devolved to his three sons. . . it remained unrepaired.

And on the road to Williamsburg:

> "the houses uniformly exhibit a mean appearance and the inhabitants betray strong symptoms of poverty"[13]

Planters headed west to more fertile ground and the "little villages" along the rivers, many now deserted, began to fall into ruin. Again, the seat of Virginia's government moved, this time westward toward the shifting population to the growing village of Richmond. Again as a sign of the times, many of the once-proud plantation mansions, if they survived at all, had to withstand the humiliation of conversion to barns or stables. For all its hard-won success in the wilderness, its billowy pomp and circumstance and air of immortality, colonial Tidewater Virginia came crashing to earth and it was not long before the simpler plows of a much-scaled-down rural society buried and scattered the wreckage.

THINGS

As the years passed, colonial Virginians surrounded themselves with an evolving material culture that from documents alone is difficult to reconstruct. After all, to cope with life many of the things people made were fragile, as temporary as apple pie or so chameleon-like they were only dimly perceived or perhaps totally invisible to the scribes of the age. All the same, it is worthwhile to look at the documentary setting within which the Virginia colonial years passed, for however meager is the supply of words there are precious few pictures and surviving objects left to offer a great deal more. Houses, for instance, were without question dominant figures on the cultural landscape, yet what people lived in is often poorly documented. Nonetheless, what little architecture there is to find in the documents and what few renderings and buildings of the period survive can present some semblance of reconstruction. Before delving too far below ground, then, what lies in the library and still stands out in the modern countryside deserves some serious attention.

At first, so the records say, during the fledgling time at Jamestown, construction of very impermanent shelters—indeed, no more than rotten canvas tents—sufficed. Documents mention also one-room wattle-and-daub huts with thatched roofs supported on "cratchets", or forked poles, or "punches sett into the Ground and covered with boards so as a firebrand is sufficient to consume them all".[14] As fragile as these structures sound, such expediencies seem to have carried on for several decades, at least during the initial months of homesteading. Well beyond the Jamestown period a sequence of crude shelter buildings seems to have been a standard part of the initial stages of frontier life, undoubtedly following the advice of those like Cornelius Van Tiennoven:

> [farmers] ought to arrive early in the Spring in March so as to be able to plant during that summer garden vegetables, maize and beans and moreover employ the whole summer in clearing land and building cottages [he recommends timber covered dug-outs]. . . to proceed the next winter to cut and clear the timber. . . for building, for palisades. . . in the course of the second summer. . . he will have more leisure to build houses.[15]

But to get started, notice that two shelters were required over the space of two summers: the temporary hut for the first year, followed by a more permanent timber house the second. Moreover, recent study suggests that the second timber house was itself considered only temporary, a make-do residence until enough capital could be accumulated to support the building of something more in keeping with a "proper" English home.

Although probably not as impermanent as the builders thought, the second-stage houses were undoubtedly built in the English timber-frame tradition, most probably not unlike that recommended for the Pennsylvania frontier in 1684, houses that could "usually endure ten years without repair" (see Figures 9 and 10).[16]

> There must be eight trees of about sixteen Inches square and cut off to Posts of about fifteen foot long which the House must stand upon; and four pieces, two of thirty foot long and two of eighteen foot long, for plates, which must lie upon the top of those Posts the whole length and Bredth of the House for the Gists to rest upon. There must be ten Gists of twenty foot long to bear the Loft and two False plats of Thirty foot long to lie upon the ends of the Gists for the Rafters to be fixed upon, twelve pair of rafters of about twenty foot to bear the Roof. . . for covering the house. . . we use clapboards of Five foot and a half long.[17]

Although the author of these specifications does not come right out and say it, the excessive length of his one-story upright support posts, (15′), leaves little doubt that they were seated deeply into the ground. That type of construction had the advantage of eliminating any prepared foundation, one of the most costly and time-consuming parts of the house-building process. With posts made of some especially durable material like cedar or locust, timber supports probably lasted longer than wood that has been directly in contact with the ground might suggest. Chimneys as well were often no more than an exterior timber frame covered with mud at the end of the house, so common and flammable that legislation was passed more than once banning their use.[18] There is some doubt as to the actual durability of these post-in-the-ground timber structures, but if they managed to stand sturdy enough beyond the estimated "ten year if the repars were made," perhaps the final more suitable "dream" house did not seem necessary.

Regardless of the durability of the second-stage structures, the final perma-nent homesteaders house rarely materialized. Historian Edmund Morgan partially attributes the lack of more substantial permanent houses to an attitude of tran-sience, at least during the early years of settlement. Morgan maintains that instead of investing in houses, many took their new-found fortune back home to England after cashing in on a few bumper tobacco crops, particularly during the boom years.[19] Architectural historian Cary Carson, on the other hand, maintains that as impermanent as they were, even the second-stage houses outlived their builders: the high death rate cut short dreams of building better.[20] But regardless of the lack of desire or opportunity, there seems to have remained throughout the seventeenth century an economic climate that priced the construction of better houses out of the reach of even the most affluent Virginians. William Fitzhugh, certainly a man with as many means as most of his peers, lamented in 1682 that the high cost of labor made a Virginia house three times as expensive to build as a comparable building in London. He therefore recommended against raising buildings of any consequence, at least for his tenants[21] According to Carson, it was not until planters diversified their crops in the eighteenth century that labor and steady capital were available for building better houses. He makes a strong case for this being true on Maryland's Eastern Shore and postulates this to be the case in Virginia as well.[22]

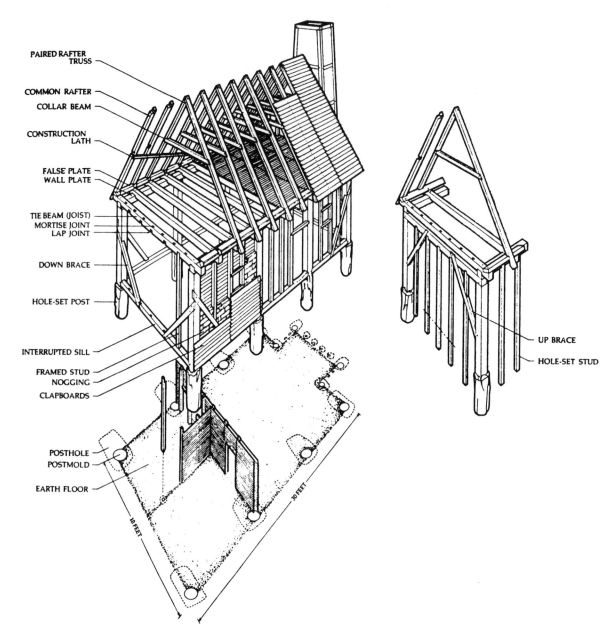

PAIRED RAFTER TRUSS

COMMON RAFTER

COLLAR BEAM

CONSTRUCTION LATH

FALSE PLATE
WALL PLATE

TIE BEAM (JOIST)
MORTISE JOINT
LAP JOINT

DOWN BRACE

HOLE-SET POST

INTERRUPTED SILL

FRAMED STUD
NOGGING
CLAPBOARDS

POSTHOLE
POSTMOLD

EARTH FLOOR

UP BRACE

HOLE-SET STUD

20 FEET

18 FEET

Figure 9   Reconstruction drawing of the "ordinary beginners" house described in the 1684 pamphlet, *Information and Direction to Such Persons as are inclined to America.* (Carson *et al.*, 1981.)

Figure 10   Reconstructed yeoman's house, based on documentary research and archaeological evidence from Virginia and Maryland; St. Mary's City, Maryland.

Although no house supported by posts in the ground like that recommended for the Pennsylvania frontier have yet been found surviving in Virginia, two still stand in Maryland.[23] The most documented, Cedar Park, near Annapolis, probably built in 1702, still has its ground posts and the remains of a timber-and-clapboard porch tower encased in an eighteenth-century brick shell (see Figure 11). The brickwork shell seems to be the reason this building has lasted now almost 300 years. Nonetheless, with some view to the future, builders originally chose enduring woods like cedar and locust for those parts of the building in contact with or closest to the ground. Fortunately, a 1736 inventory of the estate of Richard Galloway II, a merchant who presumably had the house built, preserves the floor plan as well: "on the ground floor a Hall for dining and sitting and a parlor for sleeping and two sleeping chambers above.[24] The decision to transform this timber house itself into a "third stage" permanent dwelling rather than starting a new

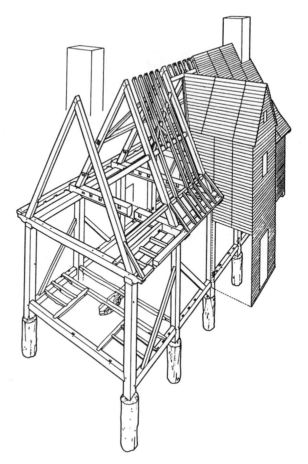

Figure 11 Timber framing at Cedar Park, Maryland; one of the two known surviving post-in-the-ground colonial houses in the Chesapeake region. (Carson *et al.*, 1981.)

brick house from scratch must have been unusual unless, of course, more timber skeletons lie hiding and undiscovered under other brick veneers. It is more likely that the addition of the brickwork was indeed unique and that is why one and only one colonial brick-encased post building survives today.

There is every reason to believe that these post-timber houses were commonplace throughout the Chesapeake region during the seventeenth century despite their almost total absence today. The archaeological evidence from Maryland and Virginia is considerable.[25] Although they tended to be built by less wealthy people as time passed, and masonry foundations for new construction replaced the earthfast posts, the popularity and basic form and materials of the frame clapboarded house persisted through the eighteenth century. As late as the 1770s Thomas Jefferson wrote:

> The private buildings [in Virginia] are very rarely constructed of stone or brick; much the greatest proportion being of scantling and boards, plaistered with lime. It is impossible to devise things more ugly, uncomfortable, and happily more perishable. There are two or three plans, on one of which according to its size, most of the houses in the state are built.[26]

The common plan to which Jefferson refers was almost certainly identical to the house James Gates contracted to build in Henrico County a hundred years earlier: "an house of 40 foote long and 20 foote wide and a partition through the middle and the Joize all to be lin'd and plain'd and 2 outside chimneys".[27] In fact, the Virginia frame houses fit such a pattern that a recent study of the houses of the common folk in rural Piedmont has led folklorist Henry Glassie to suggest that the tradition for such buildings was guided by a very rigid set of design rules, a grammar of folk architecture. Ground plans are seen as culturally determined combinations of squares and divisions of squares all growing from the addition or division of the cubit (18 inches). The location of windows, doors, and chimneys was also chosen according to cultural rules.[28]

Things were different for the very rich. In the late eighteenth century in Albemarle County, Thomas Jefferson's Monticello and a small farmhouse now known as Solitude were being built almost within sight of each other[29] (see Figures 12 and 13). They are representative of the extremes that architecture had come to in Virginia during the eighteenth century. On the one hand, Solitude represents the persistence of the hall–parlor folk tradition, and on the other, Monticello is symbolic of the mansion houses being built under the neoclassical influence of whatever "proper" architectural rules appealed to owners.

The story of the development of the opulent eighteenth-century Virginia mansions initiated by the construction of the Governor's Palace in Williamsburg is a familiar one and need not be repeated here in any detail.[30] It is perhaps enough to say that, generally, most of the plantation great houses were some variation of the palace—double-pile masonry mansions with central doorways and perfectly balanced windows, chimneys, and other details, all accented in some way by flanking or advance dependencies, terraces, and geometric gardens (see Figure 14). Wherever possible, too, the rule was to locate the mansion on some piece of high ground where it would visually dominate the scene.

But Virginia Georgian was not as simple as that: "builders systematically dismembered the new architectural concepts and fit them into traditional Virginia ones in ways that illustrate the close interdependence of local and extralocal impulses in vernacular architecture."[31] Not denying the eighteenth-century influences of the swelling ranks of the "new" house architects, architectural historian Dell Upton, by studying vernacular buildings in Eastern Virginia, concluded that Virginians, by picking and choosing from the English plans to fit their own servants and slave-holding rural society, formed a fairly predictable local tradition. This resulted at first in scaled-down versions of the hall–parlor English model and, although the outward appearance was symmetrical and regular, the Virginia tradition began to produce plans with few rooms alike in size or function inside, all dictated by the

Figure 12   Solitude, a late eighteenth-century hall–parlor, 1½-story frame house, Albermarle County, Virginia. (School of Architecture, University of Virginia.)

Figure 13   Monticello, circa 1809; a unique rendering of Virginia's plantation aristocracy. (Thomas Jefferson Memorial Foundation.)

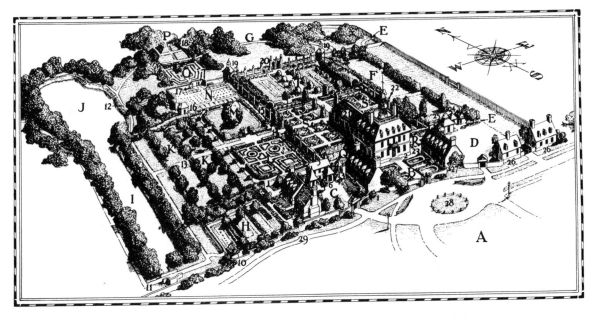

Figure 14 Bird's-eye view of the Palace grounds. (Courtesy of Colonial Williamsburg Foundation.)

owner's attempt to replicate the "civic order of public society." The "home house" then functioned as the county seat, with its public spaces—the hall and passage—kept distinctly separate from the private rooms of the family.[32]

Anthropologist James Deetz attributes this transformation of hall–parlor frame houses to balanced multiroom Georgian structures as the reflection of a major shift in American culture generally. Deetz sees the seventeenth-century "medieval" corporate society, where living space was shared and privacy practically unknown, meld into the society of the Age of Reason, where individuality and private space became sacred. Deetz accounts for the development of an American building tradition more by the changing relationship of the American colonies with England than by any local circumstances. During the second half of the seventeenth century as the result of the influence of geographic isolation and English neglect, Americans drifted away from English building models. Then as the colonies came back under British domination by the mid–eighteenth century, Deetz believes that the Georgian movement reflected rekindling of an Anglo-American culture. According to Deetz, pottery, gravestones, and music underwent the same cultural transformation.[33]

Colonial Virginia's houses may well fit predictable models, but it is clear from a few surviving estate inventories that what people furnished their houses with varied considerably, so much so that it is difficult to generalize for any one period or class. For people living in seventeenth-century timber-frame houses, the extremes could range from the case of William Harris of Henrico County, who left at his death in 1679 merely two beds, two broken guns, a mortar and pestle, a table leaf and "1 piece of old melted pewter," to the over 400 items inventoried in 1667 in the house of Jane Hartley of Northampton County.[34]

There is indirect evidence that the lot of Virginia tobacco planters in the Chesapeake area improved over the course of the seventeenth century to the American Revolution. A systematic study of over 2500 inventories dating from 1658 to 1777 from St. Mary's County, Maryland, directly across the Potomac River from Virginia's Northern Neck, showed that certain objects that one could consider to be luxuries began to increase steadily for significant numbers of people. The amount of fine ceramics, linen, spices, books, wigs, watches, clocks, pictures,and silver plate, all items that had remained at a constant level in inventories until 1716, increased at a steady rate in most households until late in the century.[35] Of course, the splendor of the mansions of Virginia's elite families is legend, with the Lee's Sulley a late but classic example:

> The house. . . is lately furnished from Philadelphia with every article of silver plate, mahogany, Wilton carpeting, and glass ware that can be conceived or that you will find in the very best furnished houses of Philadelphia. Parlour & chambers completely equipped with every luxury as well as convenience.[36]

The story of the material world of colonial Virginia's slave population is rather different. Although it is clear that there are precious few detailed records of slave life, a cautious reading of certain documents and a careful look at the few standing slave quarters, regardless of their age, can offer general glimpses of the everyday material world of the black Virginia servant. Despite the obvious bias of contemporary writers or the uncertain history of standing buildings, the personal accounts of the slaves, ex-slaves, and their descendants, the diaries and directives of the masters, the accounts of travelers, the few renderings of the period, and even Civil War and late nineteenth-century photographs can combine to suggest patterns of slave life probably more accurately than one would suppose.

The rigid and absolute structure of the relationship of the slave to master strictly defined the lifestyle of the slaves to such a degree that there was probably little opportunity for them to have more than the slightest effect on their own destiny. What impacted the slaves' situation the most was, on the one hand, the attitude and wealth of the master, and on the other, the occupational status of the slaves. House servants, for example, were necessarily a conspicuous part of the lives of the master and his family and therefore enjoyed more material amenities than did the fieldhands, but what the "amenities" were still depended on the fortune of the owner. Some house servants could live right in the master's house in relatively dry and warm basement or attic quarters in a high-style brick mansion, while others may have spent their lives in the drafty passage of a dim and cramped wooden farmhouse.[37] The wealthier planter could also provide detached kitchens and outbuildings for house servants, buildings that, because they were part of the more conspicuous landscape, were often as substantially constructed as the mansion itself. On the other hand, the field laborers and overseers usually had to live in small settlements of a less substantial and comfortable nature far enough from the mansion to be as invisible as possible.

As striking to the traveler's eye as the several Virginia plantations were, there is distressingly little cartographic or iconographic evidence showing any of them during the eighteenth century. But at least two paintings (probably done in the early nineteenth century) do add some perspective to the road maps of the day and seem to render accurately the pattern of housing for that and earlier periods. The one (Figure 15) depicts what must be a group of field hands dancing to "banjar" and drum music and otherwise "frolicing" in front of the gable-end doorways of what appear to be their very small and clustered wooden dwellings. In the distance and across the river stand the mansion house, larger outbuildings, and a line of what appear to be 7 story-and-a-half brick houses, in all probability more spacious and more comfortable accommodations for the house servants. The other drawing (Figure 16) shows a mansion on a hilltop overlooking 11 other buildings including what appear to be 3 small one-story and 1 two-story frame structures. The two-story house is most likely for the overseer or house servants, while the nearby hutlike buildings are likely for the field hands. It is interesting and probably significant to note that the field-hand structures seem to have hipped roofs and an overall appearance not unlike West Indian and some West African houses of that period (see Figure 17).

That some slaves did manage to bring African building design and construction techniques to the American plantations is clearly evident by the story of Okra,

Figure 15 A rare view of slave life at an unknown plantation (probably in South Carolina, ca. 1790), showing the contrast between the simple wooden huts for fieldhands (foreground) and the more substantial quarters for house servants (background). (Abby Aldrich Rockefeller Folk Art Center, Williamsburg, Virginia.)

Figure 16 First-quarter nineteenth-century southern plantation buildings, showing small hipped-roof slave quarters below the dominating, landscaped mansion on the hill; location unknown. (Metropolitan Museum of Art.)

a Georgia Sea Island immigrant slave who built a hut so outlandishly African in appearance that his master quickly made him tear it down.[38] But the direct transport of design to any significant extent is highly unlikely, given the circumstances of slavery. All the same, some scholars maintain that at least African spatial concepts did cross the Atlantic. For example, the arrangement of houses in clusters can be seen as similar to the Yoruba compounds of Nigeria.[39] Further, the argument goes, the typical dimensions of the small slave houses in America (10′ × 10′, 12′ × 12′) reflect African cultural preference even though the house design is essentially Anglo-American. In other words, these small buildings with their tiny rooms were as they were in Africa, the culturally defined space beyond which an African would feel uncomfortable.

Written descriptions suggest that the typical houses of slaves probably fit somewhere between "a pen made of poles and covered with pine brush" and "quarters look[ing] more like neat, pleasant New England Village[s].[40] Then, too, there are some references to barracks or dormitories such as J. F. D. Smyth seems to be describing in 1784, a single house for a group of six slaves and an overseer.[41] These barracks may have been more common during the first half of the eighteenth

Figure 17 Two-room Yoruba house in Nigeria, 1974; compare to Figure 16. (Vlach, 1978).

century when immigrants were mostly male. When the sex ratio finally reached a balance during the second half of the century, it is probable that nuclear family houses replaced dormitory units. It is during this later period that the terms *negro quarters* and *negro dwellings* begin to show up in the tax records in the Chesapeake area as well.[42] It was also during this time that the log cabin began to be the predominate slave house type, although records of them from the 1700s are scarce. Fortunately, relatively detailed records of slave quarters survive from the nineteenth century. Consequently, by carefully projecting that data backward into the colonial period one can begin to visualize the earlier slave structures.

Agricultural journal articles written by slave owners during the first half of the nineteenth century, interviews with ex-slaves done during Works Progress Administration (WPA) days, and more recent interviews of descendants of slaves and ex-slaves in Maryland begin to support one another enough to suggest what the typical single family slave house was like.[43] They all seem to agree that the standard single-family units were plain wooden buildings, one-story high with a gable roof and an exterior chimney at one gable end. *Small* meant from about 12′ × 16′ to 16′ × 18′ or perhaps as large as 16′ × 24′ in plan. *Plain* could mean either log or frame construction with a chimney made of stacked logs or sticks coated with clay. Most of these cabins had one room with a dirt floor and a loft above.

In the nineteenth century many slave owners began to advocate raising these houses on piers for ventilation and adding wooden floors. They give the impression that their experience with houses built directly on the ground with dirt floors created health problems, perhaps hinting at what had been the standard during the preceeding century.[44] However, how many houses ever conformed to this published advice or to anything else masters urged as the ideal in slave management is difficult to determine. In any event, it is likely that nineteenth-century reforms were the solutions to eighteenth-century problems.

A recent search for extant slave houses dating to the 1700s found only a handful, all of frame construction. At any rate, the few that were studied conform to the one-room loft model. It is true that two of the buildings found were much larger, but they were clearly built to function as two separate one-room loft duplexes. These central-chimney double houses are, however, more typical of the nineteenth century.[45]

An important survival of the nineteenth-century era (probably the 1830s) is a rather sizable "slave cabin" at General John Hartwell Cocke's Bremo Recess Plantation near the James River in Fluvanna County, Virginia [46] (see Figure 18). It apparently housed a single family and stands behind a main house originally built

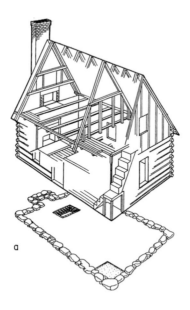

Figure 18 (a) Slave quarter at Bremo Recess Plantation, Fluvanna County, Virginia; (b) similar archaeological plan of remains of servants' house "O" Mulberry Row, Monticello, Virginia, circa 1796. (A. Gruber.)

in 1803. The building measures 25′ × 17′ overall and has three rooms: one large room on the ground floor and two rooms reached by a corner staircase in the sizable loft above. The structure also has a substantial stone-and-brick chimney with both a lower and upper fireplace. The floor, made of tongue-and-groove boards seated on half-hewn logs, has a trapdoor immediately in front of the hearth, leading to a brick-and-wood-lined compartment in the ground, presumably a small cellar for the storage of roots. In its log construction, one-room loft plan, gable-end chimney, root cellar, and corner stair, the Bremo Recess slave house appears to conform to the norm for slaves in general.

But such a large and permanent slave house was probably in many respects as atypical of the South as Bremo's owner. General Cocke was opposed to tobacco, alcohol, and slavery—certainly a very unusual stance for a member of the early nineteenth-century Virginia rural aristocracy. Because he believed in such liberal reforms as slave education, gradual emancipation, and African transport, it is unlikely that any quarters he built for his slaves would be as humble as most.[47] Nonetheless, both the documents and archaeological evidence suggest close kinship of the Bremo quarter with slave houses generally, and, had the Bremo dwelling been 20% smaller with a wooden instead of a masonry chimney, its destruction would leave remains strikingly similar to those found at the site of the log "servant house" at Monticello.[48]

In fact, a log structure at Tufton, an original Jefferson period farm at the base of Monticello Mountain, equally fits the late eighteenth-century and early nineteenth-century model. In a wooded section of the property, not more than 2 miles from the Monticello mansion, stands a nineteenth-century one-cell log cabin encased within two periods of later clapboarding. It is possible that the core of the structure dates to as early as Jefferson's lifetime although the records are mute and the archaeological evidence inconclusive. In any case, the Tufton building, regardless of its date, provides one more example of the norm.[49]

Fortunately, photographs taken during the second half of the nineteenth century of some log cabins of Virginia blacks survive (see Figure 19). There is every reason to believe that, although they show relatively "new" construction by the time they were photographed, they conform to and confirm the descriptions of the houses mentioned during the interviews of ex-slaves or by slave descendants, many of whom grew up living in or hearing stories about slave houses.[50] Photographs and accounts of life inside the houses by the slave decendants give vivid animation to the exterior photographs as well. The one ground-floor room had to provide space for practically every facet of domestic life, serving as living room, dining room, kitchen, and bedroom for the adults and the smaller children. The loft, usually reached by a movable ladder or occasionally by a corner stair, was the sleeping room or, if partitioned, sleeping rooms for the older children. Furnishings are always described as meager, usually including only a few shelves, a makeshift table, and a chair or stool or two.[51]

Like the overall quality of the houses, there apparently could be similar variation in the furnishings. On one Mississippi plantation the cabins were

> provided with beds and bedding in abundance. In others there was a show of neatness and luxury; high-post bedsteads, handsomely displayed. . . cupboards of Blue

Figure 19 Negro house near Richmond, Virginia, with the single-room loft and wooden chimney typical of slave cabins of an earlier time. (Cook Collection, Valentine Museum, Richmond.)

> Liverpool Ware, coffee mills, looking glasses, tables, chairs, trunks and chests of as good clothes as I clothe myself or Family of.[52]

On the other hand, an ex-slave painted a far gloomier picture of a slave quarter interior in Maryland:

> We lodged in log huts . . . In a single room were huddled like cattle, ten or a dozen persons, men, women, and children. All ideas of refinement and decency were, of course, out of the question. There were neither bedsteads or furniture of any description. . . the floor was as miry as a pigsty.[53]

How many masters provided the luxurious Mississippi accommodations and how many slaves were penned like cattle is probably impossible to know. It is clear, however, that neglecting "refinement and decency" could lead to problems. One

Virginia master rather vividly described what the "pigsty" approach to housing could bring:

> On my own farm a few years ago, typhoid fever. . . broke out in an old negro cabin, closely underpinned and which for many years had been used as a negro house. My family physician advised me to tear away the underpinning and have all the filth cleaned up. In doing so, I found an acumulation of foul matter in layers almost denoting the number of years it had been collecting.[54]

PEOPLE

The original Virginia adventurers may have explored Kingsmill before they settled on Jamestown Island. George Percy, Jamestown's "lieutenant governor," in his "A Discourse of the Plantation of the Southern Colony in Virginia by the English, 1601," stated that on May 12, 1607, the explorers stopped on a point of land they named Archer's Hope, the name of the creek bounding Kingsmill on the west. Although the land on the opposite side of the creek has been generally known as Archer's Hope, there is the possibility that Percy's early description refers to the point of land where the creek enters the river on the Kingsmill side:

> The twelth day [of May] we. . . discovered a point of land called Archer's Hope which was sufficient with a little labor to defend ourselves against any enemy. The soil was good and fruitful, with excellent good timber. There are also great stores of vines in bigness of a man's thigh, running up to the tops of trees in great abundance. We also did see many squirrels, conies, blackbirds, with crimson wings, and divers other fowls and birds of divers and sundry colors of crimson watchet, yellow, green, murrey and of divers other hues naturally without any art using.
>
> We found store of turkey nests and many eggs. If it had not been disliked, because the ship could not ride near the shore, we had settled there to all the colony's contentment.[55]

Although Percy's colorful writing style tends to make all his descriptions of the Virginia wilderness sound like paradise, it would still be safe to assume that the Kingsmill area was a particularly good piece of property with an abundance of the necessities for agricultural development: "good and fruitful" soil, timber, wild game and a topography that could be fortified with but a little labor."

Apparently, then, the only thing that kept Archer's Hope (possibly Kingsmill) from being chosen as the site of Jamestown was that the James River channel strayed too far from shore there. The next day the explorers came to an island 4 miles upstream from Archer's Hope, a place where ships could ride so close to land that they could be moored to the trees. Jamestown Island and not Archer's Hope, then, became the heart of Virginia settlement.

As the Virginia Company reforms cleared the way for individual land-ownership in the 1600s, settlement scattered up and down the river from Jamestown Island. Although there is no official record of it, it is logical to assume that the Archer's Hope "paradise" described by Percy drew its share of settlers. It is not until 1619, however, that the first land patents for Kingsmill appear, one to a William Fairfax for 188 acres on the western side of the property and another to John Jefferson for 250 acres to the east.[56] Both men apparently did not occupy their Kingsmill land but lived at Jamestown, and Fairfax's land was not even listed as planted in 1625. In that year, a total of 3200–3500 acres at Archer's Hope was patented, then an area that occupied both sides of Archer's Hope Creek.[57] Only Fairfax, Jefferson and Jochum Andrews, Richard Kingsmill, William Claybourne, and George Sandys, poet and treasurer of the Company, seem to have become the owners of property on the eastern side of the creek, however. Nothing written even suggests that any of these early landowners lived on their claims, so it is logical to assume that as tobacco profits began to soar in the 1620s the owners encouraged tenants to work the land. In fact, three of the place names at Kingsmill probably came from the last names of long-term tenants (Figure 20): *Farley* or *Farlow's Neck,* from Thomas Farley, a tenant who had a wife, daughter, and 40-year-old servant living at Archer's Hope in a "house supplied with 1 hogshead of English meal, 6 bushels of corn, 3 bushels of peas, 2 pounds of powder, 10 pounds of lead, 2 peeces guns, 1 armor, 5 swine and 1 pig"; *Harrop* from possibly another tenant Edward Hartop; and *Tuttey's Neck,* from Thomas Tutty, a servant or tenant transported by John Pott.[58]

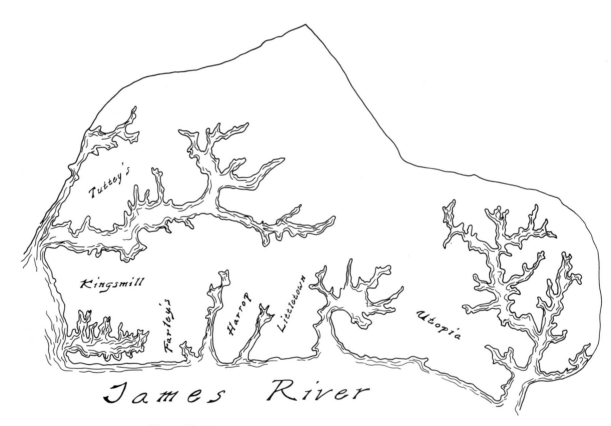

Figure 20   Seventeenth-century place names at Kingsmill, Virginia. (Sondy Sanford.)

Two areas are obviously named for individual landowners: *Utopia* for John Utie, who briefly owned the land originally patented by Jefferson, and *Kingsmill Neck* (also *Farleys* or *Farlow's Neck*) for Richard Kingsmill.[59] The central section of the property, on the other hand, acquired its own place name apart from the owners or tenants, first called *Littletown* in a patent of Richard Richards, who may have been one of the first resident landowners in the area.[60] The first direct reference to occupation by a patentee appears in 1629 when the area represented by John Browning in the House of Burgesses is described as "Harrop and the Several Plantations in the area between Archer's Hope and Martin's Hundred"; that is, modern Kingsmill.[61] From that it is clear that there were several plantations in operation on the Kingsmill land and Browning may have lived on lands he had purchased from John Utie and the estate of Edward Grindon, who had acquired George Sandys's land.[62]

Although much of the documentation of Kingsmill landownership and residency is vague for the earliest decades of the seventeenth century, it would at least be safe to say that by about 1640–1650 much of the land had been cleared and occupied, at least by tenants. But by the 1640s it appears that the land that would eventually become collectively known as Kingsmill had been consolidated into two large plantations, one by Humprey Higginson, "Gentleman," who combined Farleys or Kingsmill Neck, Tuttey's Neck, and Harrop Plantation, and the other by Colonel Thomas Pettus, one of Governor Berkeleys councillors, who combined Littletown and Utopia.[63]

Higginson arrived in Virginia in 1635, soon married into the 700-acre Tuttey's Neck land and, with the rank of captain, soon added the 320-acre Harrop tract to his growing Kingsmill estate.[64] He eventually returned to England about 1655 where he died some 15 years later.[65] Colonel Thomas Pettus, like Higginson, was of gentle birth. He was the son of a wealthy English merchant and politician of Norwich, but he was only a twelfth son, leaving him with relatively dim prospects of inherited wealth.[66] That being the case, he may have first sought his fortune in the military service, but eventually immigration to Virginia offered him his best chance of breaking the bonds of financial, social, and possibly military immobility. Best of all, however, immigration offered Pettus the chance to own land.

Exactly when Pettus first arrived in Virginia is unknown, but he was living in the colony by 1641, the first year that he served on the Governor's Council[67] He could have acquired land by the right of his uncle, Sir John Pettus, who had purchased two shares in the original Virginia Company. With that initial acquisition of 200 acres (2 shares) of Virginia soil, Pettus proceeded to accumulate additional acreage by what had then become a Virginia tradition, marrying a rich widow. By his marriage to Elizabeth Durant, who managed to outlive Kingsmill landowner John Browning, Pettus probably acquired some Kingsmill acreage along with 386 acres north of Jamestown.[68] He soon thereafter purchased a thousand acres in Westmoreland, Northumberland, and Stafford counties on Virginia's Northern Neck. How Pettus eventually acquired both Richard's Littletown and Browning's Utopia together is not recorded, but the Pettus family holdings included these two tracts—1280 acres—by the end of the century.[69] Pettus was living at "Littletown in Virginia" by 1660 when his name appears in the court records of Westmoreland County. Pettus "of Littletown in Virginia" appointed his neighbor Edward Griffin of Mulberry Island (southeast of Kingsmill) to act as his attorney in a land transaction on the Potomac.[70]

After the Colonel's death in about 1669, his son, Thomas Pettus, inherited Littletown, but he accomplished little that left its mark in historical records.[71] By 1671 he was listed as an orphan under the care of Colonel Nathaniel Bacon, who appears in court records acting on behalf of his charge for payment for the production of servants and a negro woman, and 14 crops of tobacco.[72] From this it is clear that tenants perhaps of both races, or slaves, worked Littletown land at that time. The younger Pettus was not appointed to fill his father's chair on the council and the position of vestryman for Bruton Parish appears to have been the highlight of his public service. The younger Pettus died in 1691, and an a partial inventory of his Littletown and Utopia possessions survives (see Appendix A: Table 3).[73]

Again, the marriage of a widow gave Littletown a new landowner with a different family name. When the Pettus heirs released the deed to the land in 1700 for the traditional "five shillings and an ear of corn a year," the 1200-acre Littletown and Utopia tract added yet more prime real estate to the Bray family holdings.[74] That transaction also helped to perpetuate the Bray's financial and political prominence that had begun to accumulate in the mid–seventeenth century.

James Bray II's father, James, came to Virginia in 1657, paying for the transportation of 25 others and later his wife, entitling him to patent 1300 acres. In 1671 Bray bought better land, probably with some profits from initial tobacco crops. The new land was a good choice, 290 acres at Middle Plantation, the land upon which the city of Williamsburg would be built 28 years later. By 1677, Bray had a house at Middle Plantation and, as proof of his provincial success, he was named to Governor Sir William Berkeley's prestigious council. Although he was eventually removed from his post in 1678 for his part in Bacon's Rebellion, Bray did manage to escape Berkeley's vindictive noose. As a burgess in the 1680s, he regained some political influence.[75]

Bray had three sons and a daughter before he died in 1691, enough progeny to perpetuate the family's newly won political and financial status. To the Bray children, including James Bray II, the future owner of Littletown Plantation, growing up in the home of an immigrant tobacco planter scaling the rungs of the social, political, and economic ladder made a lasting impression. On the strength of that background alone, then, James II must have brought considerable business and agricultural prowess as well as an attitude of social and political confidence to his new land (Figure 21).

If James Bray II began living at Littletown from the year of his release deed, his residence there eventually spanned the entire first quarter of the eighteenth century. During that time he carried on the political position of the family by

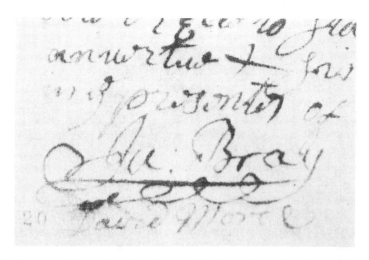

Figure 21 Signature of James Bray II as Justice of the Peace, James City County, Virginia, 1717. (Jones Family Papers, Library of Congress.)

serving as a member of the House of Burgesses, as justice of the peace for James City County and as an original alderman for the City of Williamsburg. Apparently he had inherited some of his father's other lands: in 1704 he owned 2220 acres in James City County beyond the Littletown holdings, and 1400 acres in King William County.[76] James II also had a brick house in town and was visited occasionally by the colorful William Byrd of Westover, Charles City County. In fact, they seem to have been good friends. On the night of November 16, 1711, James Bray, James Roscow, and William Byrd sat up drinking and, if they all followed Byrd's lead, got drunk—at least Byrd confessed to the overindulgence.[77]

By his will, dated November 18, 1725, James Bray II left his Littletown Plantation to his grandson, James III, who could take possession of the property when he reached the age of 21.[78] In the meantime, James II's daughter Elizabeth had the use of the place. The will also stipulated that should James III die while his father Thomas Bray II was still alive, them Littletown would revert to Thomas. Although James II left what seems to be valuable land to his son, Thomas II— probably the Bassett Hall section of Williamsburg where he lived—it is curious why James II skipped over him to leave Littletown to the grandson, James III. James II's will even provided for the cost of his grandson's "maintenance and education" through the proceeds of the sale of his brick house and lots in Williamsburg. In essence then, James II made every effort to assure a comfortable life for his grandson, but no especially equal effort for his son, as one might expect. Perhaps by this, the aging James II had become keenly interested in long-term perpetuation of his Tidewater estate located so conspicuously close to the growing social and political center of the colony at Williamsburg. His children, on the other hand, were not left property close to the capital city but in far-off Charles City County. In any event, if James II did hope to continue a Bray family dynasty at Littletown by passing its management along to his grandson, he was successful for a time. James III did live to majority, took over Littletown, and left record of a particularly thriving plantation business venture from 1736 when he began his tenure there to 1744, the year of his death. After that, according to James II's will, Thomas, James III's father, inherited Littletown until his own death ended the Bray Littletown male lineage in 1751.[79]

James II left more than the "land and buildings" at Littletown, according to an inventory taken 2 months after his death (see Appendix: Table 1.[80] He passed along a wealth of material possessions, many of which belonged to Littletown or were actually in his house there. The list leaves little doubt that by 1725 the Brays had amassed a considerable fortune beyond the value of the land alone. Besides 94 head of cattle, 91 pigs, and over two dozen slaves at Littletown, his inventory includes over 457 domestic objects. Besides the usual day-to-day necessities like beds, blankets, and pots and pans, James II left luxuries like a clock, "several pictures," 5 looking glasses, silver candlesticks and related hardware, silver tankards, silver spoons, silver spurs, silver shoe buckles, a silver cane and sword, and "2 coats of arms." Apparently life would not be without amenities at Littletown when the grandson, James III, moved in.

It appears that when James III did move to Littletown, he meant business. His surviving ledger for the decade from 1736 to 1744, in his own hand, shows that he took his inheritance seriously and made every effort through a variety of business arrangements to make Littletown pay off.[81] The document records his debits in detail and some of his credits. Although it is impossible to know the net worth of Littletown at any one time, both directly and indirectly the document provides enlightening views of the business of the plantation by identifying its products and giving some place and names to its people.

Like most of the larger plantations of the day, the ledger clearly indicates that Littletown consisted of the home plantation and outlying quarters, and that slaves comprised the bulk of the population. Although at least one tenant and indentured servant are mentioned, slaves are without doubt the main labor force. Blacks also apparently were appointed to supervisory positions, certainly "Jacko's Quarter" and "Deb's Quarter" sound like places under the supervision of blacks. Although it is unclear from the ledger exactly where Jacko or Deb lived on their respective quarters, it is reasonably certain that the quarters were located at the Tuttey's Neck and Utopia sections of the Littletown property.[82]

Tuttey's Neck was for a number of years a Bray holding by the time James III kept his ledger. Judith Bray, James II's sister-in-law, got the land by way of Frederick Jones, and James III finally got clear title to the land through a rather complicated and somewhat confusing series of property transferrals.[83] By then it appears likely that the Tutter's Neck land and Utopia were being managed by a John

Green and a Benjamin Tureman, the names this time suggesting that they were white.[84]

For their effort, both Tureman and Green got shares of tobacco. On top of that, from 1740 to 1744 Green got shares of corn, pork, and butter, probably from Utopia, and Tureman received shares of corn, wheat pears, wood, and cider brandy from Tutter's Neck. From this, it is significant to note how diversified the crops of the quarters were, particularly at Tureman's Tuttey's Neck land. It also is important to note that, unlike their earlier black counterparts "Jacko" and "Deb," the probable white overseers, Tureman and Green, did get part of the profits.

A complete census of the black population of Littletown was taken only at the time of the will of James II. In 1723, 11 men, 10–13 women, 3 boys, and 1 girl lived at the Home Plantation, Utopia and Tutter's Neck.[85] The balance of the sexes might suggest that the Littletown slaves lived together in married pairs and perhaps there were one or two full families. By the time of his death, James III owned "a considerable Number of Negro and other slaves" and "several of the Said slaves were tradesmen and House servants"[86] Bray II's widow, Frances, inherited as many as 27 slaves from the Utopia quarter section of the property alone. If the widow got her usual one third of the value of the property by acquiring one third of all the slaves, then perhaps James III's total Littletown slave population had reached 81.[87]

There is no doubt that the production of Littletown's tobacco crops would have required a sizable black work force. The amount of tobacco on hand for sale at the time of James III's death, perhaps as much as 30,000 pounds, suggests no small operation. Although it is difficult to judge overall production, in a relative sense Littletown seems to have been producing more than any single plantation in Maryland at that time.[88] Production of such a labor-intensive crop of that magnitude could only have come from the combined efforts of a considerable number of slaves.

The ledger does not make it clear how James III marketed all his crops, but reference to a bill of exchange with Robert Lidderdale suggests that Bray had ties with Robert and John Lidderdale, "merchants in London."[89] James II clearly had earlier dealings with British merchants, for some of the funds from the settlement of his estate were sent to cover his debts in England. James III may also have dealt with the same local merchants that his executors chose to sell his last crop to, Thomas Nelson in Yorktown and his Kingsmill neighbor, Lewis Burwell. Burwell's warehouse next door made him a convenient commercial contact for the Brays.

Although the extent to which corn and wheat were produced for market is difficult to determine directly from the ledger entries. The estate sale in 1744 showed over 435 barrels of corn on hand at that time, but the ledger shows that Bray sold only a total of 466 barrels in the period from 1736 to 1744, indicating perhaps that a considerable quantity of corn was consumed by the labor and livestock at home.[90] Nonetheless, the leftover corn and apparently some wheat were grown for market, probably to meet the growing demand of the expanding population of the city of Williamsburg. Also, livestock is not generally considered a vital commercial by-product of a plantation primarily organized to grow tobacco, but both James II and James III produced a considerable amount of meat for market. James III records the sale of thousands of pounds of beef, veal, mutton, lamb, and pork during the years of the entries.[91]

The Bray ledger also records a variety of other commercial ventures at Littletown. Bray III operated a water mill and produced cornmeal and "flower" there, and had one miller doubling as a shoemaker. Leather tanning was done on the property, bricks were made on a commercial scale, and cider production seems to have been more than an intraplantation activity as well. Wood brought a steady income, most of it from selling unfinished timber and cordwood, but planking, lathing, clapboards,scantling, siding, fence rails, fenceposts, framing, and barrels were also produced.[92]

It is unfortunate for historians that James III died in 1744, cutting short his ledger entries. To have only 8 years of business records of a plantation that was operated by the Brays for over almost half a century should caution against making any sweeping generalizations about Littletown's production. Nonetheless, 8 years is far better than nothing, often the sum total of the surviving records of other plantations of the period. Actually, almost a decade of agricultural production might be long enough to filter out the impact of any particularly short-run abnormal weather or sudden shifts in the economy. Even given the apparent incomplete recording and possible variation in making records at all, there does seem to be a distinct acceleration of production and diversification at Littletown after about 1740. This may have been a reaction to the depressed tobacco market in the 1730s, or it may be a result of Bray's accumulating knowledge of plantation management. It may also be that he got more serious about his planting after he married Frances Thacker who brought more land and slaves under his control.[93] Or perhaps his business sense told him that the more stable grain market was the wave of the future and, had he lived, perhaps he would have converted, as so many did, to the serious production for the new grain market. Whatever his reasons, Bray was without a doubt involved in a remarkable variety of agricultural and craft-related activities at Littletown, all of which supports the contention that Chesapeake plantations generally were not as monotonously tobacco oriented as tradition suggests.

After James III died, his father, Thomas, probably ran the place with overseers until his own death 7 years later. That ended the Bray male line, as James III died without issue. It appears that James's sister, Elizabeth Bray Johnson, inherited the central Littletown property, whereas James III's widow kept Utopia and its 27 slaves. Frances Thacker Bray in turn married Lewis Burwell of neighboring Kingsmill Plantation, but it was not until 1796 that Littletown was added to the neighboring land of Kingsmill through sale.[94]

Four eighteenth-century maps show the Littletown and Kingsmill property in useful detail: the Frye–Jefferson Map of 1754, two French army reconnaissance maps of the vicinity of Williamsburg in 1781, and several versions of a much-embellished map illustrating the capture of the Littletown–Kingsmill–Utopia area by Lt. Colonel Simcoe and the Queen's Rangers, drawn by "G. Spencer" from memory some 6 years later (see Figures 22, 23, and 24). Only the Frye–Jefferson map shows the Littletown property when it was under Bray ownership. Unfortunately, it does not show any detail other than acknowledging the Bray family as the owners. The 1781 French map has proved to be extremely accurate and detailed, down to the most minor outbuildings.[95] It shows what appears to be a main house on the edge of a bluff with two smaller structures some 1000 feet inland. One version of the Simcoe map may show the Bray mansion slightly out of place.

If by establishing a family plantation dynasty James Bray I was typical of the era, than his neighbor Lewis Burwell III, one of five generations of that name, was a virtual prototype. His grandfather, Lewis I, immigrated to Virginia in 1635 as the son of Edward Burwell, an investor in the original Virginia Company.[96] With family funds, Lewis I transported enough people to accumulate thousands of acres in the colony, principally at Fairfield in Gloucester County. He was not only a typical midcentury man of "quality," but to his great misfortune he also followed so many of his fellow planters to an early grave. He did, however, have time enough in Virginia to start a family there. He provided his eldest son, Lewis II,

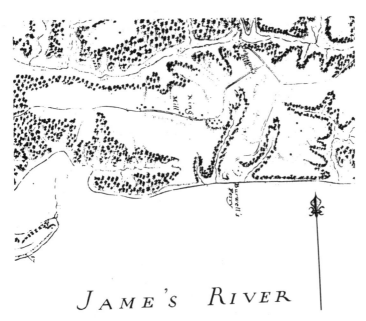

J A M E ' S   R I V E R

Figure 22 Plan of the Williamsburg area by Desandrouin, 1781.(Rochambeau #57, Library of Congress.)

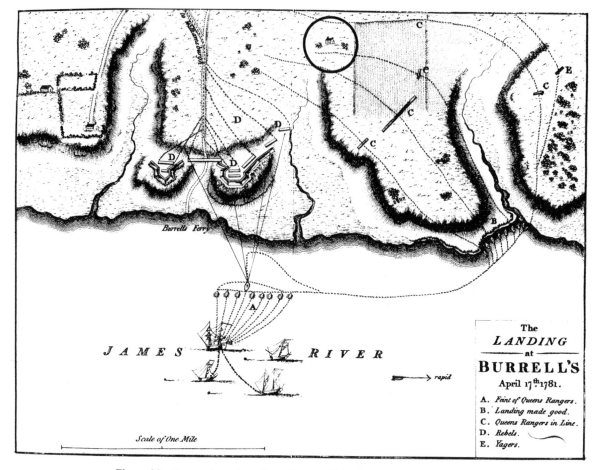

Figure 23 One version of Lt. Simcoe's map of the capture of Burwell's Landing, 1781, showing houses in the approximate location of James Bray's mansion (circle) and Lewis Burwell's mansion and dependency (upper left). (Colonial Williamsburg Foundation.)

with abundant land upon which he in turn built a respectable political career, serving as burgess and, for a short time, member of the Governor's Council, in 1701[97]

By two marriages, Lewis Burwell II had a total of nine children, and he had accumulated such a vast family landholding empire that there was plenty to go around for all at his death in 1710. His will provided for the education of two sons, James and Lewis III, training that would be "Liberal according to their Quality and Estates." Lewis III inherited land at "Farlow's Neck . . . Harrup Plantation and the Quarter land," all part of Kingsmill.[98] He could not take possession of his lands immediately, however, because he would not come of age until 1719. Mean-

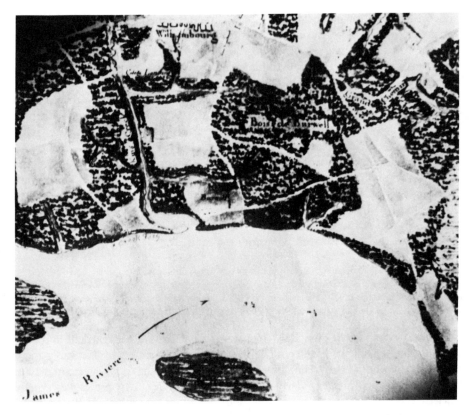

Figure 24 Map prepared for French General St. Simon, 1781, showing "Bois de Burwell" at Kingsmill. (Library of Congress.)

while he attended the College of William and Mary, training that his half brother Nathaniel urged for him in no uncertain terms. Nathaniel wrote James:

> I am very much concerned. . . to see how insensible Lewis is of his own ignorance, for he can neither read, nor give one letter a true shape when he writes nor spell one line of English & is altogether ignorant of Arithmetick so that he'll be noways capable of ye management of his own affairs & unfit for any Gentleman's conversation, & therefore a Scandalous person & a Shame to his Relations.[99]

The remedy for all Lewis's shortcomings, according to Nathaniel, would simply be a year at college learning writing, mathematics, arithmetic and Latin; then he offered to "take him home & imploy him. . . in my Office & Plantation Affairs that he might the better be capable to manage his own." The choice was simple according to Nathaniel, it was "to be a Blockhead or a man of parts." Between Lewis II's attitude that "Quality and Estate" were synonymous and Nathaniel's simple view that Virginia's population was made up of either "men of parts or blockheads," depending on their education, there is no doubt that the second generation of landed Burwell's had gained a certain arrogant confidence. They were beyond any doubt the "better sort." But to remain the better sort it is clear that they believed that one must be conversant as "befit Gentlemen" and manage their plantations with conspicuous skill. To do anything less, it seems would be to lose the hard-won elite Burwell position in Virginia's society.

Presumably Lewis III followed his brother's advice by learning those things that would assure him success in Virginia's pastoral patriarchy, but exactly when he began to put together his Kingsmill estate is in some doubt. Apparently Lewis III took up residence in the area of Farlow's Neck by 1725 when he was listed as a vestryman in the church from that parish in James City County.[100] The fact that Burwell's godfather, Stephen Fouace, sent him a letter on January 7, 1734, addressed "To the Hon'ble Lewis Burwell, at his House, Farlow's Neck, Near Williamsburg, Virginia," leaves no doubt that Lewis III was living there by that time.[101] A year and a half later the records of the General Assembly offer more definite evidence of a Burwell Kingsmill estate:

> Lewis Burwell hath laid out great sums of money in building a mansion-house, and other out-houses, and in making gardens, and other considerable improvements upon part of the said fourteen hundred acres [Farlow's Neck] intending the same for the seat of the eldest son of the family. . . to make a better provision for his younger children.[102]

In all probability, Lewis III's "mansion-house, out-houses, gardens and considerable improvements" were not brand new when the Act of Assembly mentioned them. Another governmental office that he held suggests that he may have been living at Kingsmill as early as the 1720s. Besides the post of vestryman, Burwell was appointed the prestigious and lucrative post of Naval Officer of the Upper District of the James River by Governor Gooch in 1728 (Figure 25). Besides giving him the title of colonel, the position entitled him to "extract great fees" by inspecting the cargoes of all ships entering or leaving Virginia, clearing at a point on the Farlow's Neck property shore (soon to become known as "Burwell's Ferry"), and assuring that each vessel was adhering to the "acts of Parliament and General Assembly about Trade and Navigation." The "great sums" came from a percentage of export duties on servants and liquors".[103] In all probability Lewis III acquired the naval office post because of family connections and inherited political power, but the strategic location of property near a natural landing point on the James River would also likely be a consideration for the governor. Whether or not this meant that Burwell already lived on the property or that the position encouraged him to build there is not certain. In any event, it is reasonably clear that the naval officer post, combined with his inheritance, provided him the means to support or to expand a very ambitious building scheme at that time.

There is some evidence to suggest that Burwell's ability to serve as naval officer came into some question. The subject of the letter from his godfather Fouace addressed to him at Farlow's Neck is the "grevious accusations laid to your charge," perhaps charges made public relating to the naval office. But apparently

Figure 25 Signature and Naval Office seal of Lewis Burwell IV. (Virginia Historical Society.)

Burwell answered these charges to the satisfaction of his godfather who, after reading a previous letter from Lewis, concluded, "I am fully convinced of the falsity of the charge."[104] He must also have been cleared of any wrongdoing in the eyes of his peers, for in September 1734 he was named Justice of the Peace and representative from James City County in the Virginia House of Burgess 2 years later.[105]

By 1736 Burwell had "the blessing of a good wife and hopefull children" and he let it be known that his "considerable improvements" on his Kingsmill land were intended "for the seat of the eldest son of the family."[106] It seems from this that Burwell III had reached that stage in life when immortality no longer seemed possible, and like his Bray neighbors and most of his landed contemporaries it had become his time to perpetuate the future of the Burwell estate. That same year the oldest son, Lewis IV, replaced Burwell as naval officer. Lewis III died in 1744.[107]

The life story of Lewis Burwell IV, at least until the time of the American Revolution, reads identically to that of his father. Besides his post as naval officer, Burwell IV became successively vestryman for Bruton Parish, justice of the peace for James City County, and finally "honourable Burgess" by the 1760s. But the American Revolution disrupted the Burwell continuity, as it did to the Virginia aristocracy generally. As the trouble with the mother country drew closer, Lewis

IV declined to run for reelection to the House of Burgesses (1774), which, intended or not, kept him out of the controversy over sending aid to Boston. By May 1775, Burwell IV moved west to Mecklenburg County, leaving his Tidewater plantation, by that time bearing the name — Kingsmill, to his eldest son, Lewis V.[108]

During Lewis IV's time at Kingsmill, he left a few plantation records with the accounts of his cousin Carter Burwell of neighboring Carter's Grove. In the 1760s and early 1770s Lewis IV ordered cider, butter, and mutton from Carter, indicating perhaps that Kingsmill was not producing its own food. On the other hand, Lewis IV also paid part of one bill in oats, showing that something else besides tobacco grew there.[109]

It was also during the 1760s that the name Kingsmill first appears in the records, in an advertisement in the *Virginia Gazette* for a runaway slave. Why Lewis IV chose to reincarnate the seventeenth-century name of the first land patentee is unclear, but considering the other options—Tuttey's, Farlow's, or Harrop—it seems that Burwell made the right choice. Why he felt the need to choose a name at all, and why he needed a name with some historical tradition is significant. Perhaps it was because by that time the property had been developed into one of those small riverbank "towns" that usually appeared so remarkable to eighteenth-century travelers in Virginia, and with its complex of mansion, outbuildings, and slave quarters, and its attendant ferry landing and its considerable population, it had grown to demand its own special place name. A proper name also helped to establish the Lewis Burwell family in colonial Virginia society, placing them among the ranks of the other James River estates, like Carter Burwell's Carter's Grove, William Byrd's Westover, and Hill Carter's Shirley.

Lewis IV expanded the Burwell's Kingsmill lands by acquiring the Utopia section of the Littletown property through his marriage to James Bray's widow, Frances, and Burwell's taxable acreage expanded in James City County from 1502 in the 1760s to as much as 2791 acres in the 1770s.[110] These extensive holdings, of course, required more management than its owner alone could supply. Even as early as 1755, the records mention a Frank Lester, living at "Col. Lewis Burwell's on James River," suggesting that Burwell had hired hands either to oversee his tobacco crops or to run the naval office, or both.

Land, overseers, slaves, tobacco, a family dynasty and a place name—all the familiar trappings of the Virginia "agristocracy." It should not be surprising then to learn that Lewis IV was consigning tobacco to a London agent and that he became ensnarled in the imbalance of overseas trade. By the time of his death in 1784, only 38:10 L were left of his estate after his debts were paid. Even 14 years later his heirs were back in court answering to a £202 claim on his estate by the London firm of Andrew Johnson and Company.[111]

Lewis V was handed the reigns of Kingsmill at a rather stormy moment in history—1775—and the 6 years that followed would not be good for the Virginia economy. In that war climate, it is perhaps unfair to try to assess the personality and success of the younger Burwell. Nonetheless, there is little in the records to suggest that he was anything like his forebears. He apparently lost his position of justice of the peace because he "declined to act" and he came close to murdering his brother-in-law:

> A dispute arose at dinner at Catesworth between Payton Randolph and his brother [in-law] Lewis Burwell, Who Gave, the other the Lye, on which Payton Struck him, Burwell Snatch'd a knife and struck him in the side, but fortunately a Rib prevented its proving Mortal.[112]

Also unlike his grandfather and father, Lewis V was never elected to the House of Burgesses. He also seems to have been rather opportunistic during the war, supplying rum and shelter to American troops with one hand and later stocking Cornwallis's troops with the other. Finally, it was Lewis V who ended the Burwell line at Kingsmill. He sold the property in 1783 to John Carter Byrd of Charles City County for £8500.[113]

Burwell's advertisement for the sale of Kingsmill placed in the *Virginia Gazette,* January 1781, turns out to be the most detailed description of the mansion house and auxillary buildings (see Figure 26). Apparently, by the following year Lewis V had moved to Richmond, as Kingsmill was again advertised for sale with the purchaser offered immediate possession. There is also a tenor of hard sell in the second advertisement: the "good dwelling house" had become "an elegant and convenient two story brick house." The man to see for purchase, so the ad stated, was none other than Peyton Randolph, who undoubtedly by that time rested easier knowing that his knife-wielding brother-in-law had left the neighborhood.[114]

The advertisements are made all the more descriptive when read in light of the three maps drawn as part of 1781 military activity at Kingsmill. The remarkably detailed and accurate map of the Williamsburg area from York River to James River, drawn under the direction of the French engineer, Jean Nicholas Desandrouin, shows 16 buildings at "King Mill" stretched along a road paralelling the river with mansion-flanking dependencies and auxiliary outbuildings clustered on a hilltop on the East end of the line (see Figure 23). The Simcoe map shows a series of slightly different views of the Burwell's Ferry landing area, depicting troop movements and the houses and parts of the gardens in the area (see Figures 24 and 27). The earliest version, apparently drawn some 6 years after the event, shows what appears to be a large house, an outbuilding, part of a garden or a fenced-in area, part of Burwell's buildings, and a two-story house to the east, the houses flanking landing fortifications captured during the last days of the war. The third map, drawn by an aide to St. Simon, the French General, shows a different location for buildings along the road paralelling the river and the "bois de Burwell" (see Figure 24), graphic evidence that much of Kingsmill was in woods just as the sale advertisement suggested.

The Desandrouin, Simcoe, and St. Simon maps also mark the course of Quarterpath Road, a major eighteenth-century artery linking Burwell's ferry land-

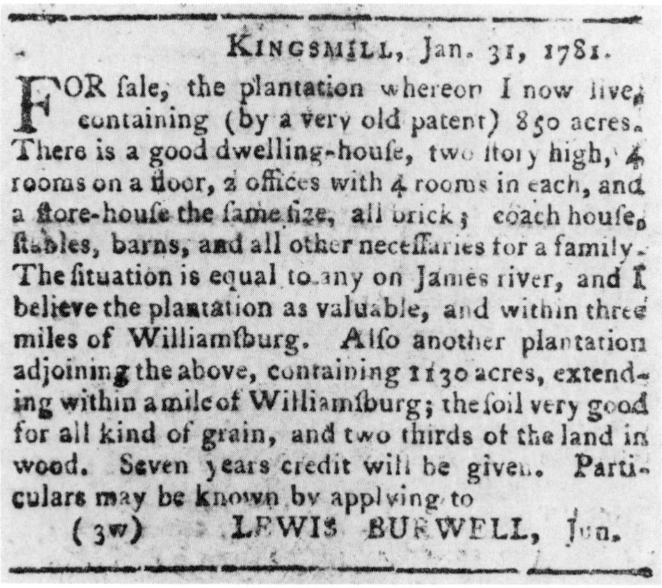

KINGSMILL, Jan. 31, 1781.

FOR fale, the plantation whereon I now live, containing (by a very old patent) 850 acres. There is a good dwelling-houfe, two ftoiy high, 4 rooms on a floor, 2 offices with 4 rooms in each, and a ftore-houfe the fame fize, all brick; coach houfe, ftables, barns, and all other neceffaries for a family. The fituation is equal to any on James river, and I believe the plantation as valuable, and within three miles of Williamfburg. Alfo another plantation adjoining the above, containing 1130 acres, extending within a mile of Williamfburg; the foil very good for all kind of grain, and two thirds of the land in wood. Seven years credit will be given. Particulars may be known by applying to
(3w)   LEWIS BURWELL, Jun.

Figure 26 Sale advertisement for Lewis Burwell's Kingsmill Plantation, February 17, 1781, *Virginia Gazette*.

ing with Williamsburg. Being the closest deep-water landing area to Williamsburg on the James, Burwell's Landing became a major port of entry for the city as the eighteenth century progressed. Also, since all ships passing that point on the James River were required to stop for inspection by the Naval Officer, the landing must have been a commercial and social hub of no small proportion.

In 1741 the noted horticulturalist, John Custis, considered the landing at "Coll. Burwells" a safe place to land and store his imported plants and seeds, suggesting that a warehouse of some substance stood on the property by that date. Seven years later the Virginia Assembly established a ferry across the James from Burwell's to Hogg Island, which continued in operation until at least 1785.[115]

Before the upsetting Revolutionary War years, the landing complex included an ordinary, or tavern, run by one Matthew Moody, Jr., who described his establishment in the *Virginia Gazette* in 1766. Moody claimed proprietorship of "a house of entertainment in the genteelest manner" and announced that "any goods stored with [him] will be taken care of, at a very cheap rate." Moody's establishment also included "[a] ferry house and a storehouse and all necessary outhouses."[116]

Samuel Coke, one-time proprietor of the Raleigh Tavern in Williamsburg, leased the landing in 1770. He advertised good entertainment for travelers, stabling for their horses, safe storage in the storehouse, and the future capability to have chairs and carts for hire "at a minute's warning."[117]

Figure 27 Detail from another version of Lt. Simcoe's maps, showing Burwell's house and gardens, 1781. (Colonial Williamsburg Foundation.)

The landing served a variety of commercial functions throughout the eighteenth century. Goods purchased from or bound for England were stored in the storehouse awaiting customer claims or the next transport. Ships and slaves were sold there on occasion, and a packet to Norfolk sailed from the landing weekly. The governor's yacht found a mooring place at Burwell's in 1771.[118]

Coke gave up the landing by 1773, at which time Burwell advertised it for rent. Apparently Thomas Cartwright had acquired the proprietary rights by January 1775, but strategic location and commercial importance inevitably entangled the landing and Cartwright in the violence of the Revolutionary War soon thereafter.[119]

A forewarning of the impending trouble appeared in the *Gazette* in March 1775, when the British announced:

A Caution to the Publick. Be it known, that his Majesty's armed schooner MAG-
DALEN, HENRY COLLINS, ESQ commander, mounting four carriage guns. . . now
lies moored opposite to Burwell's ferry, for the purpose of bringing to and searching all
vessels going up and down the James river. (Note well, masters and owners, that the King
pays *no costs or damages* in his Admiralty courts, whether your vessels, after siezure and
libelling, be condemned or not. These are *necessary expenses,* which must come out of *your
pockets,* therefore, it will behoove you to be on your guard.)[120]

The next month, a detachment of marines carried off the gunpowder from the
magazine in Williamsburg and loaded it on the *Magdalen* at Burwell's Landing.
Townspeople were outraged but cooled enough to limit their response to a peace-
ful remonstration of the governor. By November 1775, however, the ship-search-
ing policy at Burwell's led to open violence.

According to the *Gazette,* men from the British sloop *King Fisher* attempted to
board a vessel near the shore at Burwell's ferry, whereupon a rifle guard shot at
them. The *King Fisher* and three tenders then began a heavy cannonading, sending
one 6-pounder through the "storehouse at the waterside," and other shot hitting
the ferry house, "in which was a large family." A later account mentioned 10
riflemen stationed at the landing, and called the storehouse a "warehouse." In any
event, both accounts mention or imply that a waterside storage structure and a
nearby dwelling (the ferry master's house) stood at Burwell's.[121]

It is possible that the "large family" under fire at the ferry house belonged to
Thomas Cartwright, who, promptly and wisely, decided to leave Burwell's ferry
and set up business more out of the line of fire at "Mr. Thomas Doncastle upon the
main road to Williamsburg."[122] Soon thereafter American forces fortified the
landing area. A Captain Massie assumed the first command of the fortification,
followed in turn by a Captain Fox and a Captain Hobson. Troops built earthworks
along the edge of the two bluffs flanking the ferry landing beach. The troops and
forts at Burwell's, however, did not engage in any more military action until
1781.[123]

On April 17, 1781, the Queen's Rangers under Lt. Colonel Simcoe shelled
and captured the landing. The forementioned map of the engagement from Simcoe's journal showing the landing area, the two fortifications, and the course of
events illustrates his description of the action:

The troops arrived off Burrell's ferry on the 19th [April]; Lt. Col. Simcoe was
directed to land in such manner as he thought proper. The enemy had thrown up
entrenchments to secure the landing, and these appeared to be fully manned. The boats
were assembled at the small vessel on board which Lt. Col. Simcoe was, which was
anchored about two miles from the shore. Near a mile below the ferry was a small creek
which ran a little way into the land, from James river; and at the point formed by this
separation, it was determined to land. Capt. Ewald being disabled by his wound. . . the
yagers were divided between the Queen's Rangers and light infantry: Capt. Althouse's
company of rifle men was also under the command of Lt. Col. Simcoe. The boats,
preceded by the gun-boat, turned and rowed rapidly towards the point, where the
landing was to take place, assisted by the wind and tide; Major Armstrong, who com-
manded it, was desired to keep out of reach of musquet shot, and to fire his sixpounder at

the entrenchments, and particularly to scour a gully on the left, which the enemy must pass if they meant any opposition. The troops disembarked as intended; Capt. M'Kay with a detachment of the Queen's Rangers and yagers, landing below the inlet to beat up any party who might be in ambuscade there, and to give greater security to the right flank in case the enemy should attack the corps. Lt. Col. Simcoe met no opposition in his march to Burrell's ferry, from whence the enemy fled with precipitation, and where Gen. Phillips with the army immediately landed.[124]

The British, of course, did not linger to occupy their newly captured prizes at Kingsmill and by the following October the hostilities ended at Yorktown.

The military action may have precipitated Lewis V's move to Richmond, which seems to have taken place at about that same time. It could also be that the extensive Kingsmill woodlands were there to heal the soil from the adverse effects of decades of exhaustive tobacco culture. With that much acreage out of production and with the few funds left from his father's estate settlement to carry him, it was indeed a very auspicious time for Burwell to leave and try to unload the property. On the other hand, subsequent owners planted and profited from tobacco at Kingsmill. In any case, when Lewis V left Kingsmill for Richmond in 1781, the Burwell dynasty at Kingsmill ended.

The remaining years of Kingsmill's eighteenth-century tobacco production were apparently successfully directed by Henry Tazewell, attorney and United States senator in the 1790s. During Tazewell's ownership, Kingsmill had as many as 35 slaves listed on tax records, along with "18 horses 1 coach or chariot and 1 two wheeled carriage." Thereafter both Kingsmill and Littletown came together under the ownership of Arthur Allen who lived at Claremont, Surrey County, and who worked the Kingsmill tracts with tenants. Because his Kingsmill land value fell dramatically in 1844, it is reasonable to conclude that the Burwell brick mansionhouse was destroyed in that year.[125]

NOTES

[1]Edmund S. Morgan, *American Slavery American Freedom,* (New York, 1975), pp. 108–130; Warren M. Billings, *The Old Dominion in the Seventeenth Century,* (Chapel Hill, 1975), p. 8.

[2]Billings, *Old Dominion,* pp. 304–305.

[3]*Ibid.*

[4]*Ibid.,* p. 68, Jon Kukla, "Political Institutions in Virginia, 1619–1660," (Masters Thesis, University of Toronto, 1979), pp. 100–104.

[5]Morgan, *American Freedom,* p. 5.

[6]*Ibid.,* p. 112.

[7]Bernard Bailyn, "Politics and Social Structure in Virginia," in: James M. Smith, Ed., *Seventeenth Century America,* (New York, 1959), pp. 90–115.

[8]Morgan, *American Freedom,* p. 242.

[9]*Ibid.,* pp. 301, 423.

[10]Carter L. Hudgins, "The King's Realm: An Archaeological and Historical Study of Plantation Life at Robert Carter's Corotoman," (Master's Thesis, Wake Forest University, Winston-Salem, North Carolina 1981), pp. 23–34.

[11]Stiverson and Butler, eds., "Virginia in 1732," *Virginia Magazine of History and Biography,*

Volume LXXXV (1977), pp. 26–28, quoted in: Rhys Isaac, *The Transformation of Virginia, 1740–1790,* (Chapel Hill, 1982), p. 35.

[12]Paul G. E. Clemens, *The Atlantic Economy and Colonial Maryland's Eastern Shore,* (Ithaca and London, 1980), p. 23.

[13]Duke De La Rochefoucault Liancourt, *Travels Through the United States of North America,* (London, 1800), Vol. III, pp. 39–40.

[14]Susan M. Kingsbury, ed., *Records of the Virginia Company of London,* (Washington, 1935), Vol. IV, p. 259.

[15]Cary Carson *et al.,* "Impermanent Architecture in the Southern American Colonies," *Winterthur Portfolio,* (Chicago, 1981), Vol. 16, nos. 2/3, p. 140.

[16]*Ibid.,* p. 141.

[17]*Ibid.,* pp. 143–144.

[18]See Marcus Whiffen, *The Eighteenth Century Houses of Williamsburg,* (Williamsburg, Va., 1960), p. 35.

[19]Edmund S. Morgan, *American Slavery American Freedom,* (New York, 1975), p. 112.

[20]Carson, "Impermanent Architecture," p. 169.

[21]Richard Beale Davis, ed., *William Fitzhugh and his Chesapeake World,* 1676–1701, (Chapel Hill, 1963), p. 203.

[22]Carson, "Impermanent Architecture," p. 174.

[23]Carson, "Impermanent Architecture," pp. 187–189.

[24]*Ibid.,* pp. 187–189.

[25]*Ibid.,* pp. 179–196.

[26]Thomas Jefferson, *Notes on the State of Virginia,* (Philadelphia, 1794), p. 221.

[27]Warren M. Billings, *The Old Dominion in the Seventeenth Century,* (Chapel Hill, N.C., 1975), p. 306.

[28]Henry Glassie, *Folk Housing in Middle Virginia,* (Knoxville, Tennessee, 1975), pp. 21–25.

[29]Personal interviews with owner Harold Sinclair and his friends, Dick and Lois Harrington, May, 1983.

[30]See Thomas Tileston Waterman, *The Mansions of Virginia 1706–1776,* (Chapel Hill, North Carolina, 1946); and Whiffen, *The Eighteenth Century Houses of Williamsburg,* (Williamsburg, Virginia, 1960).

[31]Dell Upton, "Vernacular Domestic Architecture in Eighteenth Century Virginia," *Winterthur Portfolio,* (Chicago, 1982), Vol. 17, p. 197.

[32]*Ibid.,* p. 102.

[33]James Deetz, *In Small Things Forgotten,* (New York, 1977), *passim.*

[34]Billings, *Old Dominion,* p. 307.

[35]Lois Green Carr and Lorena S. Walsh, "Inventories and Analysis of Wealth and Consumption Patterns in St. Mary's County, Maryland, 1658–1777," (paper presented at the Newberry library Conference on Quantitative and Social Science Approaches in Early American History, n.d.), *passim;* and Barbara and Cary Carson, "Styles and Standards of Living in Southern Maryland, 1670–1752," (paper presented to the annual meeting of the Southern Historical Association, Atlanta, Georgia, Nov., 1976

[36]Thomas Shippen to William Shippen, October 24, 1797, (library of Congress).

[37]Thad W. Tate, Jr., *The Negro in Eighteenth Century Williamsburg,* (Williamsburg, VA., 1965), pp. 108–109.

[38]Muriel and Malcolm Bell, Jr., *Drums and Shadows,* (Athens, 1940), pp. 179.

[39]John Michael Vlach, *The Afro-American Tradition in Decorative Arts,* (Cleveland, Ohio, 1978), p. 126; and Deetz, *Small Things,* pp. 149–153.

[40]Edward Chappell, "Slave Housing" in *The Interpreter,* (Williamsburg, Virginia, Nov., 1982), pp. i–ii; and Eugene D. Genovese, *Roll Jordan Roll,* (New York, 1974), p. 527.

[41]J. F. D. Smyth, *Tour in the United States of America* (London, 1784),

[42]George W. Mc Daniel, *Hearth and Home*, (Philadelphia, 1982), p. 43.

[43]James O. Breeden, ed., *Advice Among Masters*, (Westport, Connecticut, 1980); Mc Daniel, *Hearth and Home, passim.*

[44]Breeden, *Advice*, p. 119.

[45]Dell Upton, "Slave Housing in Eighteenth Century Virginia," (Ms. Report, Dept. of Social and Cultural History, National Museum of American History, Smithsonian Institution, Washington, D. C., 1982), pp. 68–70.

[46]William M. Kelso, "Archaeological Survey of the Log Slave Quarter at Bremo Recess," (notes on file Thomas Jefferson Memorial Foundation, Charlottesville, Virginia, Dec., 1982.)

[47]Randall M. Miller, *Dear Master, Letters of a Slave Family,* (Ithaca and London, 1978), pp. 25–36.

[48]William M. Kelso, "A Report on the Archaeological Excavations at Monticello, Charlottesville, Virginia, 1979–1983," (mss. Thomas Jefferson Memorial Foundation, Charlottesville, Virginia,) pp. 84–88.

[49]However, test excavation produced artifacts all dating after circa 1850.

[50]Mc Daniel, *Hearth and Home*, pp. 45–103.

[51]*Ibid.,* pp. 131–186.

[52]Genovese, *Roll Jordan Roll*, p. 527.

[53]Mc Daniel, *Hearth and Home*, p. 104.

[54]Breeden, *Advice*, pp. 130–131.

[55]George Percy, "Observations Gathered out of A Discourse of the Plantation of the Southern Colony in Virginia by the English, 1606," David B. Quinn, ed., (Charlottesville, Virginia 1967), p. 15.

[56]I am most grateful for the research work of Margaret O. Peters and Martha Mc Cartney concerning the early seventeenth-century settlement of Kingsmill. I have also relied extensively on the manuscript report of Mrs. Mary R. M. Goodwin, "Kingsmill Plantation, James City County," (Colonial Williamsburg Foundation, Williamsburg, Virginia, 1958).

Susan M. Kingsbury, ed., *The Records of the Virginia Company of London,* Vol. IV, (Washington, 1935), p. 556, in Goodwin, "Kingsmill," p. 5.

[57]*Ibid.* Goodwin, "Kingsmill," p. 5.

[58](Muster, 1625) Martha W. Hiden, *Adventurers in Purse and Person,* (Princeton, New Jersey, 1956), p. 35. Thomas Farley apparently lived on the west side of Archers Hope when the muster was taken but, according to a patent of 1646, some of the land on the east was known as "Farlows" (Farley's?) Neck, suggesting that Farley either planted or moved to the land after 1625.

Nell Nugent, *Cavaliers and Pioneers, Abstracts of Virginia Land Patents 1623–1666,* (Baltimore, 1963), Vol. I, p. 161. Pott owned land to the north and probably ultimately Harrop and Tuttey's Neck. In any event, his widow, Elizabeth owned those tenements and conveyed it to her new husband Humprey Higginson in 1637.

Martha Mc Cartney, to William M. Kelso, March 31, 1983.

Nugent, *Cavaliers,* Vol. I, p. 80.

[59]Nugent, *Cavaliers,* Vol. I, p. 168, and Goodwin, "Kingsmill," p. 5.

[60]Nugent, *Cavaliers,* Vol. I, p. 178.

[61]William Waller Hening, *Statutes at Large,* (Richmond, Virginia, 1820), Vol. I, pp. 147–149.

[62]Nugent, *Cavaliers,* Vol, I, p. 168.

[63]Nugent, *Cavaliers,* Vol. I, p. 80, and Virginia State Library Acc. No. 24881 Deed Recorded Dec. 7, 1707, James City County Court in Mary A. Stephenson, "A Record of the Bray Family, 1658-ca. 1800," (mss. Colonial Williamsburg Foundation, Williamsburg, Virginia, 1963), p. 25. This is the first official record that Pettus once owned Utopia, probably by as early as the third quarter of the seventeenth century.

[64]Nugent, *Cavaliers,* Vol. I, p. 80.

[65]W. M. Stanard, *The Colonial Virginia Register,* (Baltimore, 1965, *passim.* Mc Cartney to Kelso, March 31, 1983.

[66]William W. Pettus IV to William M. Kelso, July 26, 1983. His inherited share of Virginia Company stock could not be documented but is a logical assumption.

[67]Hening, *Statutes,* Vol. I, p. 235.

[68]Nugent, *Cavaliers,* Vol. I, p. 159; Mc Cartney to Kelso, March 31, 1983.

[69]Deed December 7, 1707, James City County Court, (Virginia State Library, Accession Number 24881); Margaret O. Peters, "Littletown and Utopia," in William M. Kelso, "An Interim Report on Historical Archaeology at Kingsmill, 1972," Virginia Historic Landmarks Commission Research Center for Archaeology, Yorktown, Virginia, 1973), p. 8.

[70]*Virginia Magazine of History and Biography,* Vol. III, p. 159.

[71]Pocahontas H. Stacey, *The Pettus Family,* A. B. Rudd, ed., (Washington, D.C., 1956).

[72]H. R. Mc Ilwaine, ed., *Minutes of the Council and General Court of Colonial Virginia,* (Richmond, 1924), pp. 253, 259, 276. Mc Cartney to Kelso, March 31, 1983.

[73]Henrico County Miscellaneous Court Records, Vol. I, p. 73. Peters, "Littletown," p. 7.

[74]Mary A. Stephenson, "A Record of the Bray Family 1658–ca. 1800," (mss. Colonial Williamsburg Foundation, Williamsburg, Virginia, 1963), p. 20.

[75]*Ibid.,* p. 2.

[76]*Ibid.,* p. 5.

[77]William Byrd, *The Secret Diary of William Byrd of Westover,* Louis B. Wright and Marion Tinling, eds., (Richmond, Virginia, 1941), pp. 438–439.

[78]Stephenson, "Bray Family," p. 5.

[79]*Ibid.,* pp. 10, 19.

[80]James P. Mc Clure, "Littletown plantation, 1700–1745," (Master's Thesis, College of William & Mary, Williamsburg, Virginia 1977), pp. 109–112.

[81]*Ibid.,* p. 15.

[82]*Ibid.,* p. 38.

[83]Stephenson, "Bray Family," p. 22, and Ivor Noël Hume, "Excavations at Tutter's Neck in James City County, Virginia, 1960–61," *Contributions from the Museum of History and Technology:* Paper 53, (Washington, D.C., 1966), p. 35.

[84]Mc Clure, "Littletown," p. 41.

[85]*Ibid.,* p. 47.

[86]*Ibid.,* p. 50.

[87]*Ibid.,* p. 51.

[88]*Ibid.,* p. 61, n.

[89]*Ibid.,* p. 58.

[90]*Ibid.,* p. 65.

[91]*Ibid.,* pp. 74–83.

[92]*Ibid.,* pp. 88–98.

[93]*Ibid.,* p. 1-0.

[94]Stephenson, "Bray Family," pp. 20–21.

[95]Excavations of building sites by the author at Carter's Grove, shown on the Desandrouin Map, consistently proved the map to be accurate to within about 50 feet.

[96]Hiden, *Adventurers,* p. 108.

[97]Goodwin, "Kingsmill," pp. XIV.

[98]Will Book 14, York County, Virginia, pp. 60–64, quoted in Ann Camille Wells, "Kingsmill Plantation, A Cultural Analysis," (Master's Thesis, University of Virginia, Charlottesville, Virginia, 1976), pp. 12–13.

[99]Letter of Colonel Nathaniel Burwell, *William & Mary Quarterly,* (Series I, 1898–1899), pp. 43–44, quoted in Wells, "Kingsmill," pp. 14–15.

[100]William A. R. Goodwin, *Historical Sketch of Bruton Church,* (Petersburg, Virginia, 1903), p. 29, quoted in Wells, "Kingsmill," p. 15.

[101]Stephen Fouace to Lewis Burwell, Jan. 17, 1734, Tucker–Coleman Papers, (Colonial Williamsburg Foundation, Williamsburg, Virginia) quoted in Wells, "Kingsmill," pp. 17–18.

[102]William Waller Hening, *Statutes at Large,* (Richmond, Virginia 1820), Vol. IV, p. 535, quoted in Goodwin, "Kingsmill," pp. xxv.

[103]Earl Greg Swem, "Brothers of the Spade," *Proceedings of the American Antiquarian Society,* 58 (April, 1948), p. 181.

[104]Fouace to Burwell, 1734.

[105]Goodwin, "Kingsmill," pp. xxii.

[106]Hening, *Statutes,* IV: 534–537 in Wells, "Kingsmill," p. 21.

[107]Henry Read Mc Ilwaine, *Minutes of the Council and General Court of Virginia,* (Richmond, 1924), Vol. 5, p. 139.; Goodwin, "Kingsmill," p. xxviii.

[108]Wells, "Kingsmill," p. 25.

[109]*Ibid.*

[110]James City County Tax Lists, 1768–1769, (Virginia State Library, Richmond), p. 11.

[111]United States Circuit Court Record Book 7-G, 1798, (Virginia State Library, Richmond), p. 106 in Wells, "Kingsmill," p. 27.

[112]Goodwin, "Kingsmill," p. xxxviii.

[113]*Ibid.,* p. 34

[114]*Virginia Gazette and Weekly Advertiser,* (Dixon and Nicholson), November 16, 1782., p. 3.

[115]Letter from John Custis to Peter Collinson, n.d., (probably April 20, 1741). In Goddwin, "Kingsmill," pp. 70, 72.

[116]*Virginia Gazette,* (Purdie and Dixon), April 18, 1766.

[117]*Virginia Gazette,* (Purdie and Dixon), February 15, 1770.

[118]Goodwin, "Kingsmill," pp. 70–80.

[119]*Virginia Gazette,* (Purdie and Dixon), September 2, 1773, *Virginia Gazette,* (Dixon and Hunter), January 5, 1775.

[120]*Virginia Gazette* (Purdie), March 3, 1775.

[121]*Virginia Gazette,* (Dixon and Hunter), April 22, 1775; *Virginia Gazette,* (Purdie and Dixon), November 10, 1775.

[122]*Virginia Gazette,* (Purdie and Dixon), January 26, 1776.

[123]Goodwin, "Kingsmill," p. 83–84.

[124]Lt. Colonel Simcoe, *A Journal of the Operation Of the Queen's Rangers from the End of the Year 1777 to the Conclusion of the Late American War* (Exeter, 1787), pp. 131–134 quoted in Goodwin, "Kingsmill," pp. 86–87.

[125]Goodwin, "Kingsmill," p. 51.

3

FROM THE EARTH: SHELTER

SITES

As incomplete as they are, the documents do mention a considerable number of people associated with the Kingsmill property during the span of the two colonial centuries. All, of course, fit into two social and economic groups: those that owned the land and those that worked on it. The archaeological study of the property was approached with that in mind, so that at the end of the 3 years of digging, a comparative analysis could be made of the material worlds of Kingsmill's landlords and laborers alike. Fifteen sites eventually came under study: Littletown and Kingsmill tenements of the first half of the seventeenth century, Littletown Plantation of the Pettus family, a related settlement at Utopia, and fragments of the Harrop plantation, all 1640–1700; Bray's Littletown Plantation with its nearby quarter and other quarters at Tutter's Neck and Utopia, and a mill about 1700–1781; Kingsmill Plantation of the Burwell family with its three quarters—Kingsmill Quarter, North Quarter, and possibly another called Hampton Key; and finally the Burwell's Landing site, 1728–1790.

But the study promised to be more than a study in local history. A review of Virginia history leaves every impression that both the Kingsmill landlords and the laboring classes were typical of colonial Virginians generally. It follows then that archaeological and historical research designed to define patterns of life at every rung of the economic and social ladder at Kingsmill would produce a three-dimensional microcosmic Virginia. For the first time, an archaeological look at sites of the middle and lower classes, seen against and not overshadowed by the backdrop of the lifestyle of the elite, offered a democratic view of the colonial development of the Chesapeake region. The excavations in the field, laboratory, and library proved that these rather optimistic expectations were realistic.

George Percy and his adventurers on that day in May 1607 saw an inviting piece of real estate at what would become Kingsmill. Topographically, of course, it was much the same when excavations began as it had been then: relatively high, flat ground cut by seven or eight major ravines containing spring-fed creeks, ponds, and marshes of various sizes. The land lies on the outside radius of a severe bend in the James River, offering to settlers a clear view from its banks for 4 miles up and down stream (see Frontispiece). But the long, unobstructed stretch of river to the west also proved to be a disadvantage. There the prevailing west wind builds up tremendous waves that come crashing full speed into the shoreline at such an angle that as much as a foot of land a year is lost to erosion. Only that section slightly beyond the River Bend, part of Utopia, escapes this natural menace, and in fact the eroded soil begins settling out of the turbulence there, leaving the Utopia shore unscathed and slightly growing to the south.

But to Percy the situation was particularly secure, a location defensible with "but a little labour." And he leaves little question that the high, flat ground and original timber were especially good for agriculture. Considering all that, it is puzzling why no land claims appear until 1619. Perhaps people avoided the place because of an uncertainty of ownership. The establishment of Martin's Hundred, the enormous corporate settlement immediately east of Kingsmill, may have caused enough confusion over how far its legal boundaries extended that Kingsmill appeared already taken. A survey in 1622 finally established the eastern bounds of Martin's Hundred at Wareham's Pond, which may have opened land at Kingsmill for settlement soon thereafter.

Archaeology found clear evidence that the land was occupied during the first half of the seventeeth century, including the earliest site discovered on the Littletown section of the property. Two others were apparently occupied slightly later or longer: a site on Kingsmill Neck on the west and the fragments of a site of the same period on the same property but farther to the east (Farley's Neck?), later to become the site of Burwell's Kingsmill mansion and supporting dependencies. The remains of houses and domestic artifacts were found on all the sites, indicating that they were all homesteads. Since there is good historical evidence that tenants first lived and worked on the Kingsmill land, the sites became known for identification purposes as Littletown and Kingsmill tenements and Farley's. It is significant to note that all these early sites are located well back from the river shoreline near the head of ravines, all of which originally had freshwater springs.

Sites found to date after about 1635–1640 included the Colonel Thomas Pettus home plantation at Littletown, the small tenement or slave settlement at Utopia, a building at Kingsmill tenement, and a brick-lined well, probably all that escaped shoreline erosion at the site of Harrop House. All these sites were found to be decidedly domestic; they included the remains of houses, outbuildings, gardens, and well, and all, with the exception of the Kingsmill tenement building, were located relatively close to or on the river shore.

After the turn of the eighteenth century, new landowners chose to locate their houses along the high ridge that traverses the Kingsmill property in a southeasterly to northwesterly direction, high ground with a brilliant prospect of and from the river. The remains of a substantial brick mansion, frame and brick outbuildings, formal gardens, and wells were found on the ridge at Bray's Littletown and Burwell's Kingsmill. Two related sites of the same period were found superimposed on the remains of the earlier pioneer homesteads at Littletown and Kingsmill tenements, both apparently abandoned for a century until eighteenth-century reoccupation. Other quarters were located at Tuttey's Neck (a site excavated in the early 1960s) and another at Utopia, probably evidence of Deb's or Jacko's Quarter established during the James Bray II years at Littletown. Quarter sites on a northern section of the property included North Quarter and Hampton Key, probably the domicile of Burwell slaves during the last half of the eighteenth century. All these outlying sites were located near springs, all the buildings were of frame construction, and none of the settlements ever had a well.

The remains of leased commercial settlements dating to the eighteenth century included the ruins of a brick mill, the timber footings of an earlier mill-related building, the foundations of a warehouse, and a related house–kitchen–garden–well site, undoubtedly the remnants of the ordinary (tavern) at Burwell's Ferry Landing. The water mill was located on Kingsmill Creek where the banks were high and close enough together to permit the construction of an earthen dam. The landing location, of course, had to be on the river bank where wagons could easily descend from the higher agricultural ground to the water and on a section of the shoreline where there was a large beach area for the landing of small cargo boats.

MANOR AND TENEMENTS

Although there is considerable uncertainty about dating sites from the early seventeenth century strictly by the presumed manufacturing dates of associated artifacts, it seems reasonably certain that the initial occupation at the site known as the Littletown tenement, probably patented by either William Clayborne or John Jefferson, is one of the earliest settlements at Kingsmill[1] (see Figure 28). The removal of plowed soil from the 1-acre site revealed rectangular patterns of dark soil stains in the light-yellow clay subsoil, the remains of decayed structural wooden timbers of two eighteenth- and two seventeenth-century frame houses (see Figures 29 and 30). Larger areas of darker rectangular soil deposits and an oval soil stain nearby marked the location of small eighteenth-century storage cellars and a trashpit filled during the second quarter of the seventeenth century. The seventeenth-century house remains included two series of posthole patterns, the one composed of 10 large rectangular postholes with clearly visible post impressions (postmolds) and 9 smaller circular holes. Both formed a rectangular pattern oriented slightly east of the 1974 magnetic north, but because the original excavation of one of the larger holes cut into the stain of one of the smaller holes, it is clear that the smaller holes had been put in earlier.

Archaeological excavation of the two posthole series found that the smaller holes (averaging 1′ in diameter) contained a uniform dark soil suggesting that they

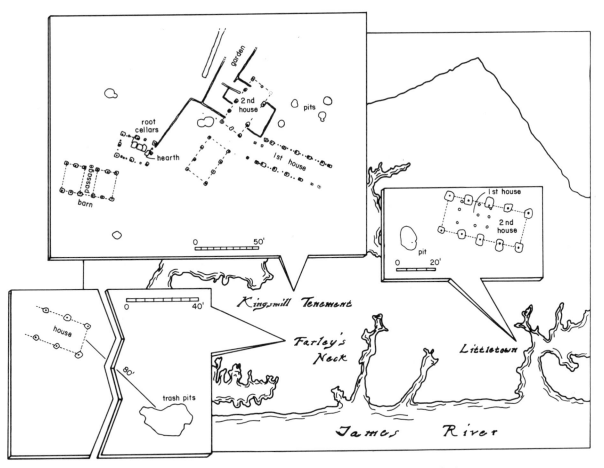

Figure 28 Early seventeenth-century tenant settlements at Kingsmill. (Sondy Sanford.)

were formed solely by the decomposition of an upright wooden timber. On the other hand, the larger series of stains (4' square, 2' deep, on the average) were formed by the initial digging of uniformly cut construction holes, subsequently backfilled around undressed timbers about 11" in diameter (see Figures 29 and 30). Moreover, three of the larger holes located on the southeastern corner of the overall rectangular pattern showed clear evidence that, over time, these timbers were periodically replaced, four times at the southeast corner, three times in the hole immediately west of that, and at least once at the third post next to that.

Considering the domestic nature of the associated artifacts and the historical evidence of homesteading patterns and earthfast houses in the Chesapeake area, there is little doubt that the rectangular patterns are the remains of two periods of houses. Although only enclosing a space of 12'6" × 16'6", the earliest series of

Figure 29 Cross-section through the main structural posthole of earthfast timber, "second stage" house, Littletown tenement. Note the dark stain left by the decayed post (left center). (Virginia Historic Landmarks Commission.)

postholes probably represents a relatively crude and impermanent two-room structure supported by nine driven timbers. That construction technique would have required relatively little time and unsophisticated framing, which in turn called for no particularly special carpentry skill.

Of course, interpreting the smaller holes as the remnants of an earlier house from the Littletown evidence alone would be highly questionable, but similar, more complete archaeological data from other sites give the Littletown interpretation more credibility. Several small "driven post"house sites were found on an obvious domestic and military site on The Maine property near Jamestown. Occupied about 1618 to 1630, the houses were probably supported by the "puches sett into the ground and covered with boards" described in 1623.[2]

Why the small Littletown structure needed two rooms, one as small as 7' × 12'6", is unclear, but a contemporary painting of the interior of what appears to be a Dutch peasant's house shows a very narrow cooking room in what seems to be a similar structure (see Figures 31 and 32). Perhaps the middle line of posts at Littletown supplied the additional support needed to carry the weight of a similar chimney hood in an equally diminutive room. Otherwise, there is no evidence of a fireplace, but any burned soil may have long since been plowed away there.

Figure 30 Posthole–postmold and rootcellar pattern of two periods of seventeenth-century earthfast houses (background right) and two contempory eighteenth-century slave quarters (background left and foreground), Littletown, Kingsmill, Virginia. (Virginia Historic Landmarks Commission.)

Once the smaller "puches" house was removed or it fell into decay, Littletown settlers erected a more permanent 41′ × 18′ building in the same location supported by five sets of frames spaced in four 10′ construction units, traditionally known as "bays." The uniformity of the size and "floors" of the postholes suggests that the supporting frames were raised in tie-beam pairs, that is in prefabricated units consisting of two opposite upright posts tied together by a connecting horizontal beam. This type of construction required either the insertion of "interrupted" sills between each tie beam if the house was to have a raised wooden floor, or intermediate horizontal braces mortised between each upright. The sills or intermediate horizontal bracing, in turn, explain the oversizing and leveling of the floors of the postholes. They had to be uniform so that the builders could jockey the posts into the joinery of each successive interrupted sill or brace. In other words, the original construction posthole had to be of a uniform depth and large

Figure 31 Coarse earthenware bowl from Littletown tenement, matching a vessel depicted by Pieter Roestraten (Figure 32); first half of the seventeenth century. (Virginia Historic Landmarks Commission.)

enough so that the prefabricated mortise and tenons would line up with the tie beams on the same horizontal plane and so that the tie beams could be maneuvered into the sill joints.

All this was not crystal clear from the archaeological evidence alone, even though the uniformity of these and other postholes from similar sites was always a clear pattern. Recent experimental reconstruction of timber houses and tobacco barns conducted by the St. Mary's City Commission supplements archaeological theory (see Figure 33). The modern St. Mary's builders found that in erecting a tobacco barn by raising tie-beam pairs the postholes did indeed have to have uniform depth and be large enough to accommodate the mortise-and-tenon joints of interrupted horizontal wall supports (the buildings had no raised floor). In fact, the modern experimental housewrights found that malleting in the sills was a necessary and recurring step in construction, something they had not planned on originally but found essential as they went along.[3]

Again, the Littletown Tenement site was plowed; thus if it had only a dirt floor, the evidence would be gone. On the other hand, the few similar sites excavated elsewhere that had never been plowed indicate that they did have elevated wooden floors supported on what must have been interrupted sills.[4] The extant post building at Cedar Park, Maryland, also has them (see Figure 11 above).

Figure 32 Pieter Roestraten painting "De Pannenkoekenbakster" (the pancake baker) showing a coarse earthenware bowl (lower left) identical to a vessel found at Littletown Tenement (Figure 31); first half of the seventeenth century. (Collection Museum Bredius—The Hague.)

Figure 33 Tie-beam earthfast construction at St. Mary's City, Maryland, showing positioning of (a) main structural tie-beam pairs and (b) malleting posts in oversized postholes to fit horizontal wall bracing, a process that explains the "oversized" holes usually found on seventeenth-century sites of earthfast buildings (see also Figures 90 and 91.)

Evidence from Cedar Park and other similar archaeological sites also can serve as a parallel for a reconstruction of the Littletown house in other ways (see Figure 34). Although the Littletown house is one bay longer than Cedar Park, it is reasonable to suppose that it had a similar hall–parlor floor plan under the sizable loft that would be created by a steeply pitched Cedar Park roof.[5] But there is negative evidence that, unlike Cedar Park, Littletown tenement did not have brick chimneys; no brick was found on the site at all. That suggests that the building had a free-standing timber and mud-daubed chimney, or merely a timber hood over a dirt hearth, a common arrangement in houses of this type. For example, excavation of the Clifts Plantation at Stratford Hall, Westmoreland County, uncovered the remains of the manor house, an earthfast four-bay building (see Figure 35).[6] Within the posthole pattern, a rectangular burned area—apparently the firehearth located between the hall and parlor—survived plowing. Other archaeological evidence indicated the Clifts house once had doors near one end, evidence perhaps that a cross-passage once existed there between the parlor and a service bay. If that were so, the Clifts plan included four rooms altogether—hall, parlor, cross-passage, and service bay—and it is possible that the Littletown house of the same size followed suit. In any case, like Cedar Park, it is likely that the walls were covered with clapboards in 5′ lengths, and it is likely that small windows pierced the clapboarding on the gables to light the loft. Windows were apparently not glazed, however; no window glass was found on the site dating to the seventeenth-century occupation.

The Littletown Tenement house stood alone, but the tenants at Kingsmill Tenement, on Kingsmill Neck, 1½ miles to the west, required much more covered space for their homesteading venture (see Figures 35–38). At least five earthfast structures stood there, ranging in size from 50′ × 18′ to 24′ × 16′. The stratigraphy again had been plowed away to a depth of an average of 1′, none of the posthole patterns ever intersected at any point and all the patterns aligned or stood at basic right angles to one another. Consequently, it was difficult to determine whether the buildings all stood at one time, if they represented a progressive series of constructions through time, or whether one building stood for a time only to be razed and then replaced by another. Associated artifacts and other features, although dating the occupation to about 1620 to 1660, failed to sort out individual time periods for buildings as well. Nonetheless, their locations relative to each other and the existence of a trench-laid fence connecting two of the structures do suggest some contemporaneity.

The remains of the largest and perhaps earliest seventeenth-century structure, presumably a house, consisted of a core section of six bays marked by large rectangular postholes and postmolds, with a series of three smaller holes on the west (see Figures 28 and 36). The bays narrowed at each end to 5′ but maintained a 10′ width across the center. Also, between most of the larger postholes, several smaller postmolds were found, apparently the remnants of smaller (6″) wall studs driven every 2′6″.

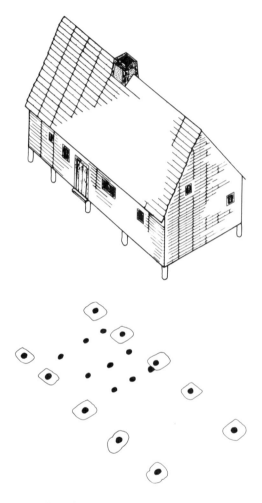

Figure 34 Artist's reconstruction of "second stage" earthfast house, Littletown Tenement, second-quarter seventeenth century.

Again, seen against the background of the construction details of Cedar Park and the Clifts archaeological site, it is reasonable to suggest that this building was like Littletown tenement, a house raised and supported by tie-beam posts. One thing is almost certain, however: The use of earthfast wall studs indicates that the Kingsmill Tenement building had an earth floor. Otherwise, the wall studs would never have had to go into the ground. That is, if an interrupted sill ever existed like

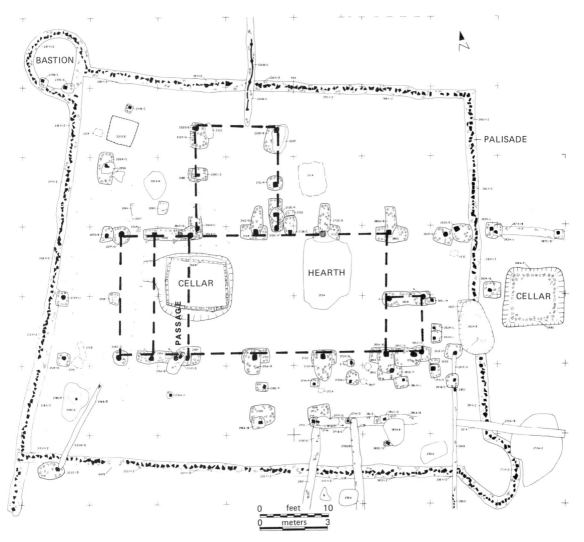

Figure 35 The "manner house on the Clifts," an earthfast house site excavated at Stratford Hall, Westmoreland County, Virginia, circa 1670. (Fraser Neiman, Robert E. Lee Memorial Foundation.)

that which survives at Cedar Park, the studs would be tied into them rather than embedded into the earth below. Thus, unless the floor for this building was supported on a groundsill laid inside the main wall line, it had no sill and consequently no suspended wooden floor. Unfortunately, no trace of the floor survived below the plow zone, nor did any evidence of fireplaces. Nonetheless, the abrupt change in the bay size at each end of the structure suggests that additional strength was

Figure 36 Posthole patterns of early seventeenth-century house sites and an eighteenth-century slave quarter (upper left) at the Kingsmill Tenement and Kingsmill Quarter site, 1974. (Virginia Historic Landmarks Commission.)

required there to support suspended end fireplace hoods. Also, the absence of appreciable amounts of brick on the site argues for timber and clay chimney work.

Changes in the stud intervals may mark the location of a door 20′ from the southeastern corner. This location would not be unlike the Clifts cross-passage door location. There may also have been a doorway on the southwestern end of the building, through a shed or porch supported there by three additional postholes.

Like the building at Littletown, the framework of the house appears to have a four-bay core section, but it also has the half-chimney bays at each end, making the main building 50′ × 18′. A hall–parlor plan with a loft above again seems logical in light of Cedar Park, as does a cross-passage service room similar to that at the Clifts (see Figure 37).

Curiously enough, no wall stud holes were found along the end wall line of the house, but their absence may be more evidence that this building was constructed by erecting prefabricated tie beams. It would have been impossible for the builders, once the tie beams were in place, to drive wall studs at each end of the house because the tie beam overhead would be in the way. On the other hand, studs could be easily driven into the ground between each tie beam where the stud

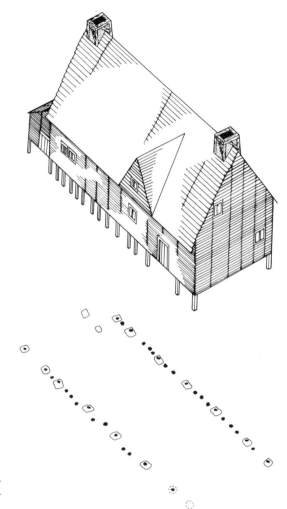

Figure 37 Archaeological plan and artist's reconstruction of "first stage" earthfast house, Kingsmill Tenement.

holes were found, along the long axis of the house—that is, until the wall plate was hoisted into place. It could also be that the lack of stud holes on each end is evidence of some totally unique construction.[7]

Excavations to the north of the earthfast post-and-stud building uncovered another configuration of postholes so close to the post-and-stud structure that it may be the remains of a building that replaced it. There a rectangular pattern of five postholes with smaller postholes centered at each end was uncovered, along with aligned slot trenches on each side. The holes undoubtedly mark a four-bay, 40′ × 18′ house of earthfast construction, and the slot trenches signal additions on the

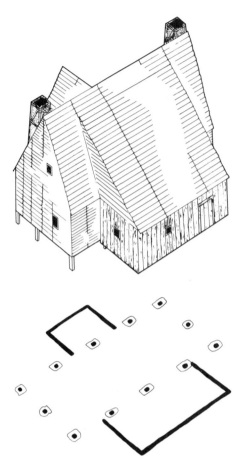

Figure 38 Archaeological plan and artist's reconstruction of "second stage" crossplan earthfast house, Kingsmill Tenement.

east and west (see Figure 38). Remnants of a ground-laid sill in the trench on the east suggests that the additions were not small fenced enclosures appended to the house, but rather horizontally laid and dressed timbers into which vertical wall boards and studs were seated. That being the case, the building formed a "cross" (crossplan) house, a fairly common seventeenth-century plan that usually employed the smaller "cross rooms" as stairtower and porch chamber on either side of a hall–parlor house.[8] It is unlikely, however, that the Kingsmill Tenement, ground-laid sill construction would support any substantial construction like a stair "tower," but rather represents simple shed additions. Also, the chimneys must have been equally insubstantial; they were probably simple chimney hoods supported by additional timbers seated in the postholes found in the center of each end wall line. Multiple series of overlapping postholes along the long wall line, like the same evidence at Littletown Tenement, suggest that the Kingsmill building stood long enough for the posts to require repairs or replacement.

Yet another posthole pattern was uncovered 50′ southwest of the crossplan house. Both large postholes and postmolds marked the structural remains and, like the largest structure at the site, smaller molds were found between the larger holes, undoubtedly marking wall stud locations. An additional posthole, too, was found at the center of each narrow end, but significantly an area of burned clay survived plowing on the east, just inside the wall line. This gives clear evidence that the centered postholes do indeed indicate chimney locations. Why the clay was burned so deeply at the site of the smaller building and not on the sites of the other structures is puzzling. Perhaps the fireplace in an exterior kitchen, if that is what the smaller building was used for, would create more intense heat for a longer period than would fireplaces used only to heat domestic dwellings. Consequently, plowing would erase the shallower burned earth but leave some of the deeper scorched soil in a kitchen undisturbed.

The smaller structure also included depressions roughly oriented with the axis of the wall lines of the building; perhaps these were the bottom few inches of shallow cellars for root storage. One of the cellars contained a clay pipe-bowl dating to the second half of the seventeenth century, making this the latest deposit on the site. Although none of the other post structures had datable artifacts in fill deposited during construction or early occupation, this smaller building nonetheless may have been occupied the longest. By the same token, the relatively diminutive size and the driven wall studs suggest that construction occurred relatively early in the occupation of the site. Perhaps it was built earlier, but, unlike the small driven-post building at Littletown Tenement, it was recycled into use as a detached kitchen and not removed. It is also possible that when black labor came to Kingsmill the smaller detached building became a slave quarter.

An additional series of postholes aligned directly with the crossplan house, a three-bay set of eight holes located 13′ southwest of the house. It is possible that the structure supported by those timbers was attached directly to the crossplan house, with the greater spaces between the two posthole patterns designed for an open but roofed passage separating the house living area to the north from a barn for animals and/or grain storage to the south. This was not an uncommon arrangement in the long houses of medieval and early modern England.[9]

Excavations at the Kingsmill home plantation (Farley's) uncovered the fragmented remains of one other settlement dating primarily to the first half of the seventeenth century, but the construction of Lewis Burwell's mansion basement there in the eighteenth century destroyed much of the archaeological evidence. Six rectangular posthole molds survived however, along with a trashpit containing artifacts of circa mid-seventeenth-century date, enough to indicate that yet another timber house once stood at that Kingsmill location. Since the southwestern end of the building was destroyed when Burwell's builders originally excavated the mansion cellar hole, it is impossible to determine how many bays the earlier house incorporated in its construction, but it is clear that each bay was 12′ long and that the structure was the standard 18′ across. The incomplete nature of the archaeological remains obviously limits any fine interpretation of this building, but it can serve to illustrate once again the total dominance of earthfast houses at Kingsmill during the seventeenth century.

It is clear from the testimony of the two relatively undisturbed tenement sites and the fragmented remains at Farley's that the houses of the second quarter of the seventeenth century were made exclusively of earthfast construction, with variation only in minor detail. There appears to have been a succession of houses, with the earliest types employing only driven or a combination of driven and prepared posthole-supported timbers. These earliest dwellings were then replaced or supplemented by the construction of houses employing earthfast structural posts seated in prepared postholes, which may indicate that a switch was made from a simple dirt floor to flooring raised on elevated sills.

House dimensions are strikingly similar. At both the Kingsmill and Littletown Tenements, full posthole plans or what appear to be core sections are about 40' long—divided into four 10'-bay intervals—and are invariably 18' wide. Also, the absence of brick from the site deposits, certain other posthole locations or variations in the spacing between posts, and, in one case, the survival of unplowed burned clay associated with adjacent posthole patterns, together suggest that all of these early dwellings had wooden fireplace hoods or wooden chimney stacks.

At about the time Littletown Tenement was abandoned, Colonel Thomas Pettus combined the Littletown and Utopia tracts, and after circa 1641 he became the first documented landowner to reside on the property (see Figure 39). His enlarged plantation required a considerable labor force and some of these laborers lived during the third quarter of the seventeenth century at Utopia. There is some question about the exact social and economic status of the laborers at Utopia; there is some reason to believe that they were tenants, servants, or even slaves.[10] Pettus had them all. There is no doubt, however, that the people who lived at Utopia were indeed a part of Pettus's labor force in some capacity and, as such, their house site provides an archaeological glimpse at the material world of the lower classes during the latter part of the 1600s.

The remains of the Utopia house show that the earthfast building tradition, as impermanent as it was, did persist throughout the seventeenth century, but certain more permanent details were added for comfort and convenience. The excavations uncovered a posthole–postmold pattern defining a three-bay dwelling, 29' × 18', with additional half-bay additions on each end (see Figures 40 and 41). It is probable that, like the half bays on the ends of the post-and-stud structure at Kingsmill Tenement, the additions to the Utopia structure were put there by the builders for the additional support needed by a timber chimney or fireplace hood. A half-basement lay under the house and was entered by means of bulkhead steps at the southwest corner of the post pattern. It is evident the basement was added to the house after it was already standing, because excavating for the basement construction disturbed one of the postholes of the main supports of the house.

The basement was lined with hard, red, undersized bricks, a type usually called "English" paving bricks. The floor bricks were laid in such a manner that any water

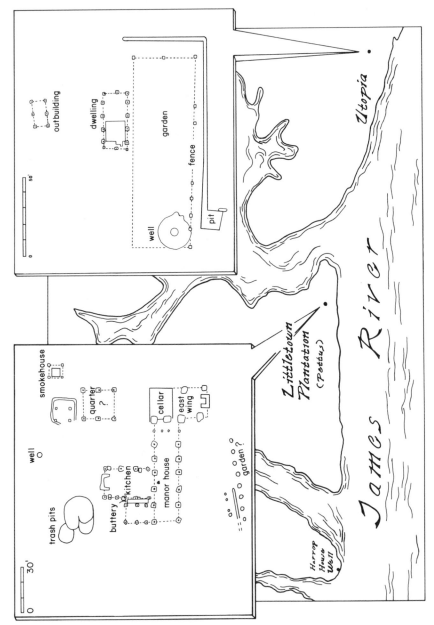

Figure 39 Archaeological plans of Colonel Thomas Pettus's Littletown, circa 1641–1700. (Sondy Sanford.)

Figure 40 Overhead view of Utopia earthfast house after excavation, showing main structural support postholes, brick-lined half-cellar, and chimney support holes at each end. (Virginia Historic Landmarks Commission.)

seeping through the walls would drain into a sump in the southwest corner. The bulkhead steps were also supported with the paving bricks. Sockets in the bulkhead walls at the edge of each riser and carbonized traces of wood indicate that each step once had a wooden nosing, and that they and the house were destroyed by fire. Soon after that, about one-third of the flooring and the east wall were removed, undoubtedly to salvage the bricks for other colonial construction.

The stratigraphy of the soil in the basement fill was typical of a fire-razed building: an occupation level on the floor, ash from the fire about that, brick rubble from dismantling the ruin above that, then humus extending to the plowed ground surface. Fragments of a Rhenish stoneware Bellarmine bottle found in the lower ash level suggest occupation between 1650 and 1670. A fragment of a glass wine-bottle seal, bearing the anagramatic name J BRAY found just above the brick-rubble level, indicates that the brick scavanging of the open cellar took place after 1700, the date James Bray acquired the property (see Figure 113).[11] No datable artifacts were found in construction deposits on the site, but the range of wine-

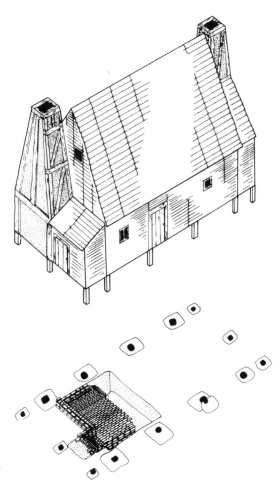

Figure 41 Archaeological plan and artist's reconstruction of Utopia house, circa 1660–1710.

bottle styles and clay pipes recovered from the cellar fill and the nearby well, and a quantified analysis of the range of manufacturing dates of the ceramics from the site, suggest an occupation span of about 40 years, circa 1670–1710.[12]

The uniformity of the shapes and sizes of the postholes again indicates that the house was razed and supported by tie-beam timber pairs, one of which needed repairing during the lifetime of the building. Also, in keeping with Cedar Park as a model, the building was probably covered with 5′ sections of clapboarding. The recovery of glass on the site also suggests that the house had glazed windows, probably informally placed wherever light was most needed on the ground-floor room and in the loft. Again, no heavily burned areas indicated fireplaces, only the half-bay posthole spacing suggests that fireplaces stood at each end. Actually the hoods may have been located in each corner of the building. At least that had to be true on the west end where half of the bay on the west served as the bulkhead entrance to the basement. Of course, the fireplace at the other end of the building could have extended completely across the width of the room. But, whatever the size of the chimneys or hoods, the recovered fired fragments of clay with impressions of wood lathing are good evidence that the structures were timber with clay daubing.

The brickwork, relative uniformity of construction, and the window glass on the Utopia site suggest that by the second half of the seventeenth century, laborers, perhaps tenants, were being provided with or built themselves more substantial dwellings than their earlier pioneering forebears. Yet the Utopia house was one bay smaller than the dwellings at Littletown and Kingsmill of a half century earlier, but earthfast main framing with its standard 18′ width was still in the lexicon of the builders. In fact, a look at the archaeological remains of the house of the landlord, Thomas Pettus, clearly indicates that the earthfast building tradition quite unexpectedly served those of higher social and economic rank as well.

There is indeed some doubt that any landowner ever lived at Kingsmill before the 1640s despite the fact that Humphrey Higginson had a patent in the mid-1630s. But archaeological evidence leaves little question that the other major resident landlord, Colonel Thomas Pettus, lived at Littletown in the early 1640s. The complex of earthfast building remains found at the seventeenth-century Littletown home plantation site are the considerable remains of the Pettus house and its supporting outbuildings, all of which provide evidence of the built environment of one member of Virginia's developing plantation aristocracy.

Digging at the Pettus site unearthed a complex series of posthole–postmold patterns, the most complicated series being the remnants of the manor house itself (Figures 39, 42–44). There, a posthole–postmold pattern of five 10′ bays defined a core structure, apparently the first building to be built on the site. The fact that, unlike most of the other post patterns, the posthole fill was either devoid of artifacts or contained exclusively prehistoric Indian pottery argues for the relative early date for the core.

Another set of postholes to the east of the core also contained no artifacts, again suggesting early construction. The postholes indicate a three-bay 32′ × 18′ plan, with a 15′ × 18′6″-deep cellar on the north lined with English paving bricks identical to those found at Utopia. The structure also had a rather massive brick chimney foundation on the south end (6′ × 10′). Artifacts found in a related set of postholes between the cellar wing and the core, together with hole size and location, indicate that lighter timbers once supported construction that eventually connected the wing with the original core structure. The core and the east-wing buildings had the same uniformly cut postholes as the other Kingsmill earthfast houses, and so tie-beam pair framing and erection must have been employed for the Pettus structures as well.

The east wing is similar to the house at Utopia, with its cellar added to the building after the construction of the superstructure. The dry-laid brick walls were

Figure 42 Archaeological remains of Colonel Thomas Pettus's Littletown manor and Quarter (upper left) showing half-cellar under east wing (upper right), core (right), additions, and buttery (center and lower left). (Virginia Historic Landmarks Commission.)

1½course thick. Postholes and a burned timber on the floor indiate that, unlike the Utopia house, a stairway from inside the building and not a bulkhead from without served as the entrance. Curiously, the construction of the cellar seems to have undermined the original two support posts and, in fact, erased the postholes entirely on the northeast corner of the east wall. It must be that the brick wall of the cellar underpinned the posts and thereafter replaced what had been the supporting earth packed around them.

A small remnant of a brick foundation within the core building was also found, suggesting that a brick chimney stood 25′ from the west end. If that is true, the stack divided the house into an equal hall–parlor plan. Traces of shallow trenches or ditches were found connecting the postholes at the west end, and between the first two postholes along the north wall line. Slight traces of the trenching survived plowing on the east as well. The trenches roughly aligned with the postmolds, but they did not extend across and in fact were cut by posthole fill. In that case, the trenches predate the post-supported building, which rules out the possibility that they mark the location of a groundsill. They may have served builders by marking off the wall line of the house just prior to construction.

Like the eventual connection of the core and the east wing, another building, a

Figure 43 Pettus manor house, east wing, showing half-cellar with few wall bricks remaining (foreground), and massive brick chimney footing (background). (Virginia Historic Landmarks Commission.)

two-bay "kitchen" with exterior end masonry fireplace, was enlarged and attached to the center of the core. In fact, three sets of postholes from three separate periods of timber supports were found: the earliest contained only Indian pottery or no artifacts; the second contained pre-1650 tobacco-pipe fragments; and the third, which tied the two buildings together, contained bottle glass dating after circa 1660. The third-period construction was itself in turn expanded with the addition of a frame room over a 4' × 9' brick and tile "cellar." The cellar also had a brick sump and brick steps on the north. Along with the tile floor, the masonry indicated that the small room was used for a dairy or buttery.

Over time then, the Littletown manor became a very large house, with over 2500 square feet on the ground floor alone. And there is every reason to believe that a steep roof like the Cedar Park model created a spacious second story as well. That being the case with the east and north wings, the structure covered 4500 square feet of living space, 3600 square feet more than Utopia and considerably more than the single houses of the earlier period at Littletown Tenement and

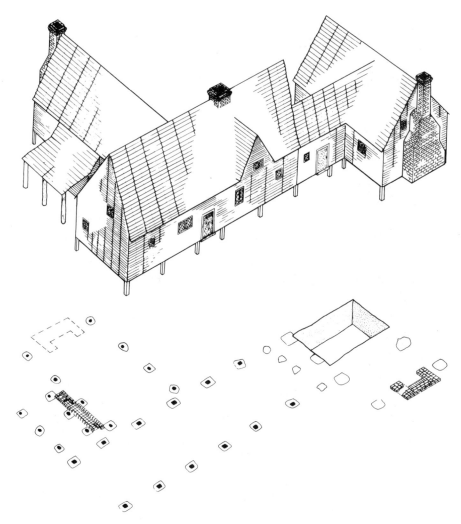

Figure 44 Archaeological plan and artist's reconstruction of the Pettus manor, Littletown.

Kingsmill. Moreover, the use of brick in chimneys, the cellar, and the buttery lend an added air of permanence in comparison to the Kingsmill houses of the early part of the century. Not only the bricks but the recovery of window glass suggest a better quality of construction. In fact, a restorable section of the turned lead and glazing of a 13″ × 15″ casement window was recovered in the destruction levels of the east wing, suggesting yet more amenities for the landlord's house (Figure 45).

The stratigraphy in the cellar contained ash, the floor was scorched, and postmolds in the core section contained the remnants of charred posts, all indicating that the building burned, probably after circa 1680–1700, the date suggested

Figure 45 Remains of casement window glazing and (left to right) fluted, marbleized delft bowl, enameled mirror or knife handle, glass wine-bottle seal ("T P" = Thomas Pettus), brass book clasp, and brass basket stirrup from Pettus's Littletown. (Virginia Historic Landmarks Commission.)

by the tobacco-pipe bowls found in a post-fire layer in the cellar fill. A fragment of a wine glass of the period 1620–1660 found in the construction backfill of the cellar wall tends to confirm a construction date of the buildings to circa 1650 and possibly as early as 1641, the year Pettus first appears in the list of the Governor's Councillors.[13]

No other archaeological evidence of Kingsmill's landlords was found, with the possible exception of the lone well shaft at Burwell's Landing. That may have been all that escaped erosion of Humphrey Higginson's Harrop House.

MANSIONS AND HOUSES

Considerably more survived, archaeologically, of the houses of the eighteenth-century Kingsmill landowners. Both Bray and Burwell built with brick. By 1700, when records suggest that James Bray II moved to Littletown, excavations at the Pettus manor site indicate that the buildings were burned and abandoned. An impressive brick mansion house took its place, 240 yards to the west, where excavations uncovered the substantial, all-brick foundation of Bray's mansion (Figure 46). It is clear that the landlords by this time abandoned the traditional earth-fast construction in favor of masonry. Also, unlike Pettus's rather casual floor plan, which grew through time to meet whatever new space needs arose, the Brays planned enough in the beginning so that their house never needed additions and little repair regardless, it seems, of changing needs.

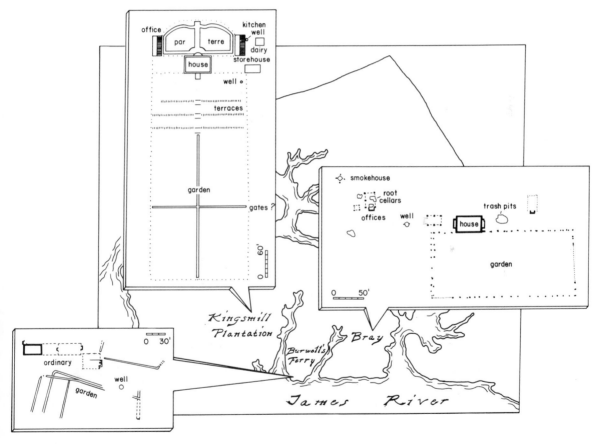

Figure 46 Archaeological plans of Bray's Littletown, Burwell's Kingsmill, and Burwell's Landing Ordinary. (Sondy Sanford.)

The Bray mansion was so substantially built that even its buried foundation could be detected from the air and by a quick probe survey (Figure 47). The buried brickwork and the backfilled full basement left a distinct dark soil and crop mark on preexcavation black-and-white photographs, and probing at that location with a simple metal rod defined exactly the extent of the footing before a shovel went into the ground. Subsequent removal of the plowzone revealed the rectangular foundation with the full English basement (3′ below grade), massive chimney footings at each end, and the brick walls of an exterior bulkhead entrance to the basement (Figures 48 and 49). The foundation measures 29′ × 53′ overall, the two-course-thick wall footing suggesting that the house stood one-and-one-half stories high. The chimney foundations indicate that the house had multiple fireplaces at each end. Masonry was not used for the subfloor of any of the flues; thus the four rectangles of clay found at the center of the brick chimney footings locate and indicate the size of the four fireplaces. From this it is certain that at least four rooms existed on the first floor, probably the hall and parlor on the south and smaller dining and sleeping rooms to the north, each heated by its own fireplace in the

Figure 47   Aerial view of the Littletown section of Kingsmill, showing soil mark at the Bray mansion site (circle). (Virginia Department of Highways.)

Figure 48 Mansion ruins at Bray's Littletown, earliest brick house at Kingsmill. (Virginia Historic Landmarks Commission.)

corner.[14] The massive size (8') of the flues on the south indicates that cooking could have been done in either of the larger rooms as well.

Other architectural evidence survived to indicate the room plan of the house. The remnants of one-course-thick partition walls in the basement were found, indicating the plan of the basement rooms. Since the partitions must have carried some of the load of the interior first floor walls as well, the first-floor plan must have been similar to the basement. That being the case, the full first-floor plan, in addition to the four heated rooms indicated by the fireplaces, may well have included a central lobby entrance on the south with a third, smaller, unheated room at the center of the house on the north, or a hall or passage through the center of the house.

In the basement, four of the rooms had simple unpaved earth floors, but the 9' × 16' room in the northwest corner was paved with square brick-tile. Its walls had traces of plaster on them and there was a 2-foot-square, brick-lined drainage sump in the northeast corner. Two small postholes cut through the tiles near the center of the room, and some of the tile between the holes appeared to have excessive wear.

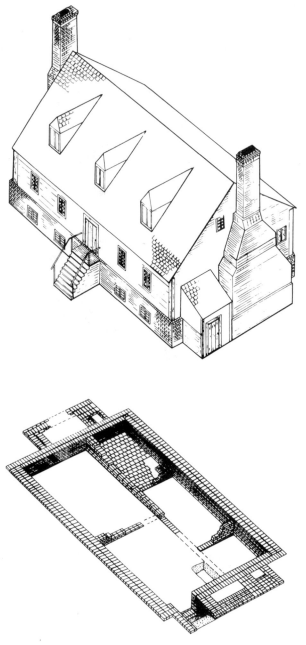

Figure 49 Archaeological plan and artist's reconstruction of the Bray mansion at Littletown, Kingsmill, circa 1700. (Leonard Winter.)

The tiles, plaster, and sump seem to indicate that the room was a wine cellar, and perhaps the holes were there to support the legs of a cask rack. On the other hand, perhaps the wear marks in the tiles came from someone working the kick pedal of a grinding wheel anchored in the postholes, indicating that the wine cellar may have become a workshop for sharpening tools later in its life.

The partition walls in the basement show where the doorways were located and the brick-tile room seems to have been the most inaccessible, further evidence that something of value, like wine, was kept there. Other doors existed at the center of the partition between the larger rooms on the south end, but one could only enter the two smaller corner rooms by passing through the smaller central room. No one could enter by the southeast bulkhead from outside and go directly to the wine cellar or other corner room. Security was an obvious consideration for the planning of these spaces. A barrel found buried on its side in the northeast corner room next to the north wall, apparently served as a sump. The only other special feature was a $4' \times 6'$ pit dug in the large room with the bulkhead, presumably a root cellar, in its traditional place near the warmer and drier fireplace area.

The basement was filled with debris from the occupation and destruction of the house. A layer of charcoal and burned plaster above an occupation level resting on the basement floor indicated that the superstructure was gutted by fire. Burned sherds of English pearlware found resting on the floor levels indicate that the house was occupied and burned as late as 1780, the date commonly accepted for the first appearance of that English ceramic type in Virginia (Figure 50).[15] Pearlware also appeared in the ashes from the fire and in the brick rubble above that—the brick rubble was the last deposit thrown into the open basement as bricks were being salvaged from the burned-out ruin. The absence of artifacts in any great quantity in the fire level suggests that the building was not occupied at the time of the fire. It is possible that the mansion had degenerated into a grain storage barn in its later years, as a considerable quantity of wheat carbonized by the fire and farm tools were recovered from the ash on the tile floor of the wine cellar.

The original builders apparently seated scaffolds in postholes during construction of the chimneys and end walls of the house, but the absence of similar holes along the north and south walls may indicate that brick work was used solely on the end walls. The entire brick foundation had been set within a builder's trench, however, and a wine-bottle glass and pipestem recovered from the backfilling of the builder's trench support a first-quarter eighteenth-century date for construction.

The two-brick-thick foundation wall, the basement partition plan, and the presence and absence of scaffold holes indicating combined brick-and-frame construction are all substantial evidence for a hypothetical reconstruction (Figure 49). Also, one version of Simcoe's 1781 map shows a two-story house with a gable roof in approximately the Bray foundation location (see Figure 24). But with such a shallow basement floor, the first floor of the house must have been 3–4' above the surrounding ground level; so, from the vantage point of the Simcoe artist, the

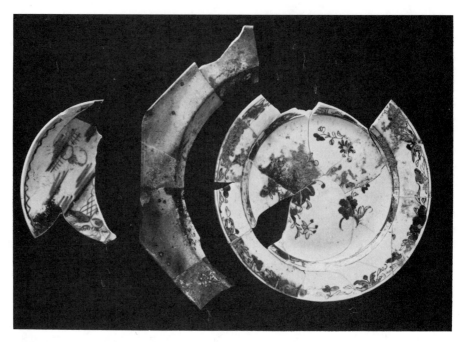

Figure 50 Burned English pearlware bowl–saucer, circa 1785 (left), octagonal creamware plate (center), and polychrome Chinese export porcelain saucer (right) found in ash deposited by the Bray mansion fire, circa 1790. (Virginia Historic Landmarks Commission.)

Bray house may have appeared to be two stories high. In any case, the two-room-deep plan must have included a considerable amount of living space and at least five rooms on the first floor. Also, dormer windows in the half story would have practically doubled the living space in the house, adding at least four lighted rooms above.

Both a sash window pulley and a considerable amount of turned lead from casement windows were found on the site. These suggest that either the house had both types of windows at the same time, or, more likely, the house underwent some renovation later in its life, work that may have incorporated a modernization of the old casement window forms. In fact, brick rubble and mortar found in a nearby trashpit, along with discarded turned-lead casement-window glass and other artifacts that suggest a deposition date of 1725–1745,[16] tends to indicate a renovation at about that time. Except for a minor repair to the wall in the basement in the southeast corner, however, there is no evidence that the original structure was ever altered.

There was no question before excavations began where Colonel Lewis Burwell's mansion had stood, because some of the brickwork and about two-thirds of the cellar were still open (Figures 51–54). Unlike the Bray mansion, the Kingsmill

Figure 51 Open overgrown basement (right) and kitchen (background) at Burwell's Kingsmill before excavation, 1974. (Virginia Historic Landmarks Commission.)

house was never quite abandoned. When the eighteenth-century superstructure burned in 1844, a smaller farmhouse soon rose from the ruins, and when that second house itself burned in the early twentieth century, part of the basement was recycled into shelter for cattle.[17] Despite all the postcolonial occupation, however, about one-third of the earlier deposits survived undisturbed at the east end of the ruin. Excavation revealed a rectangular brick foundation measuring $61' \times 40'$ with a semicircular land front entrance step footing, a rectangular waterfront entrance step footing, a bulkhead entrance on the northwest, and an entrance porch on the southeast. The building had one surviving interior chimney base, but slots or racking built into the opposite cellar wall indicate that a similar chimney stood slightly off center on the west.

The eighteenth-century mansion walls laid in English bond were four courses thick below grade, narrowing to three courses above. Original masons used a builder's trench averaging $3-4'$ in width during the cellar wall construction. However, the trench was filled immediately after the cellar walls were brought to grade. That is why postholes were found cutting through the builders' trench fill at $8'$ to $12'$ intervals: the holes were supports for scaffolds used during the construction of the upper stories of the house.

Thick ($2'9''$) brick foundation walls divided the cellar space into at least three

Figure 52 Aerial view of excavations at Kingsmill Plantation, November, 1975, (north above). (Virginia Department of Highways.)

rooms: 23′ × 34′ on the west, a 13′6″ × 17′6″ room slightly off center, and a 12′6″ × 34′ room on the east.[18] Although the nineteenth-century construction obliterated much of the remains of the walls of the central room enough original masonry survived along the east wall and the south end to show that this room was, in fact, a brick-lined vault. Enough traces of the north wall of the vault survived to indicate both the overall length of the vault and where its door had been located. No flooring material other than the natural clay was found in the vault.

The triangular chimney base on the east incorporated a 2′ × 3′ built-in shelf on the northwest side. Sockets cut into the interior cavity of the shelf indicate where wooden framing for additional shelving and doors once existed. No traces of a west chimney base survived on the cellar floor, but there is strong evidence that a matching stack stood on that end of the house. Identical racking survived on the west wall and so did traces of brick mortared into the wall at a 45° angle. Since the removal of the angled faces of the triangular east chimney would leave identical impressions in the mortar there, it is logical to assume that a similar chimney stood on the west. Also, excavations outside the cellar uncovered a Y-shaped iron rod buried at the center of the west wall, undoubtedly a ground for a lightning rod system (Figure 55). Of course, lightning rod spires must be attached to the highest

Figure 53 Burwell mansion and kitchen after excavation, November, 1975. (Virginia Historic Landmarks Commission.)

point of a building, usually at the top of a chimney stack—more reason for concluding that there was a west chimney on the Burwell house.

The archaeology identified four entrances to the mansion: at the center of the north and south facades, a bulkhead to the cellar on the northeast corner, and an original enlarged porch entrance near the southeast corner. "Bogiron" stones, no doubt quarried from natural veins of iron ore still visible in the nearby riverbank, supported the riverfront stone steps leading to the south doorway. Although the finished stone was no longer in place, enough fragments of these steps were found reused or discarded elsewhere on the site to suggest reconstruction. Finished stone with a simple fillet and ovolo profile forming a flare in plan were found in the

Figure 54 View of the Burwell mansion ruins, showing two periods of bulkhead steps into the basement (background), triangular corner chimney (right), and rubble left from mid-nineteenth-century destruction (center). (Virginia Historic Landmarks Commission.)

bulkhead steps of the later nineteenth-century building, and similar stone with finished voluting was found in the cellar fill of the house, together suggesting the flaring riverfront step design. The step design on the opposite facade was radically different, semi-circular in plan, indicated by two courses of rowlock laid brick. Fragments of stone steps with edges matching the rowlock curve were found reused in the nearby office hearth, suggesting that the rowlock bricks on the landfront originally supported stone risers (Figures 56 and 57).

The walls of the eighteenth-century brick bulkhead steps had sockets opposite the outer edges of the surviving brick, very like the other bulkhead construction at Kingsmill, each riser originally having a wooden nosing. No evidence survived of any footing of a cover for the bulkhead, but the nearby porch entrance foundation remained intact. The brickwork indicated that the original single-course foundation was enlarged by 8′ after an occupation level containing fragments of an English Agateware tankard dating circa 1740–1745 accumulated there.[19] The location of the foundation suggests that servants entered what must have been the dining room through the porch from the nearby kitchen dependency to the east.

Some of the artifacts from the destruction layers of the house give certain

Figure 55 Hand-wrought ground rod for eighteenth-century lightning-rod system at the base of the west chimney, Burwell mansion site. (Virginia Historic Landmarks Commission.)

clues to details of the aboveground construction and to furnishings. Windows had rubbed-brick surrounds, and the fireplaces were embellished with polished Italian marble. The house had shutters with offset "H–L" hinges, allowing them to set flush with the walls.

Because of the subsequent construction of the nineteenth-century house, only the extreme south end of the basement vault, the southwest corner of the west room, and the east cellar room contained original eighteenth-century fill and debris from the eighteenth-century building. An occupation level beneath burned wood and plaster, covered by 6′ of brick rubble, built up in the east room. These layers obviously accumulated successively as the result of occupation, destruction by fire, wall collapse, and brick salvage. The occupation level contained only sherds of underglaze Chinese porcelain, generally datable to the eighteenth century. Above the occupation zone, the fire that destroyed the superstructure of the house left an ash layer containing fragments of Staffordshire transfer-printed pearlware, bone china with luster overglaze decoration, and blue and gray American-made stoneware, all establishing a post-1820 date for the fire. The few scrapes of furniture hardware found in the fire level suggest that the house may have been abandoned when it burned.

Figure 56   Voluted section of mansion step. (Virginia Historic Landmarks Commission.)

Figure 57   Fragment of curved stone step originally used for landfront entrance to mansion. (Virginia Historic Landmarks Commission.)

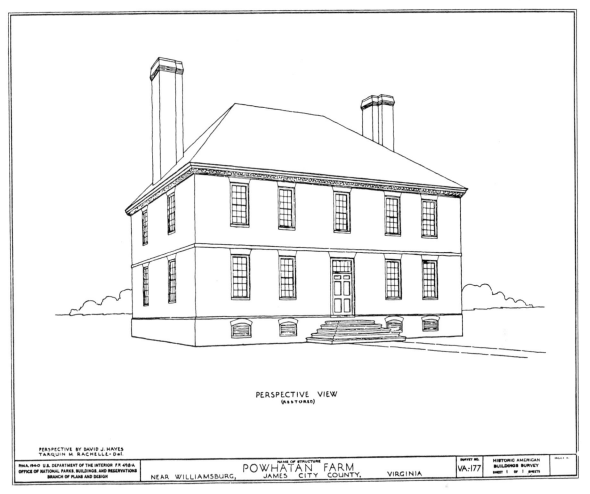

PERSPECTIVE VIEW
(RESTORED)

PERSPECTIVE BY DAVID J. HAYES
TARQUIN M. RACHELLE- Del.

PWA. 1940 U.S. DEPARTMENT OF THE INTERIOR F.R. 498-A
OFFICE OF NATIONAL PARKS, BUILDINGS, AND RESERVATIONS
BRANCH OF PLANS AND DESIGN

NAME OF STRUCTURE
POWHATAN FARM
NEAR WILLIAMSBURG, JAMES CITY COUNTY, VIRGINIA

SURVEY NO.
VA.-177

HISTORIC AMERICAN
BUILDINGS SURVEY
SHEET 1 OF 1 SHEETS

Figure 58 Elevation of Powhatan, James City County, slightly smaller in plan and probably similar in appearance to Burwell's Kingsmill mansion.

A combination of the archaeological and historical evidence and the architectural detail of two similar standing buildings of the same period—Powhatan Plantation in James City County and Westover in nearby Charles City—together provide relatively complete specifications with which a reasonably valid reconstruction of Burwell's vanished mansion can be drawn (Figures 58–60).[20] The four-course-thick foundation undoubtedly supported a "two story building" with four rooms on a floor, as advertised in the *Gazette* in 1781 (Figure 26). A reconstruction of the arch of the basement vault, allowing for a ceiling beam as thick as that used in the contemporary dependency nearby, sets the basement ceiling height at 11′, the elevation above which the four first-floor rooms stood. The basement partition

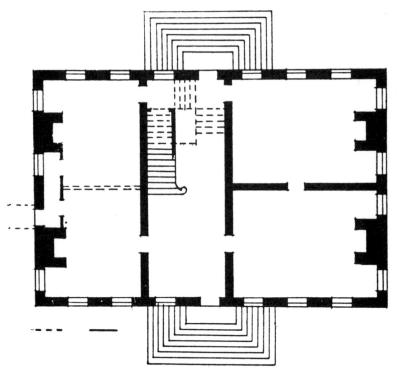

Figure 59   Plan of William Byrd's Westover, similar to room scheme suggested by the foundations at Burwell's Kingsmill mansion. (Waterman, 1946, p. 164.)

walls, certainly thick enough to support the load of first-floor walls as well, indicate the first and probably second floor plan: that is, a center passage or entrance hall above the vault, flanked by two smaller rooms with triangular corner fireplaces on the east, and larger and slightly smaller rooms with identical corner fireplaces on the northwest and southwest, respectively. That plan matches the layout of rooms at contemporary Powhatan except the building is 4′ smaller in its overall dimensions. The Burwell and Westover first-floor room plans are almost identical, except that at Westover four separate chimney stacks center the fireplaces in each room. Like Kingsmill, Westover has a side door leading to the detached kitchen from one of the two smaller rooms on the river front.

Architectural historian Thomas Waterman identifies the Westover rooms: "Entrance Hall" for the central passage, "Drawing Room" for the largest room, and "Music Room" next to it on one side of the "Hall," and "Dining Room" for the room with the side door toward the kitchen on the other side of the "Hall."[21] If Waterman is right, then the more public rooms seem to be located on the riverfront at Westover, which is only a stone's throw from shore and only slightly

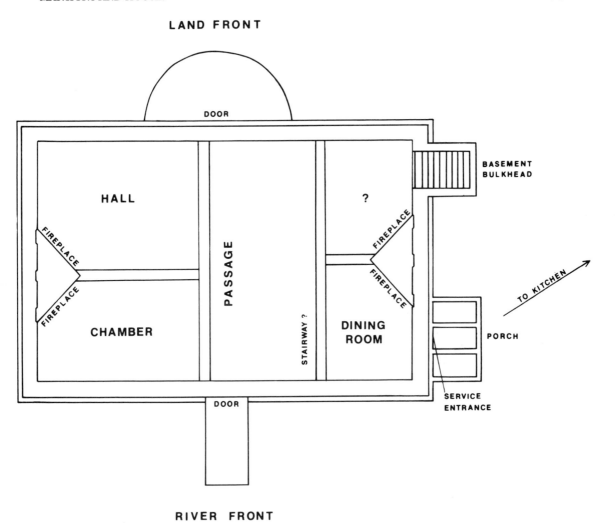

Figure 60   Conjectural first-floor plan of Burwell's Kingsmill mansion based on historical research and archaeological evidence. (Anna Gruber.)

elevated above the water. The water side of the house seems to be the emphasis. Kingsmill, on the other hand, seems to have the opposite orientation, the largest room being on the land front, with the river over 700 yards away and the house 55' above the water. At Kingsmill the land-front emphasis is natural: there is no boat landing directly below the house. Also, all of the maps of the period show that only a short road was required to connect the buildings with Quarterpath Road, the well-traveled artery linking Burwell's Landing with the Capitol at Williamsburg.

That being the case, a land-oriented room arrangement makes sense. It also follows that the largest room to the right of the land-front doorway, was used as the traditional hall where public business and social intercourse took place.

The similar Powhatan and Westover plans and the obvious two-story height of the Burwell house indicate strongly that Kingsmill mansion had a massive stairway in the passage, probably along the exterior walls of the dining room. It is also reasonable to assume that the vaulting provided the additional support for the weight of the staircase as well. But the vault probably had an additional and more significant purpose. Vaults were the only fireproof space in the house and in an age before banks, the Burwells probably kept most of their valuables in it. In fact, the archaeological evidence indicates that the Kingsmill "fireproof" worked. The small section of undisturbed fill next to the surviving section of the arch contained no ash from the house fire, indicating that the vault interior was indeed protected from the flames.

The facades of Westover and Powhatan may well have been as similar to Kingsmill as the floor plans, but it is probably the plainer and smaller Powhatan that most closely resembles Kingsmill. Balanced windows, a simple door and cornice, jack arches for the openings similar to the dependencies, and a hipped roof seem to match the archaeological and architectural evidence, although there is no record of Powhatan's original roof line. The Simcoe map of the strangely sited two-story building near the river shore shows a simple gable (see Figure 26).

The leaseholders at Burwell's Ferry both lived and conducted much of their business in the same building. The dwelling served equally as the shelter for the ordinary keeper, the ferry captain, and their families; as accommodations for travelers, sailors, and probably some slaves, and as storage space for the transshipment and storage of incoming goods.[22] A rambling brick foundation plan was defined by archaeology, and probably supported a frame construction (see Figures 46, 61–64).

Excavations on the east bluff at the landing site revealed foundations of three separate but aligned and eventually connected buildings. On the west digging uncovered a $41' \times 22'$ brick-lined basement and, 28' to the east, a $40' \times 18'$ building based on brick piers with matching exterior brick chimneys. A $16' \times 20'$ building foundation with a brick chimney was found southeast of the pier structure, and after the original construction, the smaller building was attached to the main house by means of a frame addition supported by earthfast posts. The basement structure, too, was eventually added to the pier building by adding a hyphen, but only fragments of brick foundations of that addition survived.

The $1\frac{1}{2}$-course-wide basement wall, laid in English bond on the west end of the building complex, stood within a $41' \times 22'$ construction pit that extended, for some unexplained reason, as much as 7' beyond the brickwork. Remains of a burned timber, seated in basement wall sockets, evidently served as a supporting sill for a partition forming two rooms: $12'6'' \times 14'$ on the east and $16' \times 14'$ on the

Figure 61 Remains of recent wharf, landing beach, and site of ordinary (left background) at Burwell's Ferry Landing, Kingsmill. (Virginia Historic Landmarks Commission.)

west. Other burned timbers along the north wall and an unmortared course of bricks on the sand floor of the basement suggest the location of an interior entrance stairway.

The bulkhead originally provided outside entry to the basement from the north, but later construction moved some of the stairs to the west, forming a landing halfway through the descent. It is possible that a later shed addition to the building blocked the original entry, which made the 90° turn necessary.[23] No structural remains of the shed survived below grade. Both sections of the bulkhead show similar construction, and both used sockets in the walls for wooden step nosings. A 3′ × 7′ rectangular depression on the edge of the west basement wall marked the original location of the chimney stack. Careful excavating and sorting of scattered brick rubble from the still-bonded brickwork resulted in the definition of intact sections of the fallen chimney stack resting in the basement fill. Only the inside face of the stack stayed together after impact, apparently after the rest of the body of the chimney was removed by brick salvagers. One section of the wall exterior did survive enough, however, to indicate that the stack was built of Flemish bond with glazed headers and the mortar joints were decoratively scored.

About 4′ from the base of the fallen stack, bricks still forming parts of the arch of the first-floor fireplace were found still in place. The intact opening of the second-story fireplace was also found 7′ to the east, suggesting that the original ceiling height of the first floor was 10–11′. Also farther to the east, remains of the

Figure 62   Overhead view of Burwell's Landing ordinary, showing fallen chimney *in situ*. (Virginia Historic Landmarks Commission.)

chimney weathering lay relatively intact and enough of the remains of the T-shaped chimney cap indicated the original chimney elevation to be at least 29′.

The basement contained layers of brickbats and layers heavy with wood ash just above a dirt floor. The uniformity of the ash layer and the numerous nails and abundant burned plaster indicate that the building burned, but the relative absence of burned household artifacts suggests that the building was empty at the time of the fire. Fragments of English creamware in and below the ash, a pottery type imported into Virginia only after 1769, shows that the fire occurred sometime after that date.[24] In addition to the pottery, glass fragments from the ash layer and below, coming from bottles stylistically datable to the period circa 1760–1790, established a circa 1770–1780 deposition date. Fragments of wine-bottle glass retrieved from the builders trenches were of eighteenth-century date, and the artifact date ranges from this and the surrounding area suggest a 25-year life for the building, 1750–1775.

Historical documentation supports the archeological date of the fire and, in fact, more specifically pinpoints that event in time. With the strong evidence of fire,

Figure 63 The foundation of the central section of the Burwell's Landing ordinary, showing fireplace footings (foreground and background) and brick wall piers. (Virginia Historic Landmarks Commission.)

dated by artifacts to the Revolutionary War period, there is little reason to doubt Lewis Burwell's claim against the government in 1776 that the building was destroyed during the troop occupation.[25] Of course, Burwell's claim of negligence on the part of the American soldiers stationed there could not be determined from the archaeological remains.

One-course-thick brick piers spaced 9–22′ apart and the two U-shaped-end chimney foundations defined the middle section of the ordinary complex, the relatively small piers indicating a fairly light frame construction. The survival of a rectangular stone step is the only clue to a likely floor plan, if it led to a doorway. If so, a door existed 16′ from the southwest corner of the house, perhaps indicating a large hall and smaller parlor floor plan, with both hall and parlor heated by an

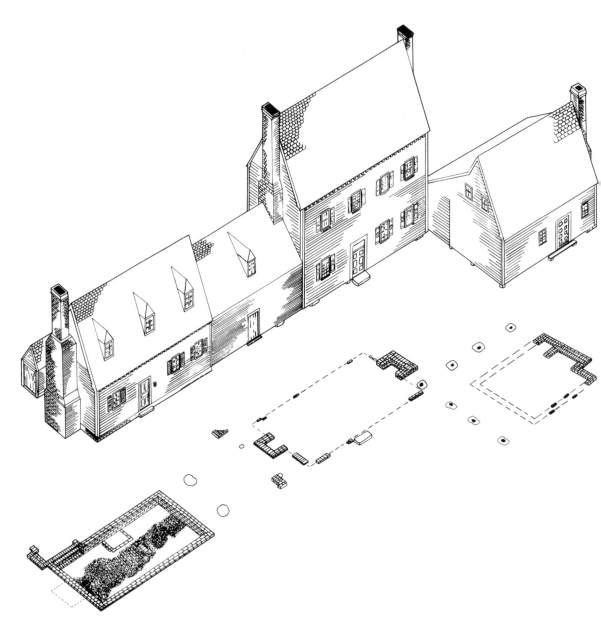

Figure 64 Archaeological plan and reconstruction of Burwell's Landing ordinary, circa 1775. (Leonard Winter.)

exterior end fireplace. The brick chimney foundations do indicate that they were no more than heaters, their openings measuring only $2' \times 4'$.

Backfilled scaffold holes at the corners of each of the chimney foundations were also found, and fragments of creamware in that fill and the fill in a construction ditch along the edge of the east chimney suggest that this section of the ordinary was also built sometime after 1769, again creamware's earliest documented use in Virginia.

Excavations between the brick-lined basement and the building on piers uncovered a section of brick wall, $1\frac{1}{2}$ courses wide, forming a corner in line with the south wall of the basement, $23'$ to the east. Traces of brick rubble and mortar also led north from the intact wall section, indicating that the wall once stood along that line before brick salvaging. It is significant to note that the scavenger's rubble and mortar debris extended on top of fill in one of the backfilled scaffold holes for the west chimney of the brick pier building. Brick paving existed to the south and large postholes were found to the west of the brick corner, all apparently parts of the footings of the structure that connected the west basement building with the brick pier central section. The brickwork on the north could have been another entrance landing, marking another doorway on the southeast corner of the hyphen. That door may have led into some sort of lobby with the west chimney stack serving as the north wall of the small room. Whatever the room arrangement, however, there seems to have been no overall initial design for the complex. That would not be surprising, for as business grew as a result of the increasing volume of commerce at the landing, so would the building.

Even what appears to have been the original kitchen, the $16' \times 21'$ frame building supported on a one-course-wide brick footing, was changed from its original plan as it was tacked onto the pier building by an enlargement using earthfast posts. The massive fireplace, originally $8'$ across, suggests that the tavern cooking took place there. Brickwork found centered on the edge of the south wall of the building marks the location of an original doorway. Another doorway must have been added to the northwest corner of the earthfast addition as well, so that there would be free passage between the pier building, perhaps the dining room of the inn, and the kitchen.

Fragments of English white salt-glazed stoneware, commonly used in Virginia during the second and third quarters of the eighteenth century, were found in the construction ditches for the chimney, suggesting a mid-eighteenth-century original construction date for the smaller building. Sherds of English agateware, popular primarily during the third quarter of the eighteenth century, were found in the fill of the earthfast holes of the addition, perhaps more confirmation that that construction was the latest. The earliest documented date for the ordinary is 1766 but there must have been someone living somewhere at the landing, perhaps in one section of the ordinary early in the Burwell Naval Officer tenure.[26]

Combining the basement building, the hyphen, the brick pier building, and the attached kitchen, the ordinary assumes a total facade over $130'$ long, enough

Figure 65   Late eighteenth–early nineteenth-century tavern, Powhatan County, Virginia, similar in plan to archaeological remains of Burwell's Landing ordinary. (Virginia Historic Landmarks Commission.)

space to accommodate a sizable number of patrons. The taverns in Williamsburg, even the popular Wetherburn's Tavern on Duke of Gloucester Street, were not much roomier. Pragmatic growth may well have been the norm for these resident businesses as well, for an ordinary built in Powhatan County with its series of aligned additions is reminiscent of the Burwell's ordinary overall plan (Figure 65). Although it is impossible to tell how many stories the brick pier building had, perhaps the Powhatan ordinary can serve as a model from which space can be determined. If so, two stories would not seem unreasonable. With over 4200 square feet of living and storage space, the Burwell's Landing structure must have been one of the major ordinaries in the area.

QUARTERS

There is little doubt that by the eighteenth century black slaves made up the majority of Kingsmill's laboring class. The nature of slavery at Kingsmill, as everywhere in the South, sorted the slaves into three groups: the servants of the landlord's house, craftsmen, and those that worked the fields. Defining the material culture of the three groups is particularly difficult because even though there is more recorded than one would expect concerning the spartan existence of slaves in general, coming to an understanding of their day-to-day lives at any given location like Kingsmill is challenging. Documents alone do not tell the story; they are, of course, primarily the chronicles of and about the literate white families there.

Nonetheless, the discovery of the remains of certain domestic structures on the Kingsmill sites, the distribution of some unlabeled settlements on the Desandrouin map of 1781 and the mention of slaves and quarters in some of the Pettus, Bray, and Burwell documents together make a strong case that some of the excavations recovered fragmented remains of the houses and artifacts of black house servants and field hands (Figures 39, 46, 52, and 66).

It is likely that the first slaves at Kingsmill worked for Colonel Thomas Pettus and lived at Littletown. On the other hand, it is extremely unlikely that before about 1670 any of the Kingsmill residents, primarily tenants, had any slaves. In that case, the structures and objects found at either the early seventeeth-century Kingsmill or Littletown tenant sites can hardly reflect slave life

Since it was common by the eighteenth century for black house servants to live in the landlord's mansions and nearby outbuildings, there is a strong possibility that Colonel Thomas Pettus's home labor force resided in the East wing of the manor, the 18′ × 32′ building that was eventually added onto the house (Figures 39, 42–44). On the other hand, it could be that only Pettus's white indentured

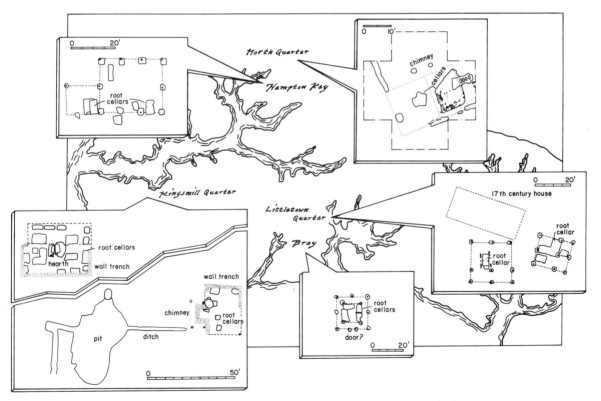

Figure 66 Archaeological plans for fieldhand slave quarters, Kingsmill. (Sondy Sanford.)

servants occupied space directly attached to the main house, while the black slaves lived in totally separate quarters, perhaps in the aligned post structure found to the north.

The sizable five-bay Pettus structure, however, included no evidence of a fireplace, which casts some doubt on interpreting it as a house at all. Still, it is clear from evidence on other Kingsmill sites that deep plowing can totally erase fireplace remains even though three other hearths survived the Pettus site cultivation. In fact, the lack of a hearth might in this case be more reason for suspecting that the building was for slaves. The wooden chimneys made of stacked sticks and mud, common to slave cabins of a later period, probably stem from seventeenth-century tradition, in which case more than other forms of impermanent chimney construction they could be erased more completely by plowing. (Figure 19).

Both positions—that slaves did or did not live in the Utopia house—can be convincingly argued. The Pettus inventory seems to suggest that whoever lived there was a leaseholder, since cattle and food remains (animal bones) from Utopia seem to conform to a tenant and not a slave diet (see Figures 125–127 below).[27] Also, the brick used in construction and the existence of a water well there, both elements elsewhere reserved for the sites of the landlords, suggest a lifestyle above slavery. On the other hand, certain local pottery types and relative numbers of ceramic forms strongly suggest occupation at the lower end of the economic scale (Figure 130). Perhaps the rather conflicting evidence is saying Utopia was indeed a leasehold, but the tenant himself had his own slave laborers living there as well. In that case, it is possible that the two-bay earthfast building site 35′ to the north of the house, like the apparent chimneyless post-house at the Pettus homeplace, sheltered the Utopia slaves apart from the masters' living quarters.

There is much less uncertainty about the whereabouts of what had become a sizable slave population at the Kingsmill Plantations in the eighteenth century; they undoubtedly worked and lived at Bray's Littletown, Burwell's Kingsmill, Tutter's Neck and the Landing.[28] The spacious attics, basements, and halls of both the Bray and Burwell mansions could have easily accommodated any number of house servants, as many of the houses of that period did, and the several substantial outbuildings located adjacent to the two landlords' houses must all have been used for quarters. The discovery of the root cellar dug below the earth floor of the Bray house basement may be additional evidence that slaves lived there (Figure 49). These cellars are almost invariably found on documented slave quarter sites of later periods and they appear at every other eighteenth-century probable slave site at Kingsmill as well.[29]

Also, at Bray's Littletown the two houses built at right angles east and west of the mansion, one of earthfast construction and the other apparently built on a groundsill, and a later, third post building aligned with the main house to the west, all must have provided shelter for the Bray family house servants. The root cellar in front of the brick chimney foundation and along the east wall of the post building farthest to the west of the mansion also may indicate the slave occupation (Figure

67). In spite of their relatively small size, these root cellars were subdivided by wooden partitions, their subsequent decay leaving dark stripes of soil on the earth floor. That they were common in early eighteenth-century Virginia and why some of them were put near the hearths is clear from the comment of Robert Beverly, who wrote in 1705: "The Way of propagating Potatoes [is to] bury em under Ground, near the Fire-Hearth, all the Winter, until the Time comes, that their Seedings are to be set."[30] It seems that Beverly is talking about the white populace but, since blacks likely did the cooking and since the cellars were ostensibly for root preservation, perhaps that way of storing food was introduced to colonial society by the blacks themselves. The fact that these small pits do not appear on the preslavery sites may be more convincing evidence that they are indeed the product of the black culture. Furthermore, absence of root cellars in the other two major Bray outbuildings is cause to suggest that they were not quarters for slaves.

In any event, the cellar idea may have been "new" but the earthfast construction, so common for even the wealthiest of the seventeenth-century Kingsmill landowners, was by that time a familiar "old" Virginia tradition. But by the eighteenth century the earthfast method seems to persist only in the construction of the lesser outbuildings. It may be that the more impermanent post construction, while it ceased to meet the housing needs of the landlords, continued to be useful, perhaps the most economical, for the construction of the slave quarters.

Earthfast construction was also employed in other domestic buildings at Littletown. One structure, relatively near the house (400' north) is close enough for the convenience of house servants, while the remains of two other eighteenth-century earthfast frame houses located on the same site as Littletown Tenement

Figure 67   Earthfast servant's quarter at Bray's Littletown includes massive brick chimney foundation, root cellars, and main structural postholes. (Virginia Historic Landmarks Commission.)

and shown to be extant by Desandrouin in 1781, were the dwellings of field hands (Figures 30 and 62). The remnants of the dwelling closest to the main house was composed of an unusual pattern of postholes–postmolds and a series of interior backfilled pits, undoubtedly root cellars (Figure 68). Both the presence of the root cellars and a number of domestic artifacts in their backfilling indicate a domestic slave site, even though no evidence of a fireplace was found. Also, perhaps the lack of a hearth can again be explained both by the insubstantial nature of the wooden chimneys so typical of slave quarters and by deep plowing. The postholes define two main structural elements, a 12′ × 12′ core element supported by four corner-posts, and a larger structure outside the core, supported with posts. The outer posts were 10′ apart except at the middle of the wall where two posts were positioned closer together, probably to form a door or gate opening. If all these postholes did indeed hold main structural posts for a single dwelling, the outer and inner room plan they created becomes unusual and difficult to understand. Of course, it is possible that the outer post line only marks the location of a fence, but the narrow 4′-wide "yard" between it and the core makes little sense. Hypothetical reconstruction of such an anomalous building is impossible, yet its conspicuous location on the main land approach to the Bray mansion must have required it to look reasonably presentable. The structure may have stood on that site early in the Bray occupation as well. The dates of the ceramics, particularly the English

Figure 68   Archaeological remains of unusual eighteenth-century earthfast house with interior root cellars, along road to Bray's Littletown mansion. (Virginia Historic Landmarks Commission.)

Agateware, suggest a backfilling date for the root cellars as early as circa 1740.[31] The two other post houses at Littletown Quarter were located along the same approach road, and this may also have influenced their outer appearance. The two were similar in plan, each supported by nine posts that in turn made a two-room or a room-and-porch floor plan above root cellars. The cellars were lined with wood, the single pit in the building on the west measuring 5′ × 3′ and in turn subdivided by vertical boards into two separate spaces, 3′ × 3′ on the north and 2′ × 3′ on the south. An earth step on the south end of the cellar was also found and there were long, narrow soil stains on each side of the pit. It is possible that the darker soil is a remnant of vertical wall boards used to secure the root storage from invasions of any animals that could get into the crawlspace under the house.

The house on the east did not align with the westernmost building. It had a rather complex series of three backfilled root cellars. One had been subdivided into four compartments by vertical boards. The artifacts recovered from the root-cellar fill give a specific date for the backfilling. A Virginia halfpenny of 1773 and a button of the 80th Edinburgh Volunteers, a unit first entering Virginia in 1781, establishes the early 1780s as the date after which the pit was filled (Figure 69).[32]

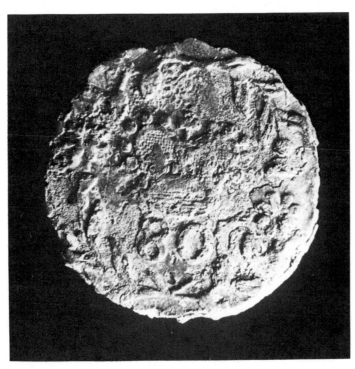

Figure 69 Revolutionary War pewter regimental button of the 80th Royal Edinburgh Volunteers who surrendered at Yorktown in 1781, found in a Littletown Quarter root cellar. (Virginia Historic Landmarks Commission.)

Wine-bottle glass in the posthole fill, however, suggests original construction earlier in the century. But beyond the dates of the construction and backfilling of the cellar, the artifacts recovered confirm the connection of the Littletown Quarter with the Bray family. Among the usual ceramics and glass fragments, a brass coach or harness boss cast in the form of the Bray family heraldic crest, a winged lion, was recovered from the root cellar (see Figure 132 below).

The Littletown Quarter earthfast houses left no evidence of fireplaces, perhaps more negative confirmation of the "phantom" slave-quarter wooden chimneys. In this case, however, their probable location is not a total mystery. If root cellars were commonly constructed directly in front of the hearth, as Robert Beverly described in 1705, the cellars at Littletown Quarter suggest they stood on the west-gable end of the west building and either the east- or west-gable end of the east building.

Other Littletown field hands may have lived at a house site discovered by archaeological testing 400′ north of the Utopia house site (see Frontispiece). There was not enough time or funds, and indeed there was no threat of construction at that location on the Busch property, so no further excavation was done. Nevertheless, spot-test digging located what appeared to be an earthfast building posthole–postmold next to a backfilled pit, probably another root cellar. From the dark organic cellar fill were recovered animal bones, ceramic fragments, and an iron hoe-blade, along with an English halfpenny of 1721. The coin and the pottery types suggest that the building was occupied and then abandoned in the 1720s or 1730s . Although not enough digging could be done to define the house plan, the root cellar and the earthfast construction replicates the other Littletown slave structures. The discovery of the James Bray bottle seal in the upper filling of the Utopia house basement close by establishes a Bray–Littletown–Utopia connection as well. It is indeed possible that James Bray II's black overseers, perhaps "Jacko," did live at Utopia as the records suggest and, in fact, one member of his family may be buried on the site. The badly decomposed bones and wooden coffin of an individual tentatively identified as a black female over 25 were found near a back-filled seventeenth-century pit at Utopia.[33] An eighteenth-century white kaolin tobacco pipe with the maker's initials *IW* stamped on the bowl was found in the coffin, pinned beneath the left arm of the skeleton, leaving no reason to doubt that the artifact was buried with the body (Figure 70). Fragments of pipes with identical *IW* marks were found buried in the eighteenth-century root cellar, evidence possibly linking the house with the black burial.

The records show that a slave quarter existed on the Tuttey's or Tutter's Neck section of the Kingsmill property that became Bray family property in 1717, and possibly Deb's or Jacko's Quarter soon thereafter. The small settlement, shown on the Desandrouin map (Figure 22) as two isolated buildings in 1781, became the focus of salvage excavations by Colonial Williamsburg Restoration, Inc. in the early 1960s.[34] The archaeologist Ivor Noel Hume concluded that the two building foundations that he found there were, respectively, the remnants of the main house of Frederick Jones, a landowner there for a few years in the early eighteenth century

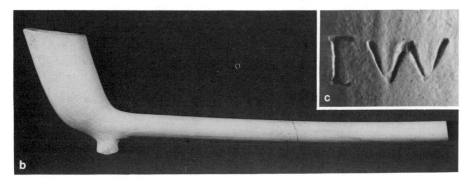

Figure 70 (a) Burial of black female (?) with English clay tobacco pipe beneath left arm and (b) bearing the same *IW* maker's mark as (c) fragment recovered from a root cellar at Jacko's Quarter (?), Utopia. (Virginia Historic Landmarks Commission.)

and with the addition of a small "kitchen" built after "1730 or 1740," a Bray slave quarter (Figure 71). The Jones connection was made by Noël Hume on the strength of initialed wine-bottle seals found there in a trash pit predating the kitchen construction, and of a reference to Jones's acquisition of 300 acres called Luttie's Neck in 1711. But Jones, who had over 4500 acres in North Carolina when he moved in 1708, probably did not occupy his land for long, if at all. Consequently, the architectural remains are more reflective of the later slave occupation.

Noël Hume concluded from his limited salvage work that the main house was rectangular in plan, measuring 42′3″ × 19′1″ overall, with massive exterior and chimneys. The brick foundation varied in thickness from 1½ courses on the east, north, and part of the west walls to only a single course on the south and the remainder of the west walls. The brickwork did not survive continuously on the east and west walls either, so the original overall plan is in some doubt. Noël Hume does conclude from the rather fragmented remains that the house could have stood no more than 1½ stories high in frame construction with a hall–parlor, or hall–through-passage–parlor ground floor plan with two rooms above. He also concluded that for its time, this house was comparable to the late seventeenth-century house of Robert "King" Carter of Northern Neck Dynasty fame and, therefore, was worthy of the rather prestigious Jones's occupation. Still, the archaeologist who had spent years examining the houses of Williamsburg points out that the building was "only just as large as the smallest houses of Williamsburg" and, lacking a basement, was actually smaller.

The so-called kitchen was smaller and of less substantial construction. Although the foundation was of brick, it was a single course thick, which is only strong enough to support a one-story building. The footing (25′ × 16′ overall) also included a massive exterior chimney centered on the north, or long axis, wall of the house. The location of the chimney there instead of on a gable end, the discovery of rectangular pits inside the footing—undoubtedly backfilled root cellars—and the recovery of well-worn and early artifacts in later contexts on the site, all indicate strongly that these buildings were indeed the homes of slaves.[35]

The two Georgian brick dependencies flanking the Burwell's Kingsmill mansion undoubtedly sheltered house servants (Figures 51–53). The fact of their remarkable survival and the opportunity to conduct archaeology within and around them offers an exceptionally complete picture of the working and living environment of the eighteenth-century Virginia domestic servant. Although they are technically merely outbuildings for the "Great House," the two flankers are impressive houses in their own right, and certainly in design and construction are far beyond the impermanent earthfast–timberframe concept so common for slave

---

Figure 71   (a) Archaeological plan and (b) conjectural reconstruction of quarter at Tuttey's Neck, a part of James Bray's Littletown, circa 1730. (By permission of the Smithsonian Institution Press from *Contributions from the Museum of History and Technology, Bul. 249,* "Excavations at Tutter's Neck James City County, Va., 1960–61," I. Nöel Hume. Washington, D.C., 1966.)

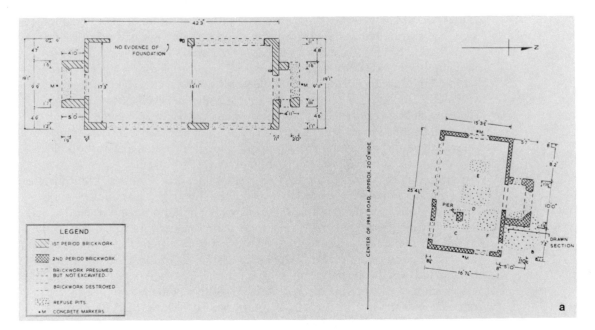

quarters on the Bray estate. When viewed from the landfront approach and fore-court, the two buildings appear identical. In fact, the houses have identical fore-court facade elements: balanced central doorways evenly flanked by two windows, matching north and south facades where small windows light the upper stories, a door leading from the south room on the south walls. One surviving chimney cap with a decorative stucco band suggests that all the chimneys looked alike as well. The Flemish bond above a simple beveled watertable band and jack arches embellished with rubbed brick over the doors and windows are also identical in the two houses, suggesting contemporary construction and further attempts by the builders to make the buildings appear to match in every exterior detail.

However, the building designs differed where they were less immediately visible, to accommodate the specific needs of the Burwells. The buildings are not exactly the same size: the structure on the east is slightly shorter and wider than its apparent twin (Figure 72). Also, no two of the room sizes are equal, nor do the sizes of the interior fireplace openings on the first story match. The doors through the central partitions are also in different relative locations and, although the framing and woodwork have only survived in the west building, probably there was variance in the interior finish as well. All of these differences must reflect to some degree variances in the use of rooms, and it follows that the proper interpretation of them can provide more insight into the daily routines of house slaves.

The *Gazette* advertisement for the sale of Kingsmill in 1781 (Figure 26) indicated that the complex included "2 offices with four rooms in each. . . all brick" undoubtedly referring to the two brick dependencies now standing.[36] In the eighteenth century, the term *offices* meant an outbuilding "specifically devoted to household work or service, [and] the kitchen and rooms connected with it as pantry, scullery, cellars, laundry."[37] The eastern dependency had to be the office used primarily as the main kitchen. The most massive of the four fireplaces stands at the north end of that building, and archaeological excavations next to the enormous hearth uncovered the foundation of what a curved scribed line in the wall indicated was a domed oven. An original water well was found within 2' of the east window of that room and the foundation of the dairy–scullery–laundry was uncovered within 22' of that. Water and food storage, of course, had to be close to the cooking hearth. Although all evidence of the original east door opening was obliterated during the days when the building was a machine shop (ca. 1900), a door must have been there to allow the cooks to pass freely from the cooking area to the well and dairy.

Double-entrance doors on the forecourt facades of each of the buildings show that the ground-floor rooms were intended for separate functions, all of which needed access directly from the outside. Traffic between rooms on the inside could be controlled by opening or closing the door through the central partition wall. Also, if the east dependency had a single stairway like the original that survives in the west dependency, by locking or opening a given sequence of doors one could

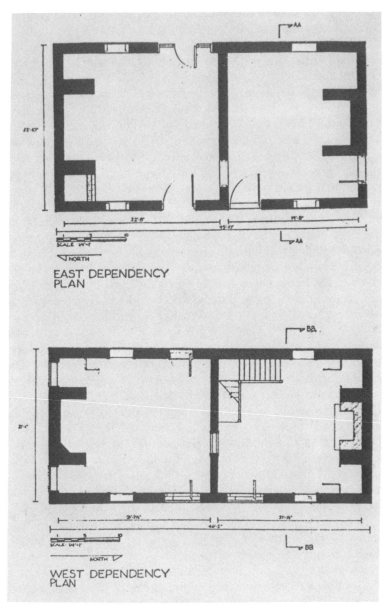

Figure 72 First-floor plans of brick dependencies flanking Burwell's Kingsmill mansion. (C. Wells, Historical American Buildings Survey.)

establish different levels and combinations of security. For example, locking the outside doors to the stairway rooms and partitions sealed three of the four rooms in each house, one on the ground floor and two above. At the same time, the more public kitchen and office rooms could remain open. This suggests a way to confine house servants by night or for house servants to maintain a certain amount of privacy for themselves.

The design of the buildings is not the strongest clue to slave occupation of the two Burwell dependencies. Archaeology uncovered backfilled root cellars in the south room of the kitchen building, one in the traditional location in front of the hearth, another in the southwest corner of the room, and a third cellar in the northeast corner. All three compartments seemed to have continued in use well into the nineteenth century (Figure 73). Fill layers in two of these cellars contained whiteware of that period, and one cellar contained bricks of a distinctive size matched only by the bricks used to support the semicircular foundation of the landfront steps to the mansion. The presence of these bricks and ash layers in the cellars generally indicates that they were no longer used after the interior woodwork and roof framing had burned, possibly by the same fire that destroyed the mansion, circa 1844. It is significant to note that the root cellars were found only in the south room and not in the more public cooking room, but surviving brickwork there suggests that it did not have a raised wooden floor. Decayed sleepers found in the south room, however, suggest that that room had a wooden floor over the cellars.[38]

The fireplaces in the west office and the stairway suggest a use of space similar to the building on the east, even though no root cellars were found. The south groundfloor hearth is almost as large as the cooking hearth in the kitchen, and the room has its two and possibly three doors to the outside. The size of the fireplace in the north room , however, suggests that it was not used for cooking and it is there that the stairway to the heated second half-story survives (Figures 74 and 75). Again, closing and locking the north forecourt door and the partition door would, in fact, close off three-quarters of the rooms for domestic servants' use—that is, the north room on the ground floor and the north and south rooms above—yet leave the south ground floor room open as a more public office.

What the "public" use was in the south room of the west building is unclear. Perhaps the larger fireplace was used to cook the meals for fieldhands who could have entered by a door on the west side of the building without invading the formal forecourt space on the opposite side. It is more likely, however, that that room served as the plantation business office for the Burwells, but it did not necessarily mean that that room or the buildings generally were at all architecturally refined, in spite of the use of the doorway, window jack arches, and interior wall plastering. Only the conspicuous north, forecourt, and south fronts seem to have been influenced by attempts to integrate the buildings esthically into the overall Kingsmill design.

One other brick building was built at the home plantation, but not as part of

Figure 73 Excavated root cellars, south room kitchen dependency at Burwell's Kingsmill. (Virginia Historic Landmarks Commission.)

the original forecourt–mansion design: the "storehouse" mention in 1781 (Figure 76). Used in many cases as a commercial store in the modern sense, these buildings existed on most of the larger plantations of the era, providing the lesser planters with a way to acquire imported goods through the established London trade networks of their wealthier neighbors.

The 19′ × 34′ partially intact brick foundation was found 100′ east of the mansion and, although it is not exactly "the same size" as the two other dependencies, it must have looked identical enough for Burwell to have advertised it that way. In that case, it is safe to assume that the foundation supported a 1½-story all-brick building on its two-course-wide footing. Also, it probably had a chimney or chimneys like the two flanking dependencies, although brick salvaging removed all of their footings. Scaffold holes found surrounding the building, necessary for the construction of brick but not frame buildings, is further archaeological evidence that this building was all brick. In fact, one version of the Simcoe map shows a building with gable-end chimneys running east–west on the northern edge of a garden plot, the same orientation suggested by the archaeological evidence.[39]

Of course, the "storehouse" of 1781 may have been used for something else

Figure 74   Original stairway, north room of office dependency, Burwell's Kingsmill.

earlier in its life and archaeology indicates that original building construction occurred about mid–eighteenth century. Artifacts recovered from the builder's trenches and scaffold holes and from a deposit beneath the brick foundation suggest a circa 1740–1750 date for its construction. Also, the south wall of the building rests on postholes from a garden fenceline that connects with the southeast corner of the mansion, a barrier that probably went in at the same time that the house was built, circa 1728–1736. This is of course yet more evidence suggesting the mid-1700 date for the structure.

Excavations also uncovered a backfilled root cellar on the west end of the

Figure 75 One of four heating fireplaces in second floor half-story of kitchen and office, Burwell's Kingsmill. (Virginia Historic Landmarks Commission.)

interior foundation, the existence of which again is suggestive of slave occupation and indicative that the chimney stood nearby. The 6'-square pit contained clear evidence that the walls had been lined with unnailed boards and as much as 1' of clear sand was found on the floor. This may be evidence of a food-preservation technique advocated by John Worlidge in a late seventeenth-century treatise on agriculture: "root crops be laid up in your cellar or such like places in heaps. . . in reasonably dry sand, will keep throughout the winter."[40] On top of the sand, fragments of burned wood survived in the fill, most probably floorboards left from the destruction of the building. Above the wood, the digging uncovered a layer of plaster and brickbats containing ceramics of the early nineteenth century, principally English pearlware and some window glass. Some of the plaster fragments had lath impressions, indicating that finished ceilings and perhaps wooden partitions stood in the building, more signs perhaps of domestic use, but certainly remnants of the destruction of the building. After that the cellar must have laid open to the elements long enough for layers of wash containing fragments of an English bone china cup with pink luster floral decoration to accumulate there. The luster fragment mended with a burned fragment of the same vessel found in the masion basement among the ashes from the fire. This suggests that the cup was broken in the mansion before it burned, then some of the pieces were thrown in

Figure 76 Partially intact foundation for brick "storehouse" near "kitchen" dependency, Burwell's Kingsmill. Note root cellar (center). (Virginia Historic Landmarks Commission.)

the nearby open root cellar hole after the superstructure of the storehouse was no longer standing. That evidence establishes the destruction of the "storehouse" building just prior to the circa 1844 mansion fire.

References to Lewis Burwell and Henry Tazewell in the bills of Humphrey Harwood, the Williamsburg brick mason, and the Desandrouin map leave little doubt that there were overseer and fieldhand quarters on the Kingsmill property some distance away from the house. [41] Although the map does not identify the cluster of four buildings on the ridge road, one-quarter mile west of the mansion buildings, it is likely that an overseer and fieldhands, or fieldhands alone, lived at that location (Figures 23 and 66). Also, the two house sites shown to the north appear to be domestic sites, and it is likely that they were slave quarters of Burwell or perhaps the houses of the field slaves of the later-day Littletown. All of these sites were excavated and all contained the remains of houses, with the nature of the remains being very consistent with the other slave sites on the property.

The excavation of the site of the four buildings relatively near the Kingsmill mansion shown on the Desandrouin map produced the remnants of two dwellings and an outbuilding (Figures 66 and 77). The construction of two of the later buildings disturbed the filling of the earthfast postholes of the two major domestic structures dating to the first half of the seventeenth century—the Kingsmill Tenements described above—indicating that the seventeenth-century structures were gone by the time the eighteenth-century settlement (hereafter referred to as Kingsmill Quarter) was established. The two major buildings at the Quarter originally had brick foundations but almost all the brickwork had been robbed from the footing when the buildings were destroyed. But soil stains, some backfilled root cellars, burned-clay areas, and concentrations of brick and mortar fragments left enough architectural data *in situ* to determine the building plans.

Concentrations of brick rubble and mortar and dark soil defined the trench left from the removal of the east, north, and west wall foundations. The core structure measured 40' × 18' overall and one brick at the northwest corner remained in place, showing that the footing was only a single course thick. Other *in situ* bricks

Figure 77 View of Kingsmill Quarter house remains, including excavated rectangular root cellars, robbed foundation trench delineated by string, and remains of H-shaped chimney (center). (Virginia Historic Landmarks Commission.)

in an area of burned clay and an H-shaped "shadow" of unburned soil mark the location of a back-to-back fireplace along the original north wall. The interior of the core structure was laced with 18 backfilled root cellars, put in everywhere a hole could be dug without undermining the double fireplace and the walls. In fact, the pits also suggest that a 12′ × 36′ addition stood on the rear of the building even though there is no other evidence of a wall line.

The root cellars, obviously dug after the house was standing, again were not a surprise on the probable slave site, but their great numbers and variation in construction detail were. They ranged in size from as small as 2′9″ × 2′ to as large as 5′ × 8′ (2′–3′6″ deep) and five of the cellars had traces of wooden walls, floors, and the remains of wooden partitions. One cellar had what appears to be a "false" brick floor, resting on earlier fill and an original dirt floor. Comparative stratigraphy, artifact dates, and the recovery of fragments from the same ceramic vessels in several different deposits suggest that either the cellars were dug, used, and abandoned in sequence over a relatively long time, or that about half of the cellars were dug and used in an earlier period, and the other half dug and used together at a later time. For example, seven cellars contained fragmented artifacts dating no later than circa 1760, the date primarily based on the style of the wine bottle found there. Each of these in turn was found next to the main wall line of the house. On the other hand, artifacts from the other pits generally dated as late as the post-Revolutionary years and contained ceramics that either directly or indirectly crossmended, suggesting backfilling at the same time (Figure 78). One pit contained a pewter military button bearing the initials *R P* under a crown (Figure 79), a type worn by the Queen's Rangers who captured Burwell's Landing on April 19, 1781. It is probable, therefore, that the *R P* button could not have been discarded at Kingsmill before 1781. This, of course, established 1781 as the date after which the cellars were backfilled.

The cellars also contained 23 Virginia halfpennies dated 1773, coinage not issued in Virginia until 1775 (Figure 80).[42] On first though, it appears unlikely that so many halfpennies would be accidentally lost and it seems illogical that anyone would discard anything as valuable as a coin regardless of its denomination. In 1789, however, a copper panic in the United States collapsed the value of all copper coins. This subsequently rendered Virginia halfpence "of too little value and popularity to circulate freely."[43] For a time after 1789, therefore, it would not be too surprising to find worthless coins mixed with the daily garbage. Inversely, one could consider the presence of so many copper coins as further evidence for a late 1780s date for the cellar deposits. Also, the last layer of fill in the latest group of cellars all contained considerable brick rubble and mortar that must have been deposited during the dismantling of the building. The rubble, in turn, covered layers of organic fill that contained the deposits of domestic refuse. The artifacts within these two layers not only crossmended among the later pits but within each pit, presenting the strong possibility that the pits were filled with trash at the same time or just before the building destruction. In some cases the later pits also

Figure 78 Excavated root cellar, Kingsmill Quarter, showing bottles, ceramics, faunal remains, and tools *in situ*. (Virginia Historic Landmarks Commission.)

contained sections of butchered animal bones and skeletons obviously discarded with flesh still on them.

There is relatively little evidence to suggest what the superstructure looked like, but some detail seems clear. The 1½-story frame core building was divided into two 20′ × 18′ rooms by the H-shaped chimney centered along the north wall. The house addition 12′ to the north was probably a lean-to shed added to the original

Figure 79 Pewter military button with the initials of the Royal Provincials under a crown. This type, worn by the Queen's Rangers who captured Burwell's Landing on April 19, 1781, was found in a root cellar at Kingsmill Quarter. (Virginia Historic Landmarks Commission.)

structure. After the addition, root cellars were put in, first along the outer walls, then around the chimney stack. The cellars must have been entered through doors in a raised wooden floor above, but it is difficult to imagine a wooden floor so laced with trapdoors. In any case, it is logical to conclude that cellars were not put where the trapdoors would have to support heavy traffic inside the house. In that case, where cellars were *not* may mark the location of where doorways *were*: that is, along the west half of the south wall, and the northwest and northeast corners.

Excavations 75′ southeast of the larger eighteenth-century building uncovered remains of another salvaged brick footing, traces of an exterior end fireplace, and six interior root cellars. The brick salvage trench outlined a building 28′ × 20′ with the 8′ × 9′ fireplace located off center along the west wall line. Two bricks in place in the building's southwest corner show the footing had been $1\frac{1}{2}$ courses wide.

Each of the six root cellars was backfilled with domestic refuse. Fragments of an English scratched-blue stoneware pitcher found in a cellar in the northeast

Figure 80　A representative collection of coinage from the Kingsmill Tenement/Quarter site, including numerous Virginia halfpennies, 1773. (Virginia Historic Landmarks Commission.)

corner of the kitchen crossmended with fragments from the fill in a cellar in the main building, indicating a contemporary filling date. However, two other cellars in the smaller structure contained fragments of English pearlware, again, a pottery type believed to have reached Virginia no earlier than 1780.

If the existence of root cellars is evidence of slave occupation, and the recurrance of the pattern certainly argues strongly that such is the case, then the sheer numbers of cellars alone at Kingsmill Quarter leave little doubt that slaves lived there. The numbers also suggest that gangs of fieldhands must have shared the two buildings, each with its own separate storage below ground, with all the fieldhands living together in structures more like barracks than single-family homes.

The Kingsmill property-wide survey of 1973 also located a backfilled basement at the location where the Desandrouin map shows three buildings, a larger structure south of two smaller buildings close to the Williamsburg–Hampton Road (Figure 23). The buildings, perhaps the "New Quarter" Humphrey Harwood repaired in the 1780s, are likely Burwell slave quarters, but like the other out settlements shown by Desandrouin, there is no label proving that to be so.[44] Nevertheless, Burwell slave ownership and the comparable archaeology at Littletown and Kingsmill Quarters tend to identify these scattered houses as the dwellings of fieldhands.

The site, hereafter referred to as North Quarter, was determined by initial testing to be relatively small (800 square feet), and, unlike other Kingsmill sites, there was considerable lead time to do the archaeology before the Busch construction.[45] Thus the plowzone in this case could be removed and screened by hand in small units, providing a more precisely defined artifact provenience. Consequently, analysis of the artifacts could isolate concentrations and voids in artifact distribution, indicating where doorways, windows, paths, trash areas, and chimneys had been located even if those features could not be found by study of the architectural remains and subplowzone deposits alone. In fact, once the plowzone was removed, relatively few structural remains were found: a backfilled half-basement with earth steps on the east, two small root cellars on the west, two postholes (probably scaffold holes used for chimney construction on the north), a section of robbed foundation walled on the south, two drainage ditches leading from the northwest and southeast corners of these features, and a relatively intact section of a brick partition in the basement fill (Figure 81). The orientation of the south wall of the basement, one of the drainage ditches, and the robbed wall line, together with the location of the scaffold holes and the other ditch indicate that the building was 25′ × 16′ overall. Moreover, the width of the robbed wall trench and the fallen partition wall suggest that a one-course-thick footing was used for the entire building, the size of brick footings of sufficient size to support only frame construction.

The half-basement, probably dug beneath the building after it was already standing, is rectangular on three sides, but the north wall makes an oblique angle with the other sides, and the orientation of what appears to be an enlargement of the small root cellar to the west tends to make an opposite, odd angle on its north wall. This rather irregular cellar construction may have been caused by the fact that a triangular chimney stood on the north wall line of the house and that the cellars had to be shaped to avoid undermining the existing brickwork of the fireplace. In fact, the scaffold holes could align with a chimney in that location and it would be logical for the partition to attach to the apex of the angle of the triangle putting a corner fireplace in each of the rooms above.

A concentration of brick and mortar in the plowzone in the general area of the scaffold holes and a concentration of nails to the north also suggest that a chimney stood there.[46] (Figure 82). The nail concentration may be there as a result of the deposition of ashes coming from hearth cleaning where packing crates, with their nails still in the wood, were burned as kindling. It is also possible that the postholes on that side of the house were not scaffold holes at all but were used instead to seat chimney timbers. In that case, nails used to build all or part of the stack may have accumulated on that side of the house as a result of the destructive chimney fires

Figure 81 Overhead view of excavated house site at North Quarter. (Virginia Historic Landmarks Commission.)

that so often plagued that type of construction. In fact, the photographs and interviews with blacks who lived with wooden chimneys in the nineteenth century make it clear that periodic destruction was a fact of life, so much so that they purposely built them to lean away from the buildings against wooden props (see Figure 19). Whenever the stacks accidentally ignited, the props were knocked away, allowing the burning stack to fall from the house, saving it from the flames. New similar construction would follow, with the ruins, ash, and nails of the original stack often left to accumulate in the yard.

The basement was typically filled with layers of washed clay and dark organic soil containing domestic refuse (Figure 83). The dates of the artifacts become more recent from bottom to top, indicating that the cellar was filled over a relatively long period of time. Sherds of creamware and a Virginia halfpenny of 1773 were found in the lowest level, indicating the date after which the cellar began to gather its backfill and perhaps a construction date in the 1770s. English handpainted pearl-ware and French Military buttons of a unit number *8* found in the upper backfill suggest a post-1781 filling, the year French troops came to the Yorktown area,[47] (Figure 84). It would, at any rate, be safe to say that the building was occupied

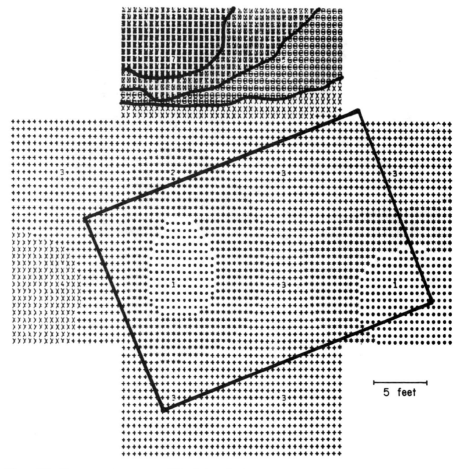

Figure 82 Computer-drawn map of North Quarter house site (rectangle) and excavated yard, showing concentrations of plowzone nails (top) near probable chimney location. (D. Sanford, University of Virginia.)

during the last quarter of the eighteenth century. The two other cellars were merely small pits, ostensibly for root storage, the largest retaining enough brick at the bottom to suggest that it had had a dry-laid brick and brickbat floor.

Although no traces of the other two buildings shown at the North Quarter site by the Desandrouin map were found by testing, it is possible that they were outbuildings employing earthfast construction. That being the case, only total stripping of the plowzone would likely define the location, an operation beyond the means of that excavation.

The development of a piece of the Busch property subsequently named Hampton Key uncovered the remains of the building shown on the Desandrouin

Figure 83 Cross-section through backfilled cellar, with bulkhead entrance steps at center left; North Quarter. (Virginia Historic Landmarks Commission.)

map to the south of North Quarter. Excavations there defined another dwelling site of the second half of the eighteenth century, another probable slave house employing earthfast building techniques. Posthole patterns and backfilled rectangular root cellars were found when the plowzone was removed. Ten major structural postholes and postmolds defined a three-bay building, 24′ × 28′ with an apparent 14′ × 12′ addition (Figure 85) to the west. The postholes encompassed two periods of root cellars.

The main posts in the core section were on slightly more than 9′ centers and there was a posthole along each end of the building at the center, 12′ apart. The centered post must have been necessary to support the end plate and roof ridge since the building was 6′ wider than the standard 18′ for earthfast construction on the other Kingsmill sites. On the other hand, like remains of the post buildings at Utopia and the Kingsmill Tenement, it is possible that the end-centered posts were necessary to give additonal support to chimney hoods. In fact, no other evidence was found for fireplace locations. The domestic nature of the artifacts from the cellar fill indicates that the building was a dwelling, and again, the recovery of English creamware and a 1773 Virginia halfpenny date the occupation to the last quarter of the eighteenth century.

Another map of 1781 shows that a "race ground" was located in the general vicinity of the area now known as Hampton Key and several artifacts, notably curry combs, bits, and horseshoes, were recovered from the backfilling of the root cellars

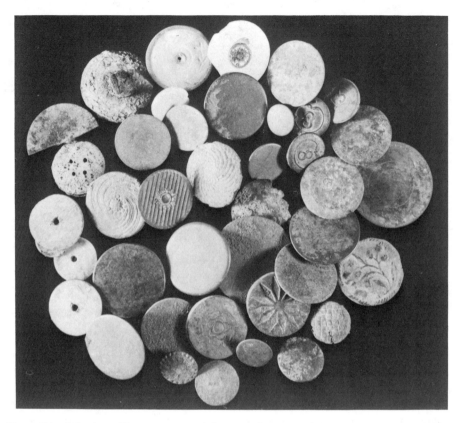

Figure 84 Collection of buttons recovered from North Quarter dating to the second half of the eighteenth century. (Virginia Historic Landmarks Commission.)

(Figure 86). It is possible that a slave was living there to attend to the horses and whatever "track" existed.

OUTBUILDINGS

There is no doubt that the most distinguishing characteristic of Virginia's colonial rural landscape was its villagelike appearance, so much so that travellers of the day rarely failed to comment on it. With so much land and so many people devoted to staple-crop production, it is little wonder that the land took on that look. The archaeology of the settlements at Kingsmill with their multitude of building remains gives the same impression. Of course, just the Kingsmill houses are almost enough in themselves to have created a pastoral villagelike landscape to the eye of a colonial visitor, but along with the numerous other buildings required by plantation society's goal of self-sufficiency—that is, the slave quarters and the

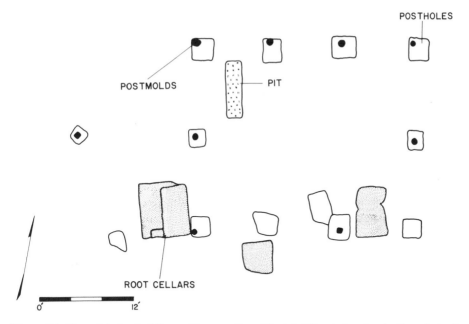

POSTHOLES

POSTMOLDS — PIT

ROOT CELLARS

0'   12'

Figure 85   Plan of timber building at Hampton Key. (Virginia Historic Landmarks Commission.)

shelters for animals, crops, food preparation, and storage—Kingsmill may well have even taken on the appearance of a "micro-megalopolis." The archaeological remains of the kitchens, dairies, storehouses, poultry houses, barns, and granaries, although largely only part of the settlements of Kingsmill's landlords, together give a more complete picture of the more pragmatic side of plantation life and, at the same time, trace the durable but changing role of the earthfast building tradition.

There is little question that the archaeological remains of kitchens indicate that they doubled as dwellings for servants and slaves; therefore, these buildings are more a part of the story of Kingsmill's residential architecture. Of course, where and how the cooks lived is significant, but where—in a comparative sense—cooking was done by the landlords and the laborers is an equally important part of the story. Even the tenants on Richard Kingsmill's property eventually moved the cooking out of the house and into the post-and-stud building 50' from the dwellings, perhaps as early as 1650 (Figure 28). On the other hand, Colonel Thomas Pettus seems to have assigned the cooking to a close but separate building at first, but toward the end of the occupation enlarged the structure until it was attached directly to the core section of the manor house (Figure 44). The enlargement campaign also resulted in the addition of the indoor dairy or buttery, a logical addition to the food-preparation building. But the people at Utopia, either servants or tenants, must have done their cooking right in the main house and, except

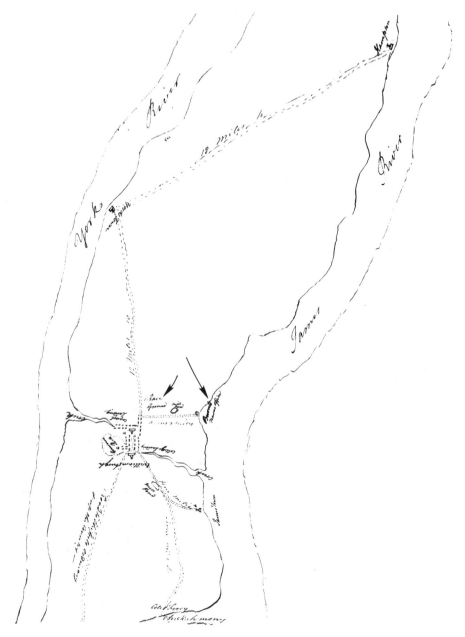

Figure 86 Map of Williamsburg area, 1781(?), showing "Burwell's Naval Office" and "Race Ground" at Hampton Key site (arrows).

for the tiny post building to the north, needed no other outbuildings that were substantial enough to leave archaeological remains.

The massive sizes of the two fireplaces on the south side of the Bray mansion and the root and "wine" cellars in the basement strongly suggest that, during the earlier years at least, food was prepared in the house (Figures 48, 49, and 67). But later, cooking moved to one or both of the earthfast buildings to the west. It may be that these buildings became summer kitchens as well as doubling for slave houses.

Certainly all of the cooking chores at Burwell's Kingsmill were carried out in the flanking brick dependencies, particularly in the building on the east side of the house where the enormous fireplace, oven, root cellars, adjacent "utilities," and doorway pattern all indicate food-preparation activity (Figures 72 and 73). In fact, remains of a path drain in the yard east of the house seem to mark the walkway between the south door of the kitchen building and the side door into what was probably the dining room of the mansion. A route for the waiters was also screened from the view of the forecourt by a wooden fence between the northeast corner of the house and southwest corner of the kitchen.

All other outbuildings on the Kingsmill property except some other "kitch-ens" and the Burwell dairy were of earthfast construction. Pettus and Bray built identical earthfast smokehouses with posts at each of the corners of a 9–10′ square (Figures 39, 87 and 88). Both structures also had square dry-laid brick fireboxes 5′6″–6′ on a side positioned within the building so that there was a working area on (the door?) side. No traces of smokehouses were found on any of the fieldhand sites with the possible exception of the four-posthole 9′-square building site found at Kingsmill Quarter. Unlike the Pettus and Bray structures, however, the Kings-mill Quarter structure had no brickwork or any layers of charcoal and animal bones associated with it.

Tobacco storage houses and barns were of great importance to the plantation economy of Kingsmill, and at least seven earthfast building sites found during the course of the excavations mark the location of these essential buildings (Figures 28, 87, and 89). Of course, it is clear from some of the seventeenth-century descrip-tions that grain was often stored in lofts in the houses of the poorer tenants, but even as early as the Kingsmill Tenement occupation, separate covered space for grain storage was constructed by the planters (Figure 28). The posthole–postmold pattern of the five-bay building on the south edge of the settlement leaves little question that that building was a granary. The 10′ gap between posts forming the central bay probably marks the location of a covered space through which carts could be driven to unload their cargo into flanking cribs. Granaries and corn cribs of that design can still be seen in the Virginia countryside today.

Colonel Thomas Pettus probably housed slaves in the post building on the east of the settlement, but he could have stored grain in the loft as well (Figure 39). The discovery of posthole–postmold patterns 180′ west of the house site suggests that he had at least three other storage buildings, likely barns, granaries, and/or

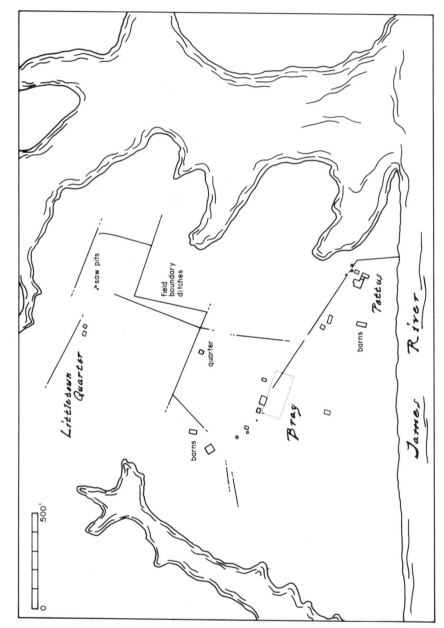

Figure 87 Plan of Littletown, showing outbuilding sites and boundary ditches. (Sondy Sanford.)

Figure 88 View of earthfast smokehouse with remains of brick firebox, Bray home plantation, Littletown. (Virginia Historic Landmarks Commission.)

tobacco barms as well (Figures 87 and 89). The posthole–postmold lines were found to be on the same general axis as the house, usually an indicator that they dated from the Pettus period and that they were probably all standing at the same time. No datable artifacts were found associated with building deposits, perhaps more reason to suggest that the structures were for produce storage.

The building site closest to the river was built in five bays and was the largest of all, 50′ × 20′. The aligned holes were about 3′ in diameter with postmolds 1′ in diameter spaced irregularly 9–13′ apart. Such an irregular spacing of the main structural posts (tie-beam pairs) would have made it difficult to incorporate any flooring sills between, so perhaps the irregularity proves that the building had only a dirt floor. The two other buildings were smaller, the one a two-bay (18′ × 24′) and the other (18′ × 42′) of four bays. The two larger buildings were built at right angles to the third and their construction seems to indicate that they were used for different purposes. The larger of the two consisted of a series of 10 postholes averaging 2′6″ square with postmolds 6–9″ square. Like the largest building near the river, the postmolds were basically aligned on the long axis, but the spaces between posts varied from 9′ to as much as 13′. Again, if these irregularities mean that the building had no floor sills between the tie-beams, the building would

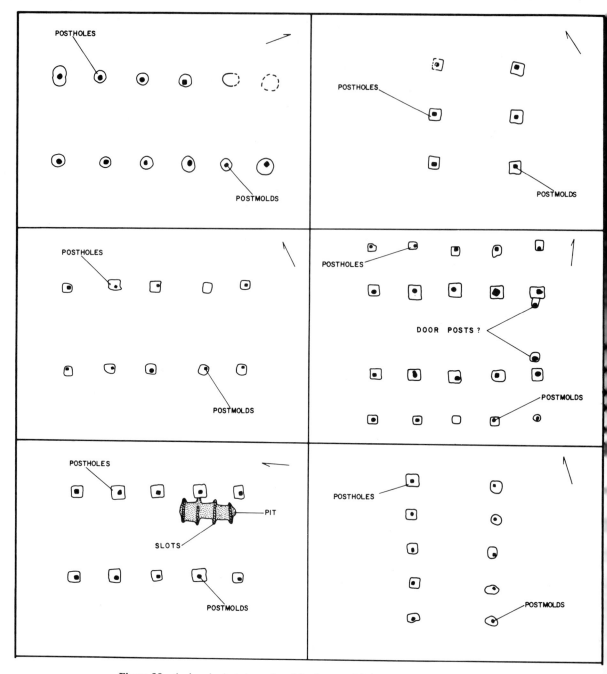

Figure 89   Archaeological plans of earthfast barns at Littletown. See also Figure 87. (Virginia Historic Landmarks Commission.)

probably have had no raised floor. It follows then that this building, like its larger riverward counterpart, was more utilitarian in nature.

The remains of the third structure consisted of only six postholes with postmolds indicating that the main structural posts were all 10″ square. Unlike the other two buildings, the posthole–postmolds were of a uniform depth, alignment, and spacing throughout, more characteristic of seventeenth-century house construction elsewhere at Kingsmill. The care taken by the builders to evenly form the postholes that would in turn ensure exact alignment of the posts in all directions may well be evidence that this smaller building had a raised floor supported on the interrupted sills that required consistently positioned posts. This does not suggest that this smaller outbuilding was a dwelling; no domestic artifacts were found. But farmsteads like Littletown needed the dry, varmint-proof space a raised and tight wooden floor would create for food storage, particularly grain and corn. Conversely, tobacco barns, where the leaves are suspended on racks, can get by with simple dirt floors and they were usually relatively large (20′ × 40′ or 60′), "the whole covered with clapboards"[48] (Figures 90 and 91). It follows then that the two larger and more casually built buildings west of Pettus's manor house were tobacco-curing and/or -storage barns.

Two more post patterns in the Littletown section of the property, northwest of the Bray Plantation domestic area, indicate the locations of additional colonial outbuildings (Figure 87). Sets of postholes of two different sizes remained of what almost certainly had been a barn there. The central core section consisted of 10 large postholes (four bays), containing postmolds 10″ square to 1′3″ in diameter, placed on consistent 10-foot centers. The regularity of the posthole spacing again may suggest wooden flooring. Smaller posts, 6″ in diameter to 9″ square, placed 10′ from the core section, apparently supported sheds on either side, making the structure 40′ square overall. Two additional postholes, centered along the east wall line, spaced 12′ apart, probably supported door posts.

Only a handful of artifacts—all rose-headed nails—were found associated with the building, suggesting that the building dated only generally to the colonial period. That structure's north–south orientation, 40° to the east of the otherwise aligned buildings at the nearby Bray domestic site, however, argues that the structure was not a part of the Bray complex. If that is true, it is likely that the barn was yet another storage building of Pettus's Littletown.

But the other post pattern did align with Bray Plantation buildings, 380′ to the northwest, probably the eighteenth-century Bray Plantation barns. Ten rectangular postholes, with 10″-square postmolds placed on 10′ centers, marked the location of the main structural beams. A 4′ × 12′ pit, probably a root cellar, was found in the southeast corner of the building. The exactly spaced and aligned postholes and the root cellar both suggest that the structure, in fact, had a wooden floor, but an almost total lack of artifacts hinders attempts to determine the function or date of the structure. Its alignment with the other Bray buildings, however, does suggest an eighteenth-century date. The root cellar, a feature found almost

Figure 90　Earthfast tobacco barn, St. Mary's City, Maryland. See also Figure 33 above.

Figure 91　Reconstructed seventeenth-century tobacco-barn interior, St. Mary's City, Maryland.

invariably in the dwellings of Kingsmill's laborers, found in this case in a building used for grain storage, is puzzling.

Another post pattern (19' × 32'), outlined a timber building with irregularly spaced structural posts, located between the Bray Plantation mansion and the river. The fill in a related posthole contained a fragment of a glass wine-bottle datable to the period circa 1740–1760. Again, the dimensions of the structure and its probable dirt floor suggest that it served as one of Bray's tobacco houses.

The one utilitarian outbuilding with a brick foundation, most likely the remains of Lewis Burwell's dairy or scullery or laundry, was found in the east kitchen yard (Figures 46, 92, and 93). A nearby well supplied both the laundry and dairy operations and a 1½'-wide brick drainage tunnel, found still extant extending from 55–177' to the north, must have drained waste water from the floor of the 20' × 17' structure into a nearby ravine.

There is no doubt that the building, probably a frame 1½-story structure, was contemporary with the Burwell complex, although no datable artifacts were found in the construction trenches. A fragment of coarse earthenware, a type made in Yorktown during the second quarter of the eighteenth century, found in the fill of

Figure 92 Surviving south and west wall foundations of dairy, Burwell's Kingsmill. (Virginia Historic Landmarks Commission.)

Figure 93 Cross-section through drainage tunnel, Kingsmill dairy. (Virginia Historic Landmarks Commission.)

the drain, suggests that the building was standing early in the Burwell occupation.[49] The Desandrouin map shows a building in that general area as well, and it apparently stood until 1862, the date a Civil War map shows a structure in that same location.[50] The Desandrouin map shows yet another Burwell building at a location where excavation uncovered a segment of a brick foundation, but not enough of it survived to suggest the building's plan or its function.

Excavations at Burwell's Ferry Landing uncovered the eighteenth-century remains of a partially eroded brick foundation at the river's edge, almost certainly the warehouse so often referred to in *Virginia Gazette* notices (Figure 94).[51] The surviving sections of the east and north walls were two courses thick, laid in English bond. The remaining walls (one-half of the north and west walls) were detected by tracing the rubble-filled trench left by brick salvagers. Erosion had totally destroyed the south wall and portions of the east and west walls as well. A one-course-wide footing or pier bonded into the east wall 23′6″ from the surviving northeast wall. The 23′6″ distance from the undisturbed corner is the same as the width of the building. That being the case, the footing probably supported a central partition beam dividing the building into two equal-size rooms. Also, two changes in the wall bonding immediately south of the partition suggest a door location, 4′6″ in width.

Artifacts in soil layers in, around, and under the warehouse foundation gener-

Figure 94 The Burwell's Landing warehouse foundation during excavation, showing two-course brick construction and a later post bulkhead. (Virginia Historic Landmarks Commission.)

ally date the lifespan of the structure. A wash layer beneath the brickwork containing seventeenth-century locally made clay-pipe fragments and square-case bottle glass establishes a post-1640 date for construction. But these artifacts were probably washed down from the seventeenth-century Harrop site on the hill to the west long after that early date. Wine-bottle fragments recovered from the salvage trench, however, indicate a post-1770 date for the dismantling of the structure. And it is probable that the building was "Burwell's Naval Office" shown on a map of 1781 (Figure 86). It would be safe to assume that the buildings spanned the Burwell Naval Office years, 1728–1775.

NOTES

[1]The dating is partially based on tobacco-pipe bowl shapes and measuring the diameters of the pipestem holes, although those data can be somewhat unreliable: I. Noël Hume, *A Guide to the Artifacts*

of Colonial America, (New York, 1970), pp. 296–307. Nonetheless, the absence of the post-1650 wine-bottle glass from the site strongly suggests pre-1650 occupation. It is possible that a trash pit accidently uncovered by a bulldozer during construction at a military training camp on the Utopia section of Kingsmill found to contain artifacts predating 1640 and an iron seige helmet marks remains of another early site. No structural remains survived there.

[2]This conclusion was drawn after discussion with Cary Carson, Colonial Williamsburg Foundation historian, and historical archaeologist Carter Hudgins, and in light of recent discoveries of early post building patterns at the Maine Site near Jamestown: Alain C. Outlaw, "Excavations at the Maine, James City County Virginia," (mss. Virginia Research Center for Archaeology, Yorktown, 1979).

[3]Discussion with Gary Wheeler Stone, Chief Archaeologist, St. Mary's City Commission, St. Maries Citty, Maryland, December 12, l980.

[4]James M. Smith, *Archaeology of Yorke Village and the First and Second Parish Churches, Yorktown, Va.,* (Williamsburg, Virginia, 1978), pp. 31, 46.

[5]I am grateful to Dell Upton for the sketches he provided of possible reconstructions of the Kingsmill earthfast houses.

[6]Fraser D. Neiman, *The Manner House Before Stratford,* (Stratford, Virginia, 1980), pp. 12–18.

[7]I have suggested elsewhere (William M. Kelso, "Rescue Archaeology on the James," *Archaeology,* September/October, 1979, pp. 15–21) that the absence of stud holes at each end of the building could be evidence of a type of construction known as "cruck," which employs curved one-piece sections of trees to form the rafters and walls. In that case studs might have only been necessary along the longer wall lines; that is, to support the wall plates. Although this type of construction still may be the correct interpretation, the reconstruction shown as Figure 37 seems the most logical.

[8]Bacon's Castle, Surry County, Virginia, is the best example.

[9]Eric Mercer, *The English Vernacular House,* (London, 1975), pp. 34–44.

[10]Cary Carson, "Impermanent Architecture in the Southern American Colonies," *Winterthur Portfolio,* (Chicago, 1981), Vol. 16, nos. 2/3, p. 180.

[11]See above (Chapter 2, note 74 and Figure 112 below.

[12]Noël Hume, *Guide to Artifacts,* pp. 63, 303, and Stanley South, *Method and Theory in Historical Archaeology,* (New York, 1977), p. 214.

[13]Noël Hume, *Guide to Artifacts,* pp.191, 303.

[14]I am grateful for the interpretative comments of Mr. Paul Buchanan and Ivor Noël Hume during their visit to the site in August, 1972.

[15]I. Noël Hume, *A Guide to the Artifacts of Colonial America,* (New York, 1970), p. 128.

[16]*Ibid.,* pp. 65, 114–116.

[17]Mary R. M. Goodwin, "Kingsmill Plantation, James City County Virginia," (Colonial Williamsburg Foundation, Williamsburg, Virginia, 1958), p. LXIV.

[18]I am grateful for the comments and visit to the excavation by Paul Buchanan, and for Camille Wells's thoughts on the meaning of the ruins offered in Camille Wells, "Kingsmill Plantation: A Cultural Analysis," (Master's Thesis, University of Virginia, 1976).

[19]I. Noël Hume, *Guide to Artifacts,* p. 132.

[20]Again this interpretation owes much to the thesis of Camille Wells (see note 18 above).

[21]Thomas Tileton Waterman, *The Mansions of Virginia,* (Chapel Hill, North Carolina, 1946), pp. 154–164.

[22]I am grateful for the historical research of Mrs. Margaret Peters of the Virginia Historic Land-marks Commission pertaining to the landing ordinary.

[23]I appreciate the visit to the excavation and the thoughts that day of Ivor Noël Hume, Fall, 1973.

[24]I. Noël Hume, *Guide to Artifacts,* p. 126.

[25]Wells, "Kingsmill Plantation," p. 30.

[26]I. Noël Hume, *Guide to Artifacts,* pp. 114–116, 132 and *Virginia Gazette,* Purdie and Dixon, April 25, 1766.

[27]Cary Carson *et al.,* "Impermanent Architecture in the Southern American Colonies," *Winterthur Portfolio,* (Vol. 16, nos. 2/3, (Chicago, 1981), p. 180; and Henry M. Miller, "Pettus and Utopia: A Comparison of the Faunal Remains from Two Late Seventeenth Century Virginia Households," (Paper presented at the Conference on Historic Sites Archaeology, September, 1978, Winston-Salem, North Carolina).

[28]See above Chapter 2.

[29]Small cellars appeared with regularity on the sites of "servants houses" during recent excavations at Thomas Jefferson's Monticello: William M. Kelso, "A Report of Archaeological Excavations at Monticello, Albemarle County, Virginia, 1979–1983," (Thomas Jefferson Memorial Foundation, mss. Monticello, Charlottesville, Virginia, 1984), pp. 49–150.

[30]Robert Beverly, *The History and Present State of Virginia,* ed. by Louis B. Wright (Chapel Hill, North Carolina, 1947), p. 145.

[31]I. Noël Hume, *A Guide to Artifacts of Colonial America,* (New York, 1970), p. 132.

[32]William Louis Calver and Reginald Pelham Bolton, *History Written with Pick and Shovel,* (New York, 1950), p. 113.

[33]I am grateful for the preliminary analysis of the skeleton by Leonard Winter, then assistant archaeologist with the Colonial Williamsburg Foundation.

[34]I. Noël Hume, "Excavations at Tutter's Neck in James City County, Virginia, 1960–61," *Contributions from the Museum of History and Technology* (Paper 53, Washington, D.C., 1966).

[35]This is my own reinterpretation of the evidence presented in Mr. Noël Hume's site report given in light of discoveries made years after the report was written. I. Noël Hume, *Tutter's Neck,* pp. 46–48; William M. Kelso, "A Report on the Exploratory Excavations at Carter's Grove Plantation, James City County, Virginia, June 1970–September, 1971," (Colonia Williamsburg Foundation, Williamsburg, Virginia, 1971), pp. 37–41 and Note 3 above.

[36]*Virginia Gazette,* Dixon and Nicholson, February 17, 1781.

[37]*The Compact Edition of the Oxford English Dictionary,* (Oxford, 1971).

[38]Fraser D. Neiman, "Archaeology of Burwell's Kingsmill: The Kitchen and Storehouse" in William M. Kelso, "An Interim Report, Historical Archaeology at Kingsmill, the 1975 Season," (mss. Virginia Historic Landmarks Commission, Research Center for Archaeology, Yorktown, Virginia, 1977), pp. 38–46.

[39]Neiman, "Burwell's Kingsmill, Storehouse," pp. 46–58.

[40]*Ibid.,* pp. 46–58.

[41]Humphrey Harwood Ledgers, (mss. Colonial Williamsburg Foundation, Williamsburg, Virginia), Ledger B, folio 67.

[42]I. Noël Hume, *Guide to Artifacts,* pp. 162–163.

[43]Eric P. Newman, "Coinage for Colonial Virginia," *Numismatic Notes and Monographs,* (The American Numismatic Society, 1956), p. 36.

[44]Harwood, Ledgers, folio 67.

[45]The discussion of the archaeological remains at North Quarter is drawn from my own field observation and from Nicholas Luccketti, "North Quarter Salvage Excavation Interim Report," (mss. Virginia Historic Landmarks Commission, Research Center for Archaeology, Yorktown, Virginia, 1979).

[46]I am indebted to archaeologist Douglas Sanford, Assistant Archaeologist, Thomas Jefferson Memorial Foundation, for the computer analysis of North Quarter artifacts.

[47]There is however, no known record of a French unit Number 8 at Yorktown. Personal communication with James Haskett, Historian, Colonial National Historical Park, National Park Service, Yorktown, Virginia, Fall, 1973.

[48]William Tatum, *Essay of the Culture and Commerce of Tobacco,* (London, 1800), quoted in Harold B. Gill, Jr., "Tobacco Culture in Colonial Virginia," (mss. Colonial Williamsburg Foundation, Williamsburg, Virginia 1974), p. 21.

[49]Norman F. Barka, "The Kiln and Ceramics of the Poor Potter of Yorktown: A Preliminary

Report," in Ian M. G. Quimby, *Ceramics in America,* (Winterthur Conference Report for 1972, Charlottesville, Virginia 1973), pp. 272–273.

[50]Captain H. I. Abbott, Campaign Maps, Army of the Potomac Yorktown to Williamsburg, Map No. 1, September 1862.

[51]Mary R. M. Goodwin, "Kingsmill Plantation, James City County, Virginia," (Colonial Williamsburg Foundation, Williamsburg, Virginia, 1958), pp. 70-90.

4

FROM THE EARTH: FOOD AND DRINK

GARDENS

The vegetable or kitchen garden was a vital part of rural life in all periods and at all levels of the social and economic scale. By the eighteenth century, gardening, at least for the landowners, began to be something more than pure necessity. The pleasure-garden concept, already so popular in Europe and England, began seriously to take hold across the Atlantic, and clearly the rash of Georgian estate planning in Virginia included attempts at formal landscape architecture. These landscape efforts usually left only faint traces in the ground, making attempts to understand that part of Kingsmill archaeologically difficult. But just as the otherwise vanished earthfast timber buildings were found by identifying the soil stains left from the installation and decay of wooden posts, so too could lost garden plans be recovered by tracing patterns of soil stains from planting and fencing.

Although no subplowzone soil stains outlining enclosures were found dating to the early settlement period at Littletown Tenement, the series of ditches near the earthfast building complex at Kingsmill Tenement shows that a garden did exist (Figure 28). There, continuous ditches about 9″ wide by 6″ deep were found, one of them 75′ long connecting the northernmost house to the corner of the smaller post-and-stud dwelling. Since no individual postholes could be seen in the uniformly dark earth in the ditches or slots, it does not appear that the barrier that stood there was any version of a post-and-rail fence. Rather, it is more likely that either saplings with woven branches or vertically placed boards were seated side by side in the slots, a common pragmatic solution to seventeenth-century fencing. Boards buried side by side in the ground would be the most effective deterrant for burrowing animals as well. Although not enough of the entire fence plan could be traced beyond the immediate vicinity of the houses, there is the distinct possibility that the Kingsmill Tenement "garden fence" also doubled as a defensive palisade, giving some security to the building compound and the garden, much like the Clifts Plantation palisade at Strafford (see Figure 35).

Pettus's tenant or servant at Utopia constructed a more substantial barrier, a post-and-rail garden fence on three sides of a 130′ × 40′ area on the river side of the house (Figure 39). Postholes with postmolds 6–9″ in diameter were found 10′ apart, marking the course and location of the major support timbers for the barrier. On the east and south, a continuous ditch 1′6″ wide followed the fenceline along the exterior, terminating in a 13′ × 15′ pit or pond. A description of fence construction in the Kingsmill area in the 1790s leaves little question about what the posthole-ditch archaeological evidence did and did not mean:

> Spots of several acres are seen enclosed with fences which are even sometimes well executed by means of a mound of earth a couple of feet in height forming a kind of wall on which are planted stakes that are afterwards interwoven with pine branches. But traveling America the traveler cannot refrain from asking in his own mind why the people do not plant quick hedges, which afford a better security and are at the same time an ornament to the lands.[1]

It is puzzling that the posthole-ditch patterns did not continue on the west and north. It could be that the woven stakes were not seated as deeply near the house and/or a plain split-rail "worm fence," which required no posts in the ground, filled the void.

The fence is oriented to the axis of the house, but the enclosure seems to have been erected with no regard for symmetry. In fact, its size may have been dictated by the location of the well, the builders extending the enclosure just far enough to the west to make sure that the well wound up inside. Also, the south wall postholes appear to have been aligned so that the fence connected to the southwest and southeast corners of the house, in which case the garden was completely enclosed by the fence and the house. This meant that the garden could be entered directly from the house without troubling with a gate. The convenience of the garden along with its well also suggests that cooking took place in the house itself.

The landlord, Pettus, also enclosed garden space on the river side of his house, the plan partially recovered by archaeology (Figure 39). The remains of the enclosure was similar to Utopia, a line of postholes inside a ditch, again reflecting Liancourt's observation of elevated stake fences with interwoven pine. Although woodland and time did not allow complete excavation, it appears that the garden fence continued to the southeast, 180′ from the house, where it made a turn toward the river. If the enclosure was centered on the house site, then perhaps the total enclosed space was double the distance of the house to the southeast "corner," making the north side of the garden 360′ long. The southern extent of the enclosure, of course, could not be determined because the 1′-per-year erosion of the shoreline at that point has destroyed the fenceline postholes and ditches. Nonetheless, if the garden did extend completely to the seventeenth-century shoreline, it is possible to suggest that the garden was as large as 360′ × 200′, the distance of the postholes to the modern shoreline plus the conjectured amount of shoreline missing since circa 1650. This amounts to an enclosed space of about 2 acres, a considerable garden to manage and maintain and a considerable investment in fencing alone. Although not enough was excavated within the enclosure to detect any planting pattern, there is some reason to doubt that such a relatively large acreage could be reserved for vegetables alone. It is more likely that the garden, so visible from the river, was somewhat formally laid out. There is a puzzling seventeenth-century reference to the remarkable orchard at a "Littletown," but the location seems to be several miles away.[2] It is possible that the narrator was, in fact, viewing the garden at Pettus's Littletown directly on the James, but his description became garbled over time. If that is true, the Pettus garden may have included the showpiece orchard.

There is much less speculation about the landscaping efforts of Kingsmill's eighteenth-century landlords (See Figure 46). Both at Bray's Littletown and Burwell's Kingsmill the traces of decayed post-and-rail fencing mark relatively formal garden plans and, in the case of the Kingsmill home plantation, an overall landscape design.

Removal of the plowzone south of the Bray mansion revealed two lines of postholes and postmolds, forming a rectangle 105′ × 235′, slightly over ½ acre (Figures 46 and 95). The north fenceline connected to the south corners of the

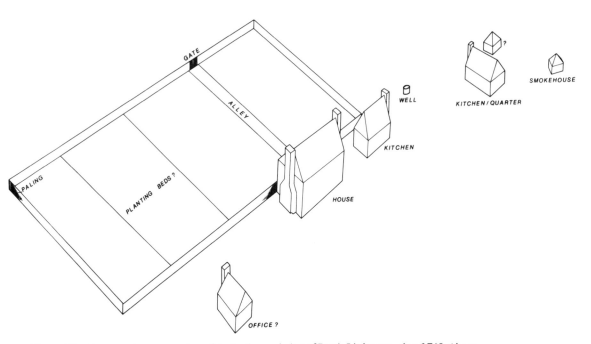

Figure 95 Conceptual reconstruction of the landscape design of Bray's Littletown, circa 1740. (Anna Gruber.)

house so that the south door opened directly into the garden and the house itself became a section of the barrier. The posts, set on 10–12′ centers, formed two lines on the west and north, indicating that the garden existed long enough for the fence to decay and be replaced one time. That could indicate a 40-year lifespan for the barrier. If the enclosed garden were in existence for that period of time, then it probably served all of the Brays who lived there between 1700 and 1744.

The intervals between postholes remained constant except at a location 60′ from the southwest corner of the enclosure where two posts stood only 4′ apart. This undoubtedly represented a gate location that aligns with the center of the house, 105′ to the north. In all probability, therefore, the gate stood at the end of a walkway leading directly from a central doorway in the house. This divides the space into a rectangle 105′ × 60′ at the west end of the enclosed space. If the rest of the garden was arranged symmetrically and geometrically, than perhaps the major planting areas were divided into even rectangles, four in number, similar in size to the area marked by the housedoor cross-walk. If the walks were so systematically laid out, then the east wall of the conjectured east dependency would align with the easternmost crosswalk as well. That being the case, the garden begins to take on aspects of a relatively formal design, suggesting that the garden was created to be both practical and esthetic. Like the Pettus enclosure, the garden would have been a conspicuous element of the landscape when viewed from the river, and in all probability decorative as well as edible plants were growing there in geometric patterns.

Owing to the fact that the topsoil was removed from most of the open field surrounding the Bray site, all subsurface features could be traced in their entirety (Figure 87). Consequently, all of the buildings that left disturbances below the subsoil level could be detected and a series of interconnecting ditches were also apparent. These ditches all appear to date to the eighteenth century and are basically oriented to the compass axis of the Bray home plantation buildings. It is reasonable to conclude, therefore, that the ditches were most probably put in to divide the Bray fields. They seem generally to mark off the land into $2\frac{1}{2}$-acre plots, perhaps separated by the types of raised fences seen in the neighborhood by the contemporary Liancourt. These separate planting areas may have been a part of Bray's relatively early attempts at field-crop rotation, as well. A curious notation in the ledger book of 1736–1744 shows what appears to be the mathematical calculations for experiments with rotating tobacco, clover, and wheat, a system adopted by Thomas Jefferson later in the century (see Figure 96).[3]

The extent to which the Lewis Burwells designed a formal garden to enhance Kingsmill mansion and forecourt outbuildings is crystal clear. In fact, before excavation, the remnants of the terraces on the river side of the house indicated that the land had been sculpted, which, viewed from the river, must have created a virtual pedestal for the house. The excavations of the garden spaces below the terraces and in the forecourt revealed the details of a formal garden that in scope probably rivaled the best of the Virginia Georgian estates of the period.

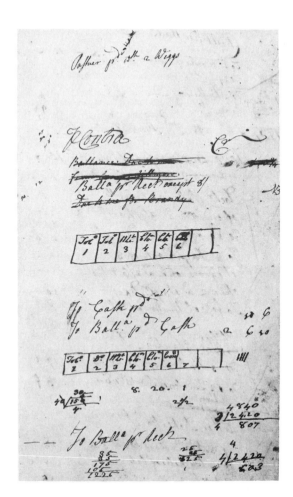

Figure 96 Page from 1736–1744 Bray Littletown ledger, showing calculations (?) for rotating the planting of tobacco, wheat, and clover. (Colonial Williamsburg Foundation.)

The discovery of the postholes of a major garden fenceline—issuing originally from the south corners of the mansion, then moving to the north corner, extending 50′ east and west, then turning 480′ toward the river—shows that the Burwell riverfront garden encompassed two acres, the south front yard of the house, the terraces, and an area 200′ × 320′ on the level plain below. The initial period of fenceposts, 10″ square and repaired at least once, were seated in holes 3′ × 3′, suggesting a solid paling of monumental size, perhaps as large as the fence Jefferson had instructed his overseer Edmund Bacon to build in 1809:

His first work is to pale in the garden, with a paling 10. feet high. the posts are to be of locust, sufficiently stout, barked but not hewed, 12 f. long, of which 2½ f. are to go in the ground. it will take about 300: placing them 9. f. apart. the rails are to be of heart poplar or pine. the stock is to be slpit into 4. quarters thus ⊞ then each quarter is to be split diagonally thus ◺ so as to make 2 three square rails out of each quarter. they are to be of

the size usual in strong garden paling. I do not know what that is. there will be 3. to each
pannel & consequently 900. in all.

  The pales are to be of chestnut, riven, & strong, 5. f. 3. I long, to be dubbed on one
another on the middle rail like clapboards, so that 1. nail shall do, & [the] two lengths of
pales will make the whole height. I suppose they will be generally from 5. to 7. I. wide, &
should be so near as not to let even a young hare in. there will be about 7500. wanting.
they are to be sharpened at the upper end thus ◖ and not thus ◖ as usual.[4]

The deer and rabbits were undoubtedly as great a problem to Lewis Burwell as they
were to Jefferson and there could be little other reason to dig such massive
postholes or to use such large timbers for the posts unless the rails and paling
boards were similarly massive.

  The postholes were generally on 10′ centers, except where a 4′-spacing
marked gate locations. A 4′-wide gate stood at the end of a central alley 460′ from
the house. Similar hole spacing marked gates on the east and west, 160′ from the
the south fence, probably placed at each end of a major crosswalk. The alley and
crosswalks then divided the planting space into four major plots, each bed being
160′ × 200′. If this garden were laid out like its contemporaries, there must have
been walks along the base of the terrace and the fence, which may have narrowed
the beds somewhat. The "schematic" Simcoe map of the property does indeed
show a garden divided into rectangles much as the archaeological evidence suggests
(if one discounts the east–west orientation) (see Figure 26). With the crosspath
and central alley, the enlarged garden plan becomes three equal-size modules of
approximatly 160′ each: the mansion riverfront yard–terrace, the area between the
base of the terrace and crosspath, and the area between the crosspath and the
southern end of the enclosure. It is significant to note that the 160′ distance
between the flanking dependencies is identical to the north–south dimensions of
the garden modules, suggesting that an overall grid pattern dictated the garden
design.

  Three sets of steps, built with granite slabs ranging from 2′ 3″ to 4′ 6″ with 1′
6″-wide risers, descend the slope of each terrace. (Figures 97 and 101). The dismantling of part of the top steps uncovered a shell-mortared brickbat foundation
resting on either natural clay or thin layers of construction debris. Both the shell
mortar and the recovery of fragments of wine-bottle glass stylistically datable to the
first quarter of the eighteenth century suggest that the steps were put in at the same
time as the mansion outbuilding complex. The origin of the stone is difficult to
determine, but it has been suggested that the granite material could have come
from Wales or northern Scotland.[5]

  The first-period fenceline also extended to the east of the central garden
enclosure, forming an enclosure 103′ × 63′ on the east side of the terraces.
Although the northern line was partially covered by the construction of the storehouse, evidently this eastern enclosure continued in use after the storehouse was
constructed and a riverfront gate relocated.

  It appears that the eastern enclosure ceased to exist after circa 1770. But

Figure 97 Granite steps on terraces south of Burwell's Kingsmill mansion. (Virginia Historic Landmarks Commission.)

during its existence and after, the area became a domestic refuse disposal site. A considerable deposit of discarded artifacts and food remains were deposited along the fenceline eventually covering abandoned postholes (see Figure 113). Sherds of creamware dating after 1770 were found in the initial trash layer covering the fenceline postholes.

Foundations, fencepost lines, and ditches in the forecourt area on the land front of the mansion defined a formal parterre, which included a marl walk extending from the semicircular entrance steps axially to an entrance gate 65' to the north and both east and west to connect the mansion with the dependencies (Figure 98). The walk continued past the dependencies to form an ogee curve on each side of the entrance gate.

Other details add to the formal plan. A series of postholes (fenceline) lay outside the ogee curve of the walk on the east and, probably, the west sides of the entrance. A ditch paralleled the walk from the southwestern corner of the kitchen to a point midway between the gate and the dependency: it was probably a planting ditch for a boxwood (?) hedge.

Another detail suggested that originally the walk was defined by a series of brick pillars, one base surviving northwest of the office dependency near a related brick drain (Figure 99). The discovery of carved portland stone sections of decorative urns and the survival of the landfront fence employing identical urns based on brick pillars at Westover Plantation in Charles City County establish the distinct

Figure 98 Forecourt garden area, showing entrance-gate postholes, second-period fenceline postholes, curved planting ditch, and brick foundation of marl path. (Virginia Historic Landmarks Commission.)

Figure 99   Brick drain for garden path (right) and brick garden pillar base (left). (Virginia Historic Landmarks Commission.)

possibility that the original Kingsmill forecourt enclosure was of an identical construction and ornamentation (Figures 100 and 101).

The fill in the postholes of the enclosure along the eastern ogee curve contained brickbats, mortar, and sherds of creamware, suggesting both a post-1770 date for the construction and that brickwork had been removed in the area at the time of construction. It is possible that the "takeing down Pillers" on August 22, 1778 listed in the ledger of Humphrey Harwood, the Williamsburg brickmason and contractor, referred to the removal of the formal brick posts when they were replaced with wood.[6]

The only other traces of gardens associated with the landholding classes were the remnants of the enclosures on the east and south of the Landing Ordinary building (Figure 46). There, two periods of ditches, probably again the remains of Liancourt's "raised stake fences" and a later paling in the same location, as well as another separate enclosure, were found south and east of the kitchen. The garden that was enclosed by the first and second period of raised fencing apparently was subdivided into plots 50′ wide. The 60′ × 110′ space enclosed by only a single period of raised fencing to the east of the building was probably similarly subdivided. Of course, considering the necessity of having a livery stable at the landing, these enclosures may have been merely to pen horses and were never planted. Possibly, the garden to the south, an area quite visible from the river, was formally

Figure 100 Carved portland stone pedestal, found at Burwell's Kingsmill, is similar to eighteenth-century pedestals below decorative urns at Westover Plantation, Charles City County, Virginia. (Virginia Historic Landmarks Commission.)

laid out as the ditches suggest, whereas the single fence toward the land approach was kept for horses.

That slaves were allowed to have their own kitchen gardens is a well-documented fact, but clear archaeological evidence of slave gardens did not appear on Kingsmill's slave sites, with the possible exception of North Quarter (Figure 66). The same ditches that may have served to shed water away from the house at the northwest and southeast corners of the house may have, in fact, been the ditches for raised fences. There is no way of knowing the size or planting arrangement, in that excavations could not be extended into that area. However, it is interesting to note that distribution studies of the refuse disposal clearly locate concentrations of garbage within what may have been the kitchen garden. Nineteenth-century slave owners encouraged the composting of the domestic refuse from slave quarters and it follows that the material then went on the gardens.[7]

WELLS

Seven wells were found during the course of the Kingsmill excavations and it is clear that only the landlords or the more permanent leaseholders went to the

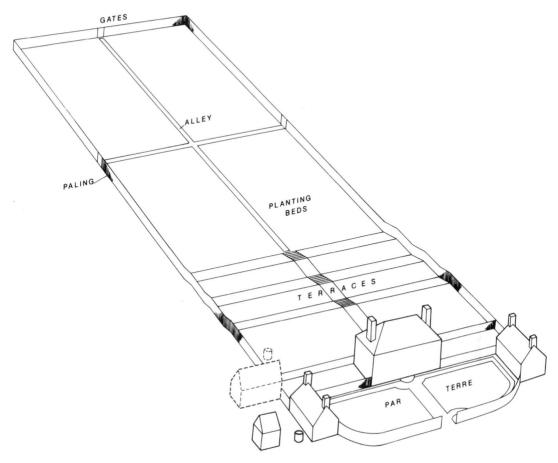

Figure 101 Conceptual reconstruction of the landcape design at Burwell's Kingsmill, circa 1760. (Anna Gruber.)

trouble and expense to dig them. Natural springs and, apparently, simple rain barrels served the needs of the people at Kingsmill and Littletown Tenements, and the overseers and/or slaves at Tutter's Neck, Hampton Key, and the Kingsmill, Littletown, and North quarters. Backfilled, bricklined, or once-bricklined shafts were found at Harrops's, Pettus's, and Bray's Littletown, Utopia, Burwell's Landing, and Burwell's Kingsmill.

It should be no surprise that all of the wells were found reasonably close to the house sites, 2' at a minimum to 80' maximum from the buildings used for cooking (Figures 39 and 46). It should also be no surprise that the wells were located conveniently close to the gardens.

All of the wellshafts were originally lined with brick, which had either been removed when the well fell into disuse or had been left essentially intact during backfilling. Depth varied from a minimum of 33' at the ordinary to at least 67' at

Utopia, always depending, of course, on the original depth of the colonial water table. Where the brickwork survived, wedge-shaped well bricks were used in the construction of the shafts for the major section of the wall, while rectangular bricks were often used for shoring at the bottom. The upper 10′ of the Burwell kitchen wellshaft was constructed of mortared rectangular brick for additional strength. There was some variation in brick sizes between the two seventeenth-century wells; at Harrop and Pettus they tended to be longer and molded to a less-severe angle than their eighteenth-century counterparts. The seventeenth-century wells, therefore, had a slightly larger diameter than those dating to the 1700s.

The archaeological evidence suggests two construction methods. The most obvious was to install a brick lining from the bottom up, within a predug shaft. A safer but probably more difficult method known as *steening* was to line the shaft from the top down as the excavation of the shaft proceeded, as impossible as it at first may sound. This rather arduous feat was accomplished by first positioning a circular wooden platform, or ring, on the undug shaftsite, building up a reasonable section of brickwork above ground, then from the interior of the brick cylinder, digging out and undercutting the wooden ring enough to allow the preconstructed section of brickwork to sink to ground level by its own weight. At that point another section of brickwork was added and the shaft undercut and sunk as before. The whole process would be repeated until the shaft was complete.[8] The discovery of rings in the Pettus, Bray, and Landing Ordinary wells then indicates that half of the wells at Kingsmill were built by this top-down method. Apparently, then, there was some concern for the safety of the well diggers, but not at the other sites.

With the exception of the Burwell kitchen well, all of the shafts had been robbed of some of the brickwork from 5′ to 7′ below the colonial ground level. This appears to have been done while the abandoned shaft was still open, which, in turn, explains why brick salvaging in wells rarely ever went to any appreciable depth. Working to remove bricks while suspended or reaching down an open wellshaft, some over 50′ deep, could rather quickly become discouraging. The robbing of the brickwork invariably resulted in the erosion of the unlined shaft, producing an ever-widening crater-shaped hole (Figure 102). That being the case, remains of what had been the aboveground well-curbing were usually destroyed. Nonetheless, some evidence of the posts once supporting the bucket hoists was found, as well as sections of the posts and part of a drum (Figure 103). The shaft at the landing still contained the well bucket preserved beneath the modern water table (Figure 104). It was attached to the main rope with a chain held to the bucket with nails and staples. Two worn, half horseshoes were found attached to the bucket chain, acting as weights to tip the bucket as it hit the water. The discovery of the shoes on the bucket also suggests an explanation for the relatively consistent discovery of other metal implements, all with holes in them. At the Harrop well, as many as two dozen hoe blades, most still in perfectly usable condition, were found at the bottom, and an unbroken mortising axe and harrow tooth were found near the base of the Pettus wellshaft (Figure 3). Like the improvised horseshoes, they all

Figure 102   Cross-section through wellshaft at Utopia, showing the over-size hole created by erosion and the alternating layers of seventeenth-century domestic refuse deposits and rain-washed clay (light bands). (Virginia Historic Landmarks Commission.)

must have served as makeshift bucket weights until whatever was used to fasten them to the bucket wore out, leaving them lying at the bottom. Recovery of these and other objects accidentally lost down the deep shafts was evidently too much bother at the time they were lost.[9]

The quantity of other intact and relatively complete objects in the final 6–10′ in Kingsmill's wells suggests that, as the wells were in use, objects were accidentally lost and fragile things like bottles remained intact because of the cushioning effect of the standing water. That must have been what saved the unbroken bottles found at the bottom of the Bray well, one still containing its original contents; but their accidental loss, unlike the numerous intact bottles recovered from the Pettus shaft, did not occur as they were being filled on the edge of the curb (Figure 105). The

Figure 103 The partially dismantled and backfilled well at the Landing ordinary. Note posthole supports for windlass. (Virginia Historic Landmarks Commission.)

Figure 104 Bucket from Burwell's Landing ordinary well with chain and horseshoe counterweight still attached. (Virginia Historic Landmarks Commission.)

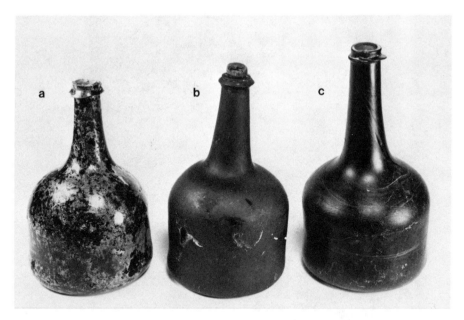

Figure 105 "Wine" bottles from Bray's Littletown well (1735–1750), one (a) recovered from the cooling vault 18′ below the surface, the others (b, c) at the bottom 37′ below. (b) and (c) were probably lost from the vault during the second quarter of the eighteenth century. Survival of the cork in (b) preserved its original contents—milk. See also Figure 106. (Virginia Historic Landmarks Commission.)

Bray shaft, unlike the others, had a unique and innovative feature; the builders incorporated a brick-lined vault 4′ into the east wall, some 18′ beneath the colonial ground surface (Figure 106). Sockets in the wall at the depth of the vault suggested that a narrow curb, or catwalk, had been there to facilitate the deposit of or removal of the vault's contents. A bottle found on the floor of the vault suggested that the room was used for a "cooler," taking advantage of the relatively cold ambient temperature of the soil at that depth. The difficulty of access to the opening, however, must have on occasion resulted in loss of whatever was to be stored or was being removed from the room. Consequently, other bottles wound up at the bottom of the well, some 37′ below, protected from breakage by the water. That the room acted as a small dairy is unquestionable. One of the bottles with the cork still in place contained milk. Of course, other bottles could have contained any other liquid that needed a cooler temperature for preservation or needed to be cooled for drinking. Regardless of the contents of the vault, the Bray well-builder certainly devised a novel if not cumbersome method for cold storage, so far without precedent on other colonial sites.

The contents of the shafts found above the accidental loss level were largely soil and fragmented sections of the dismantled or collapsed brick shafts, material thrown in to eliminate a hazard in the yard, other trash, and/or unsalvagable bricks

Figure 106   The intact "wine" bottle found on the floor of a brick vault in the side of the Littletown well and other bottles below suggest that the compartment was a "cooler" 18′ below the ground surface. (Virginia Historic Landmarks Commission.)

thrown in after the well no longer supplied water. This suggests that the houses nearby were in their last days or were already abandoned.

   The upper few feet of fill in the wells usually contained artifacts dating later in time than the majority of the shaft fill, almost certainly garbage and trash thrown into a low place in the yard formed when the loose fill in the shaft settled over time. That certainly happened to the Burwell kitchen well where the accidental dislodging of the unmortared bricks 45′ below ground led first to an attempt to patch the break, then ultimately to the abandonment of the well altogether, relatively early in its life. Consequently, the hole became a natural trash disposal just outside the kitchen window, and settling of the fill over the years did result in later depositions at the top. When the Burwell shaft collapsed, circa 1760, judging from the bottle styles and mid–eighteenth-century delft and white salt-glazed stoneware in the backfill, it was equally convenient to toss the daily garbage out the window into the open hole until it could take no more (Figure 107).

Apparently the other wellshaft found at Burwell's Kingsmill replaced the kitchen well, and its backfilling material indicated that it lasted as late as the present century. Located southwest of the storehouse, itself an addition to the building complex built after the flanking dependencies, the new location probably reflects a change in the use of yard space. Also, if the storehouse did house slaves, then it makes sense that the new well would have been located close by. It still would be reasonably convenient to the kitchen, closer to the house than the original shaft, and now inside the terrace–garden enclosure.

Apart from structural failure of the brick walls of colonial wells, the archaeology of the Kingsmill shafts suggests that either the drawing of the water or periodic cleaning below the water table resulted in removal of earth from and below the bottom. This resulted in an undermining of the brickwork and the wooden footing rings. A variety of solutions to the problem were found, ranging from the installation of makeshift brick boxes of a smaller diameter than the origi-

Figure 107 Burwell well, beneath kitchen window. (Virginia Historic Landmarks Commission.)

nal shaft or, in the case of the well at the ordinary, sinking a wooden barrel below the level of the brickwork.

The Pettus well found 40′ north of the main house first appeared as a large, backfilled circular pit (Figure 108). The brick lining, constructed completely with wedge-shaped well bricks, had been dismantled below the modern grade, after which erosion appeared to have washed in the sides. The shaft was 44′ deep, and at the 26′ level the opening widened about 6″. The bricks were based on a wood ring, or curb, at the bottom. The well fill consisted of three major deposits above an initial filling of sandy clay that contained artifacts of the second half of the seventeenth century. Above that, trash from the first half of the eighteenth century accumulated, then a 15′-thick layer of clean clay had been deposited. A layer of yellow sandy fill and brickbats was deposited on the clay, probably debris scraped from the surface of the surrounding area—perhaps to level the site for cultivation.

The lowest fill contained artifacts of the period 1650–1690, including a copper tobacco-can lid embossed with the figure of an owl smoking a mid-seventeenth-century tobacco pipe (See Figure 109), iron tools, and an intact bottle of the period 1685–1700. The layer above contained eighteenth-century artifacts, including a wine bottle with the J. Bray seal (identical to those recovered from the Bray site), a half-size bottle embossed with an *IM* seal, a bottle of the period 1730– 1735 with the seal of the Williamsburg merchant S(amuel) Cobbs, a pair of leg irons with one anklet chiseled off, and a saber hilt, probably made in America during the period 1750–1775. The layers and the dating evidence (particularly a tobacco pipestem marked with the maker's initials *IF,* circa 1690–1700) suggest that the initial deposit accumulated during the last decade that the well was in use (ca. 1690–1700).[10] They also indicate that the abandoned well was used for a trash pit probably by residents from the nearby Bray Plantation during the years circa 1720–1740, after which the shaft was backfilled and the site leveled.

One other layer, a deposit of mixed clay sloping in from around the brick lining, is significant. Apparently, this well was constructed within a large in-sloping construction hole (builder's trench), at least at the top. No datable artifacts were recovered from the construction deposit that would indicate when the well was made. However, its location and the deepest artifact deposit indicate that it served the occupants of the nearby post buildings during the second half of the seventeenth century.

The archaeological excavation of the seventeenth century wellshaft at Burwell's Landing (Harrop's) involved two basic operations: the removal of the dangerous cliff above the exposed shaft and the excavation of the fill in the shaft, necessitating the partial dismantling of the brickwork. The excavation of the overhanging cliff was done with a backhoe while the actual removal of the fill immediately above the brickwork and within the shaft was done by hand labor (see Figures 2, 3, 4, and 108).

The well extended 38′6″ below the modern grade, was 4′ in exterior diameter, and had a shaft 2'8" across. Of the brick lining, 29'6" survived. It was constructed with unmortared rectangular bricks (chinked with brick fragments) and compass bricks (wedge-shaped bricks) for the upper 6', and compass bricks alone (35 to a course) for the remaining 23'. The upper 5'6" of the lining had been removed, probably just after the well was abandoned. The construction hole along the outside of the shaft varied from 6" to 1'6" wide.

The stratification in and above the well consisted of six major deposits. During the well construction, the space between the outside of the brick shaft and the inside edge of the well construction hole (the builder's trench) had been backfilled with mottled yellow clay containing bits of shell and brick (builder's fill). One artifact recovered from this layer, a clay tobacco pipestem fragment with a diameter of $\frac{3}{32}$", could indicate a late seventeenth-century date for the construction.[11] During the time when the well was in use, a layer of dark-brown clay and silt accumulated, filling in the first 1'9" of the shaft. Pipestem dating suggests that this layer built up during the 1720s. The upper portion of this layer contained the 24 iron blades, a pewter porringer, and a pistol-grip, bone-handle fork of the late seventeenth–early eighteenth-century period (Figures 3 and 4). When the well was abandoned, at least 15'6" of the remaining open shaft was filled with domestic trash and soil containing a considerable amount of wood ash and nails, perhaps debris from a fireplace. A wine bottle of the period 1730–1745 dates this deposit to after circa 1730, with the rest of the artifacts dating in the period 1700–1730.

Above the major trash deposit and continuing up to the 3'8" mark, a layer of extremely compact brown and yellow clay with brick fragments and fragmented artifacts of the period 1650–1680 was found, above and below a 2'2"-thick layer of wine-bottle glass. The bottles were all made of light olive green glass and were all of apparent Dutch manufacture, circa 1770–1790. It is probable that the later glass was deposited during the construction of the Revolutionary War fortification on the site, with the earlier seventeenth-century material inadvertently thrown into the well with fill dirt during the same construction operation.

The soil layers above the wellshaft consisted of a 3'-thick section of an earthwork sandwiched by a layer of prefort and postfort topsoil. These three layers had to be removed by machine together because they were entangled with roots from the two cedar trees that had formed the forementioned dangerous cliff overhang. No artifacts could be recovered *in situ* to suggest the date for the construction of the earthwork. It could be the remains of a Revolutionary War defense or a Civil War fort, both known to have existed at the landing.

The well probably served the Harrop House known to have been located along the river on the western edge of the Littletown property in 1700. It is probable, however, that the house site itself was located between the well and the river, in which case the house site has been completely eroded away.

Excavations 70' west of the main house at Utopia uncovered a 22'-diameter backfilled hole, which at a depth of 30' narrowed to a 5' diameter, the usual size of

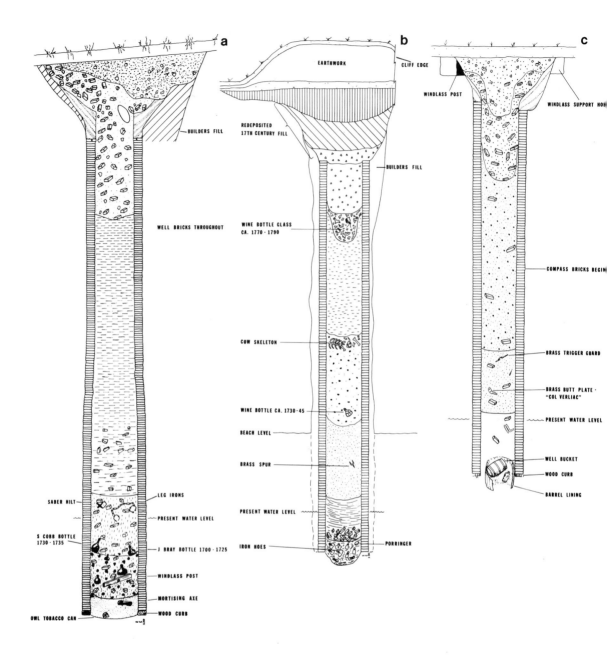

Figure 108 Cross-sections through five wells excavated at Kingsmill, 1972–1975. (a) Pettus; (b) Harrop; (c) ordinary at Burwell's Landing; (d) Bray; (e) kitchen at Burwell's Kingsmill.

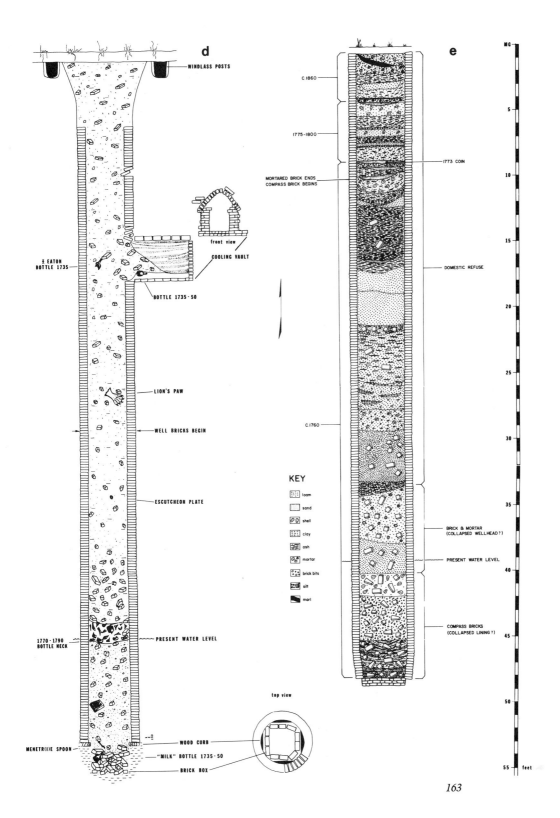

d

WINDLASS POSTS

¼ EATON
BOTTLE 1735

BOTTLE 1735-50

LION'S PAW

WELL BRICKS BEGIN

ESCUTCHEON PLATE

1770-1790
BOTTLE NECK

PRESENT WATER LEVEL

MENETR(I)E SPOON

WOOD CURB

"MILK" BOTTLE 1735-50

BRICK BOX

front view

COOLING VAULT

top view

KEY

loam
sand
shell
clay
ash
mortar
brick bits
silt
marl

e

C.1860

1775-1800

MORTARED BRICK ENDS
COMPASS BRICK BEGINS

C.1760

1773 COIN

DOMESTIC REFUSE

BRICK & MORTAR
(COLLAPSED WELLHEAD?)

PRESENT WATER LEVEL

COMPASS BRICKS
(COLLAPSED LINING?)

MG

5

10

15

20

25

30

35

40

45

50

55 — feet

163

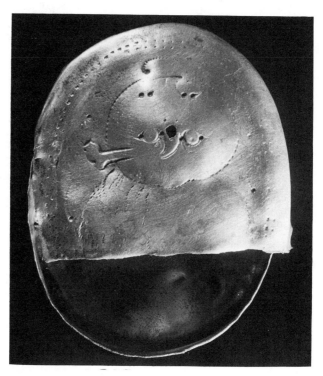

Figure 109   Mid–seventeenth-century copper tobacco can recovered from the Pettus Littletown well. (Virginia Historic Landmarks Commission.)

excavations encasing brick-lined wells (Figures 102 and 108). The brick lining had been removed, however, to a depth of at least 67′, the level at which the danger to excavators cancelled further digging.

Alternate deposits of domestic refuse and sandy silt filled the well to a depth of 13′. This implies that the upper section of the open shaft was periodically used as a trash pit, and that between trash deposits rain eroded the shaft walls, causing the silt layers to accumulate.

The artifact-bearing strata contained numerous English clay pipe fragments, several of which were stems bearing the initials *IF* flanked by *X*'s molded in relief. *IF* pipes have been found elsewhere in Virginia in 1688–1710 contexts.[12] The pipestems, along with a distinctive type of earthenware, undoubtedly made at the late seventeenth century Challis pottery near Jamestown, suggest a backfilling date for the well in the period of circa 1680–1710 (Figure 130). Fragments of the same locally made coarseware pan were found in the backfill of both the house cellar and the well, establishing that both were filled concurrently.

The Bray wellshaft was found 80′ west of the mansion. The windlass postholes survived, spanning the 7'-wide eroded shaft. The brickwork went to a depth of 55', yet the backfill material consisted of only three major deposits: a layer of sand and bricks on the bottom, containing material from the period 1735–1750, including two intact bottles (one of which was half filled with milk) (Figure 105); turned window lead (from casement-type windows); and the pewter spoon with the name DAV[I]D MENETR[IE] (Figure 110). From that level to the top of the brick shaft, the fill consisted of various deposits of what appeared to be masonry debris from the destruction of a building, probably the nearby mansion, and a layer of concentrated bottle glass, 44' beneath the surface. The rubble contained wine-bottle fragments from the period circa 1771–1790, a sheet copper lion's paw or gambe (Figure 133) presumably from the coat of arms of the Burwell family of nearby Kingsmill, and post-1770 creamware, the bottles and creamware showing the well had been abandoned and backfilled contemporaneously with the abandonment and destruction of the mansion; that is, circa 1770–1790.[13]

Most of the fill in the cooler contained more of the same rubble fill. However, a layer of silt and an occupation layer were found directly on the floor. An intact bottle of the period 1735–1750 was also recovered from the "cooler" backfill, indicating use during the mid–eighteenth century (Figure 106).

The remainder of the shaft was filled to the surface with black loam and brickbats containing artifacts dating to 1770–1790. Apparently the well had been completely backfilled when the site was abandoned; that is, when the cellar of the mansion was filled in circa 1770–1790. The fact that two identical fine-quality escutcheon plates with molded lion and unicorn designs were found, one in the rubble fill in the well and one in the rubble fill in the cellar, also points to a contemporaneous filling.

The artifact dates suggest that the well was in use at least as early as 1735 (the bottle dates) and until circa 1770–1790. It is possible, however, that the date of the deepest deposit merely reflects the date after which the well was last cleaned and that the shaft had been constructed at the same time that the mansion was built, circa 1700–1725.

Figure 110   Pewter spoon, bearing the name DAV[I]D MENETR[IE?], a well-known Williamsburg house builder, found at Bray's Littletown. (Virginia Historic Landmarks Commission.)

The Burwell kitchen well still retained its brick lining to within 6″ of the present ground surface (Figures 107 and 108). Excavations determined that the shaft was 5′4″ wide overall, with an open shaft 3′9″ in diameter and 48′5″ deep. Rectangular shell-mortared bricks and brickbats shored the upper 10′ of the shaft. Wedge-shaped compass bricks supported the remainder of the shaft, which was in turn based upon three courses of horizontally laid compass and rectangular bricks. The entire shaft had to be dismantled during excavation, due to the fact that the southern side had collapsed from a point 28′ from the top to within 3′5″ of the bottom. Near the bottom, rectangular bricks were found laid at the base of the fallen wall section, an apparent unsuccessful attempt to stop the collapse in its early stages.

Well stratigraphy consisted of two major deposits: fill left behind the shaft wall during construction, and the material that filled the abandoned wellshaft. Dismantling the shaft walls revealed, at a depth of 10′, brickbat infilling of what appeared to be eroded areas in the construction hole. Some artifact material seems to have been deposited with the in-filling. Sherds of a white salt-glazed stoneware mug, generally datable to the period circa 1730–1740, imply that the well was built at the same time as the mansion outbuilding complex, circa 1728–1736. Also, the presence of the in-filling establishes that the shaft was originally excavated to the bottom, then bricked in by the builders.

Near the bottom, shaft fill contained compass bricks from the collapse of the shaft lining. Rectangular bricks and brickbats, apparently from the dismantling of the well head, and another deposit of rectangular bricks, all covered by domestic refuse, ash, and decomposed organic material, extended to the present ground surface. A considerable quantity of wine bottles, stylistically datable to circa 1760, and examples of mid–eighteenth-century delftware and white salt-glazed stoneware suggest a circa 1760 date for the collapse, abandonment, and initial filling of the shaft.

Trenching 35′ southeast of Burwell's ordinary located the backfilled well. The windless postholes, 9′ apart, were found flanking the backfilled shaft (Figure 103). The brick lining was dismantled to a depth of 5′, but below that it remained intact, incorporating rectangular bricks to the 17′ level, then wedge-shaped compass bricks to the 32′ level. Below that, a barrel shored the remaining section of the shaft to the bottom, 34′ below the surface. A circular wood ring, 2″ thick, supported the brick shaft at the base, evidence of the "top-down" method of construction.

Filling material consisted of dark loam with brickbats above a sandy fill, which in turn covered an 11′-thick trash deposit toward the bottom. The trash layer contained a square case bottle of the last quarter of the eighteenth century, suggesting a well backfilling date of post-1775.[14] No artifacts were recovered in a construction context, but it is reasonable to assume that the well was contemporary to the circa 1750 ordinary structure.

WASTE

There can be no question that abandoned wellshafts became rubbish disposals. But, where wells were not yet abandoned or where there were no wells, other means had to be found to dispose of material waste. Judging from the great number of artifacts in the plowzone, it seems clear enough that much of the domestic refuse was simply scattered across the yard, but at every site, regardless of economic and social status, rubbish-filled pits were also found in the vicinity of the houses. The pits, however, do not appear to be a part of any conscientious effort on the part of the inhabitants to bury garbage and trash. It seems more likely that the pits were dug for some other reason—perhaps to quarry clay for fill and masonry work—then, like the abandoned wellshafts and cellar holes, the open holes became convenient receptacles for waste. The trashpit found below the subsoil level at the Littletown Tenement, for example, may well have been a borrow pit, perhaps dug to acquire clay to coat the wooden chimney or chimney hood in the house (see Figures 28 and 30).

The shape, location, and regularity of the three pits made by the people living at the Kingsmill Tenement, on the other hand, and of an entirely different nature (Figures 28 and 111). They were distinctly round in shape, 4–8′ in diameter, and averaged 4′ deep with relatively flat bottoms. The pits, first appearing as backfilled wells, were filled with organic soil containing considerable amounts of ash, artifacts, and faunal remains—obviously domestic refuse coming from the nearby house. The uniformity of the original digging of the circular holes suggests that they were made for a specific purpose when they stood open. Since none of the seventeenth-century structures on the site had even the smallest root cellar, it is possible that the pits were originally used for root storage, protected perhaps by wooden covers or straw. This method of preservation, over the winter, is still used by many gardeners in Virginia today.[15] Once the circular pits were empty, like the abandoned wellshafts elsewhere, they became a logical place to dispose of garbage and trash.

The laborers of Thomas Pettus who lived at Utopia apparently did not need exterior pits for root storage; the one brick-lined half-cellar must have sufficed (Figures 39 and 40). The only feature at the site that could qualify as a waste "pit" was the rectangular hole at the terminus of the "raised" fence at the southwestern corner of the garden. Very little trash accumulated when this pit was backfilled and it is possible that the pit merely silted up as water drained along the fence ditch. Since this pit was not primarily for trash disposal, it is not clear how refuse was disposed of before the abandoned wellshaft began to be filled.

The people living on the Pettus home plantation disposed of rubbish in three ways: by filling holes in the yard of the house, by scattering refuse directly across the surface of the yard, and by dumping trash over the edge of a ravine just to the east of the smokehouse (see Figure 39). Unlike the Kingsmill tenants, exterior pits

Figure 111 North–south cross-section through one of the six storage pits found at Kingsmill Tenement, showing lenses of domestic refuse and ash. (Virginia Historic Landmarks Commission.)

were not necessary for food preservation or later for trash; the bricklined cellar under the east wing and the below-grade dairy or buttery next to the kitchen wing of the house were apparently enough to store the Pettus's food.

How the other landlords got rid of their waste could not be determined. The river erosion seems to have destroyed the yard areas at Harrop, and the Farlow's Neck site at Burwell's Kingsmill was so severely disturbed by the eighteenth-century construction that, save for an irregularly dug and filled pit 80′ to the southeast of the fragmented housesite, nothing was found (Figure 46).[16]

The people at Bray's Littletown, on the other hand, dug and filled pits in the vicinity of the mansion–kitchen–slave quarter and the well (Figure 46). The largest of the holes, not far from the east chimney foundation of the house, was enormous, measuring 15′ across and as deep as 5′ near the center (Figure 112). Judging from the irregularities in the shape and walls, it seems that the large Bray pit was created merely to get the clay out; the house already had a full basement and a root cellar. The clay could have been used for a number of purposes, but it seems likely that that clay ultimately became bricks, a commodity recorded by James Bray III as one of the products of Littletown in the 1740s.[17] Certainly wine bottles and white salt-glazed stoneware recovered from the pit, along with numer-

Figure 112 Cross-section through an enormous pit backfilled with domestic refuse and debris from the construction and destruction of masonry building(s) found near the Bray Littletown mansion. (Virginia Historic Landmarks Commission.)

ous wine-bottle seals bearing the logos of James and Thomas Bray, suggest backfilling during that time (Figure 113). The uppermost levels of fill also contained debris from the construction or alteration of a masonry building, brickbats, mortar, plaster, and turned lead and glass from casement windows. In fact, the recovery of the pewter spoon from the backfilling of the Bray well marked DAV[I]D MEN-ETR[IE] (Figure 110), the well-known Williamsburg area master builder, suggests that the construction debris might have got into the pit during construction or renovation work that Menetrie might have directed there.

As self-defeating as it may seem, the slaves living near the Bray mansion continually filled their root cellars with waste, but they also filled two smaller irregularly shaped pits in the yard. One, filled in during the second quarter of the eighteenth century, was found as close as 5′ to the kitchen building, and another of similar shape was found 7′ east of the well (Figure 46). Pipebowls and English delftware dated the kitchen-pit fill to 1710–1750, but the pit to the south seems to have been filled very late in the occupation of the site, perhaps as late as 1770–1790, as suggested by the shapes of the wine bottles found in it.

No eighteenth-century pits backfilled with domestic refuse were found at Burwell's Kingsmill, but only 20% of the site was excavated. Other features found determined that the forecourt area on the landfront and the terraced area on the riverfront were formally landscaped, and there is no reason to expect borrow pits or rubbish disposal there (Figure 46). A considerable deposit of trash and garbage

Figure 113 Wine bottle and seals bearing anagram of J.[ames] Bray (II?) (d. 1725) and his son T.[homas] Bray (d. 1751); types found in the major trash pit near the Bray's Littletown mansion and at Utopia. (Virginia Historic Landmarks Commission.)

was found to the east of the storehouse, however, built up along an east–west fenceline enclosing that yard area. There may still be a number of backfilled pits in that vicinity as well, though the limited excavations failed to locate them (Figure 114). Concentrations of rubbish were also found at the base of the terrace in what would have been the enclosed garden, and two rectangular pits were found just north of the storehouse foundation. These later pits may have originally been root cellars beneath a lean-to addition to the storehouse, but they were not filled with any appreciable amount of artifacts or food-related material. It may also be that these pits were used for some craft, perhaps the processing of flax or hemp, for example.[18] Before flax-breaking machines came into general use, the flax bundles required soaking in "pools". The uniformity of the pit walls and bottom argues against their being originally mere borrow pits. At any rate, the manufacturing dates of ceramic fragments from the pit backfill indicate that, whatever their function, the ceramics were used after the Burwells sold the property. The dating is

Figure 114 Domestic waste at Burwell's Kingsmill was found concentrated along and within what had been an enclosed area in the side yard, south of the kitchen. (Virginia Historic Landmarks Commission.)

based on the presence of nineteenth-century transfer-printed pearlware in the backfill.

At the same time that the slaves living at Kingsmill Quarter periodically dug and backfilled the multitude of root cellars beneath the floors of their two houses, they were taking some of the refuse out into the south yard and throwing it into a huge (18′ × 30′ at a maximum) irregularly dug pit (Figure 66). The irregularly shaped hole connected with what appears to be a sizable ditch draining into it. The ditch and pit then created a pond for standing surface water before its backfilling, but its purpose is puzzling. It is difficult to see the stagnant pond as the source of drinking water for the Quarter although, again, no well was found on the site. Even if the pond were created only for the convenience of hogs, a likely explanation, it is difficult to imagine the quality of domestic life in the midst of such a potential mosquito breeder.

Many of the ceramics from the root cellars under the house cross-mended with the very considerable amount of artifacts and faunal remains found in the pond's backfill, showing that the occupants at the Quarter typically expended little effort to remove garbage and trash from the immediate vicinity of their houses. The dates of the artifacts suggest a long, slow accumulation, continuing until the houses were torn down in the late 1780s. Symbolic of the long use of the pond for waste disposal was the recovery of the handle of a copper pan or skillet with the *LB* monogram of Lewis Burwell, dated *1738,* along with an octagonal bottle embossed with the seal of the Williamsburg merchant John Greenhow, dated *1770* (Figures 115 and 116).

The trash-disposal pattern at Tuttey's Neck largely dated to the period when the land was owned by the Bray family. There the major rubbish area was found to be 60′ to the northeast of the main house, although one of five subsurface deposits was found as far away as 125′ to the southeast (Figure 71). Again, although the archaeologist originally believed that the pits predated the construction of the smaller kitchen building that stood over one of the pits and encompassed four others, it is almost certain that some of the more-regularly shaped features were root cellars dug beneath the floorboards when the smaller building was standing, a consistent Kingsmill slave quarter pattern. In fact, the one odd-shaped pit under the small building foundation probably helps prove that the symmetrically shaped holes inside the footing were root cellars and that the irregular holes originally were dug for some other purpose; that is, the irregularity sorts out borrow-pits-turned-rubbish-pits from root-cellars-turned-rubbish-pits. In fact, the irregular pit contained artifacts of an unquestionably earlier date than the others, particularly a wine-bottle seal of "Richard Burbydge, 1701," while the cellars held pipestems and tobacco pipebowls of a style and type suggesting a circa 1740 backfilling date.[19]

Figure 115 Cooking pan (?) handle bearing the logo *LB* of Lewis Burwell, dated 1738. (Virginia Historic Landmarks Commission.)

Figure 116 Octagonal bottle with the seal of the merchant, John Greenhow, Williamsburg, dated 1770, indicating that the "pond" at Kingsmill Quarter in which they were found was used for waste disposal for a relatively long period of time. (Virginia Historic Landmarks Commission.)

Besides the backfilling of the cellars and root cellars, no trash deposits in pits below the subsoil level were found at North Quarter or Hampton Key (Figures 66, 81, and 88). Nonetheless, because the plowzone at North Quarter could be screened in controlled units, concentrations of artifacts could be defined by computer analysis to show that the nails, ceramics, and discarded animal bones—that is, garbage and trash—were consistently thrown in specific places (Figures 82, 117, and 118).[20] The computer-drawn contour maps show a distinct concentration of the ceramics and bone at each end of the house, which supports the suggestion that doorways were located there and that a partition divided the house into at least two rooms, as other architectural evidence indicates. The concentra-

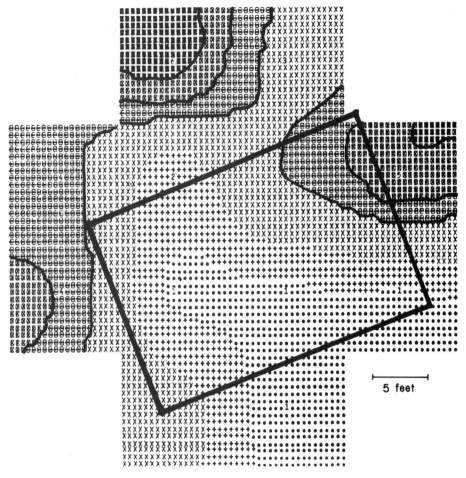

Figure 117 Computer-drawn map of North Quarter site, showing concentrations of ceramic fragments in plowzone. Compare to Figure 118. (D. Sanford, University of Virginia.)

tion of bone and ceramics on the west end certainly pinpoints a major waste-disposal area and the analysis also showed that ceramics were concentrated in a different place (northeast of the house) than the bone (southeast of the house). This may suggest that there was some effort made to separate garbage (the bone) from the trash (ceramics), perhaps in an attempt to create a compost pile in the garden on the southeast of the house. It may seem unlikely to compost so close to the house, but again Virginia slave owners encouraged composting.[21] Regardless of any logic behind the scattering of rubbish in the yards near houses, it is clear from the North Quarter study of plowzone artifacts that the relatively small number of pits that happened to be deeper than the plowzone found on the other

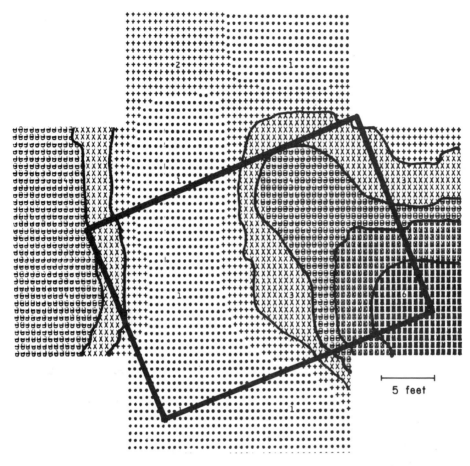

Figure 118 Computer-drawn map of North Quarter site, showing concentrations of bone fragments, by weight, in plowzone. Compare to Figure 117. (D. Sanford, University of Virginia.)

Kingsmill sites do not necessarily indicate complete refuse-disposal patterns. In fact, in most cases the very appreciable amount of artifacts in the plowzone on those sites certainly suggests yard scattering as well as pit filling.

It would be reasonable to expect to find enormous trash deposits at the sites of public eating and lodging facilities like an ordinary, considering the fact that so many different people occupied the site through time. Therefore, it was puzzling to find so few trash deposits below the plowzone at Burwell's Landing (Figure 46). Besides the backfilled basement of the west wing and the backfill of the wellshaft, refuse deposits were found only in the backfill of the raised garden fence ditches. There was, however, a considerable amount of artifacts in the plowzone, but not apparently more than at any other sites. Perhaps at a public ordinary more care was

taken to clean up around buildings in an attempt to make the place more commer-
cially attractive. The formal landscaping seems to suggest that some thought was
indeed given to the appearance of the establishment and perhaps this affected how
trash was disposed of as well. On the other hand, accounts of ordinaries by eighteenth-century travelers make it clear that most tavern owners paid absolutely no
attention to cleaning up their grounds.[22]

POTS, BONES, AND STATUS

The thousands of fragmented artifacts found buried amid Kingsmill's abandoned buildings, cellars, wells, trashpits, and gardens are, of course, important
beyond their use as dating tools for the archaeological features. Like the buildings
and the landscape, they affected and reflect the Kingsmill society generally. The fact
that these artifacts were found in relatively tightly dated contexts on sites occupied
by people at all rungs of the social and economic scale renders their comparative
analysis particularly illustrative of the evolving colonial society. Cultural change
through time, social relationships within the colonial class structure, and any effect
that Anglo-American and Afro-Americans had on each other are all reflected to
some extent in the artifact collections. Of course, a complete analysis of the vast
Kingsmill collection can never be done. Practically each student and certainly each
generation asks its own questions. Nevertheless, some current analytic devices
provide what seem like logical ways to order the material qualitatively and quan-
titatively. Taken together, the methods do seem to define some interesting
patterns.

But judging fairly the quality of objects across the space of time is an extremely
difficult and necessarily subjective exercise. Quantifying things is an activity only as
valid as the set of rules one uses to generate and manipulate the figures. Yet the
combination of the two approaches, the one drawing more on the criteria of the
humanities and the other on the methods of science together produce what seems
to be a clearer picture than any one procedure could do alone (Figure 119). It
seems reasonable, therefore, to look both at the Kingsmill artifact collection for
signal objects that in their very presence directly reflect specific cultural behavior,
regardless of their quantity. At the same time, it is useful to compare relative
numbers of objects common to all sites because their sheer numbers point to
equally valid cultural conclusions.

Like most other domestic archaeological sites, ceramics and discarded animal
bones were found in great numbers on all the Kingsmill sites, so this element of the
artifact assemblage lends itself most readily to quantified analysis. And food, with
all its attendant trappings, had meaning in eighteenth-century Virginia beyond
mere subsistence (Figure 120). The traveler Liancourt leaves no doubt that osten-
tation at the table was a Virginian's delight, even beyond concern for his house:
"You find therefore, very frequently a table well served and covered with plate, in a
room where half the windows have been broken for ten years past, and will

Figure 119 Identifying and quantifying ceramics requires technical and historical knowledge only possible through a synthesis of artistic and scientific thinking. (Virginia Historic Landmarks Commission.)

probably remain so for ten years longer."[23] This is no casual conclusion either; it was Liancourt's general impression of Virginia after traveling the state for months from Norfolk to Williamsburg, Richmond, and Charlottesville, and up the Shenandoah Valley into Maryland. It seems, then, that a particular emphasis on the analysis of table artifacts is a valid test of Virginia's culture, and that spending what may seem like an inordinate amount of time working with pottery and bone is not occasioned only by the fact that they happen to survive in the ground long enough to dominate the archaeological collection.

A functional analysis of the Kingsmill ceramics, quantifying the collection by vessel form, seems to point out differences in lifestyle through time and across the social and economic scale. This is particularly true considering the pottery of Pettus's Littletown and Utopia. If one accepts the premise that the relative number of plates (flatwares) compared with serving bowls and drinking vessels (hollowares) can reflect, respectively, a regular diet of roasted prime cuts of meat for the rich and a diet of stews and porridges for the poor, then the dramatically opposite flatware–holloware ratios of the wealthy Pettus family and the poorer Utopia occupants seem remarkably accurate (Figure 121).[24] By the same token, if

THE DINNER.

Symptoms of Eating & Drinking

Figure 120 Virginians considered formal dining and all of its attendant trappings a significant part of their lives. (Colonial Williamsburg Foundation.)

mere tenants did live higher on the hog earlier in the seventeenth century as a result of the boom tobacco years, the higher percentage of flatware to holloware found at the Kingsmill Tenement is not surprising.[25] Further, if one assumes that relative differences among site collections in the percentages of serving, storage, and preparation vessels reflect the value placed on the appearance of the table and the means to accumulate surplus food for storage, then the presence at the Pettus site of the more valuable Chinese porcelain and matched dinnerware sets, and the relatively higher percentage of storage vessels, compared to the lower incidence or even the total absence of similar vessels at Utopia, equally reflects differential wealth (Figure 122).[26]

The numbers change dramatically in the eighteenth century. Of the sites where vessel form could be tabulated, the holloware–flatware ratio becomes about

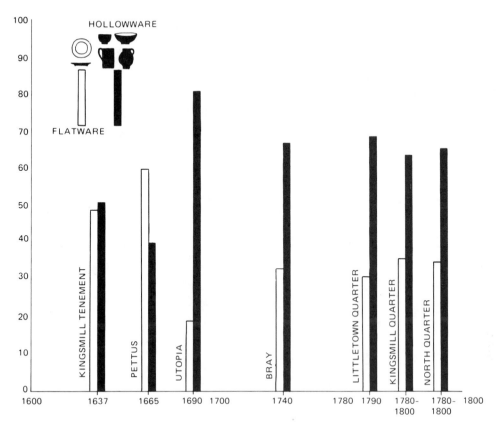

Figure 121   Comparison of percentages of flatwares to hollowwares.

2:1, which stays consistent for landowners and slaves alike. Also locally made pottery tends to appear and have its heyday in the later seventeenth century, then practically disappears by the end of the eighteenth century, (Figure 123) and storage and preparation vessels also practically disappear. But just as flatware and preparation and storage vessels decrease during the colonial period, the opposite is true for the average percentages of drinking vessels (Figure 124). Cups quadruple from the seventeenth to the eighteenth century. The reason for the rise in popularity of this form, of course, is the growing eighteenth-century rage for tea drinking.[27] The increase in the presence of Chinese porcelain on the eighteenth-century sites is also obviously related to the popularity of tea and, undoubtedly, to the increase in the China trade that probably resulted in lower porcelain prices. Related to the increase of porcelain and refined earthenwares in the eighteenth century is the distinct decline of the use of the less-durable tin-enameled English delft tableware.

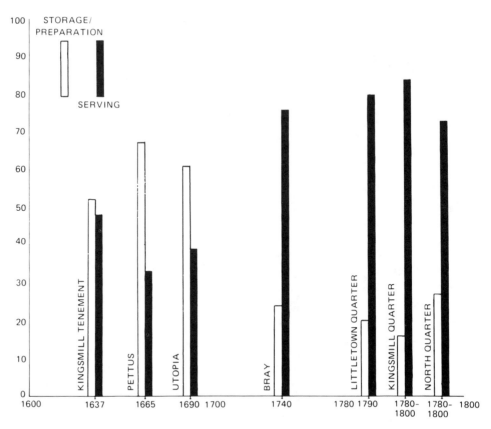

Figure 122   Comparison of percentages of storage/preparation vessels to serving vessels.

Quantitative analysis of the remains of what was eaten off or out of the ceramic vessels is equally informative. Over 8000 individual bone elements were identified from deposits at Kingsmill Tenement, Utopia, Pettus' and Bray's Littletown and Burwell's Kingsmill, and Kingsmill Quarter, and a comparative study of the results clearly shows change in diet and animal husbandry through time, distinctions between the landlords and the laborers, as well as other trends.

Generally, the deposits show what one might expect. As society evolved from its frontier roots to the stable plantation aristocracy, diet changed from a mixture of wild game and an unsystematic slaughter of domestic stock to almost total reliance on a well-managed processing of cattle, swine, and lamb (Figures 125–128). But there appears to be some variation in the pattern from site to site, perhaps owing to some economic status. For example, Pettus evidently had the means and labor to pen his swine, monitor their ages, and slaughter only when the meat was at its prime. The Utopia hogs had no consistent slaughter age, possibly because they

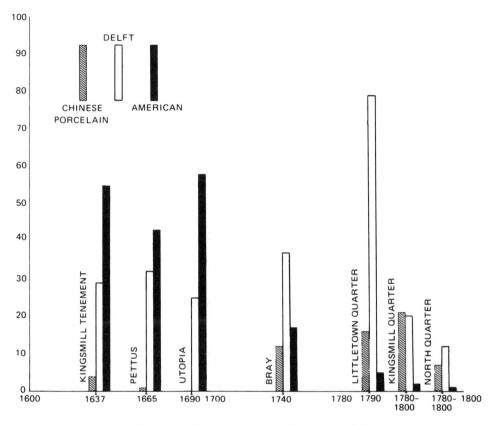

Figure 123 Comparison of percentages of pottery vessels by type.

ranged free, making it impossible to determine reliably the best slaughtering time. It is also significant that the age when sheep were slaughtered at Burwell's Kingsmill, consistently at the prime age of 18 months to 2 years, indicates that they were not raised primarily for their wool. By the same token, the people at Pettus's home plantation, Utopia, and Burwell's Kingsmill butchered very few young cattle, indicating that dairying and beef production were the major goals of animal husbandry (Figure 126). Conversely the Kingsmill tenants of the early seventeenth century killed their cattle earlier, indicating a different management process. Also, the butchery practices seem to indicate that meat was cut into much smaller pieces, probably for stews and porridges in the 1600s, while the wealthy planters of the next century, particularly Burwell, relied on roasts and large cuts of boiled meat.[28] The records indicate that slaves seem to have eaten meat rarely, but when they did eat meat the faunal remains suggest that it was served in the stews and porridges, as one might expect. Also, it seems that slaves ate less beef and more pork and mutton than did the master (Figure 125).[29]

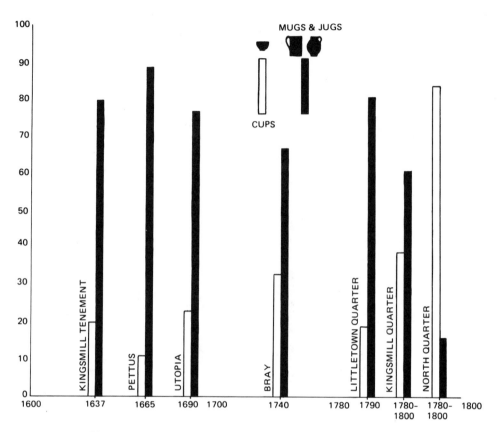

Figure 124 Comparison of percentages of cups and drinking vessels.

The quantification of the faunal remains from the six backfilled "storage pits" at Kingsmill Tenement are interesting in comparing the percentage of domestic to wild game (Figure 110). They range from completely domestic remains in one pit to a mixture of domestic and wild to completely wild remains. From this it is possible to conclude that the diet varied radically on a seasonal basis, with wild game the fare during the best hunting and fishing seasons.

The bones reflect more than mere subsistence. For instance, 13 whole cat skeletons were found in the Bray well fill, numerous cottontail rabbit skeletons in the Pettus well, and the skulls and leg bones of at least three horses in the well and cellar fill at Utopia. The rabbits probably accidentally fell into the abandoned Pettus shaft showing that it stood open at ground level for sometime, and the cats possibly met a similar fate. But the remains of so many cats may suggest that, without the modern technique of spaying, their population posed quite a problem for the colonial Kingsmill society.[30]

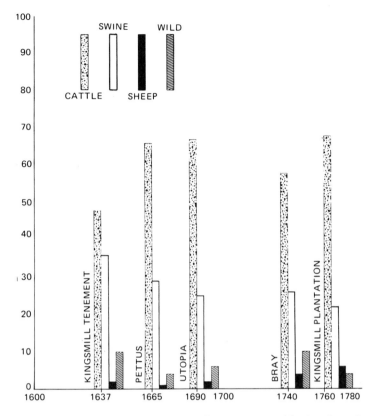

Figure 125 Comparison of percentages of meat represented by faunal remains.

The recovery of only the skulls and leg bones of the horses is puzzling, but perhaps the complete absence of other horse bones solves the riddle. Skulls and foreleg bones were traditionally put in new houses in East Anglia in England to ward off evil spirits and bring good luck. Perhaps the bones suggest that the people at Utopia, who otherwise left their identity so in doubt, were immigrants from that region.[31] Or perhaps these bones point to slavery instead. Coins and horseshoes were often used by the highly superstitious blacks, and perhaps they adopted this white superstition as well.[32]

Other unique artifacts recovered from the various Kingsmill sites are, regardless of their quantity, equally reflective of given aspects of society. The recovery, for example, of jewelry and luxury items (Figure 129) from the early seventeenth-century site at Kingsmill Tenement, like its types and forms of pottery, suggests a relatively flamboyant lifestyle not unlike the "boomtown" described by the historian Morgan.[33] Conversely, the recovery at Utopia of the crude colono-

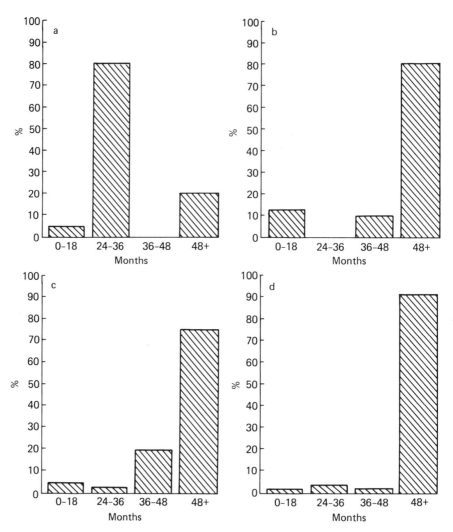

Figure 126   Comparison of percentages of the slaughtering ages of cattle, based on the analysis of the faunal remains from each of four Kingsmill sites. (a) Kingsmill Tenement; (b) Pettus; (c) Utopia; (d) Kingsmill Plantation. (Henry Miller.)

Indian pottery (the local clay, open-hearth-fired vessels made in European forms) and the poorly made, lead-glazed earthenware from a Virginia kiln (Figure 130) graphically suggest a more spartan existence. The presence of the colono-Indian wares at sites dating after the influx of African slaves also suggests what might be a certain impact of Indian culture on the blacks. It is uncertain if slaves ever made the pottery, but it is logical to suggest that Indians taught the art to their fellow slaves.

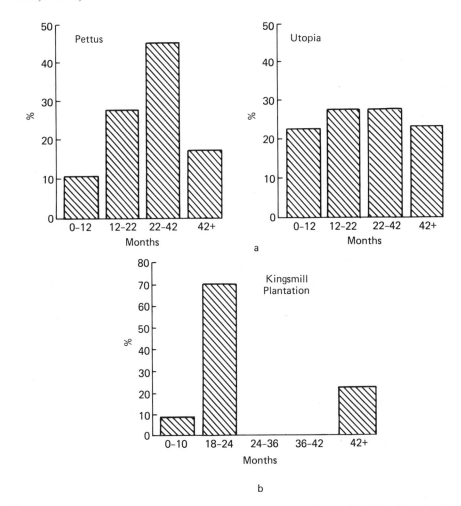

Figure 127 Comparison of percentages of the slaughtering ages of (a) swine and (b) sheep, based on faunal analysis from three Kingsmill archaeological sites. (Henry Miller.)

Also, numbers of clay tobacco-pipe bowls, handformed in local clay and decorated with Indian-like designs, were found in mid- to late seventeenth-century sites at Kingsmill, certainly a sign of trade, and perhaps even evidence that whites learned to make their own pipes in the Indian style (Figure 131). In fact, the pipes occasionally bear English initials, a bowl marked *TP* (Thomas Pettus?) was found at Utopia. Also, pipes from English molds but made of the reddish Virginia clay were found, proving that there was a certain amount of English-style pipe manufacturing going on in Virginia as well.

There can be no clearer archaeological evidence of status consciousness than

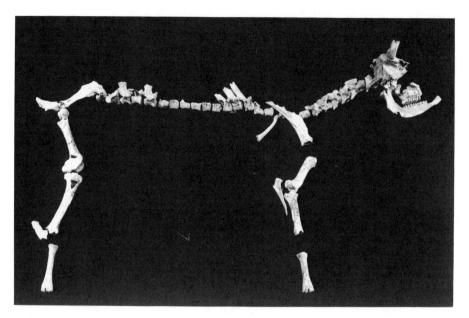

Figure 128 Surviving bones of a small, mature cow buried in the Harrop well, circa 1730–1745. (Virginia Historic Landmarks Commission.)

Figure 129 Link from bracelet with chalcedony stone and enameled knife (?) handle (2½″) from Kingsmill Tenement. (Virginia Historic Landmarks Commission.)

Figure 130 Assemblage of locally made pottery: Challis, Virginia-type lead glazed earthenware jar (upper left) and milkpans (right), and colono–Indian wares (lower left) from Utopia. (Virginia Historic Landmarks Commission.)

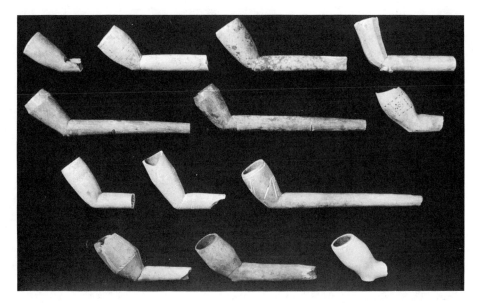

Figure 131 Assemblage of colono–Indian clay tobacco pipes from Kingsmill Tenement. (Virginia Historic Landmarks Commission.)

the fragments of the Bray family coat of arms found in the Littletown Quarter root cellar and the Bray's Littletown well (Figures 132 and 133). If the mansions of the Brays and Burwells were intended to announce that they had "arrived" and that the families' prominent social and political positions would be perpetual, then conspicuous display of symbols like the family crest on their coaches or in their halls should not be surprising.

There is no record of the Burwell arms with a lion's paw or gambe at the College of Arms in London, yet the tomb of Lewis Burwell in Gloucester seems to show one as the family crest.[34] But the existence of unofficial arms in Virginia is clear from the comments of Thomas Jefferson. When Jefferson's mother persisted, he wrote a friend in London requesting a rendering of the Jefferson family crest, regardless of whether the Jeffersons were entitled to the distinction, for, he wrote,

Figure 132   (b) Brass-winged lion harness or carriage boss found at Littletown Tenement; (a) rendering of identical crest of the Bray family from the Book of Standards, College of Arms, London. (Virginia Historic Landmarks Commission, and Rodney Dennys.)

Figure 133 Sheet-copper lion's "gambe" (paw) from a late eighteenth-century deposit in the Bray's Littletown well, and the arms on the tomb of Lewis Burwell, Abingdon Church, Gloucester County, Virginia. (Virginia Historic Landmarks Commission.)

he had heard that in London a coat of arms could be had for the right price as easily as "any other coat."[35] Apparently, the pressure to have a family coat of arms, any coat, was common, which suggests their significance in the eyes of the Virginia aristocracy.

The deposit of the lion's paw in the Bray well and not at Burwell's home at Kingsmill and the deposit of the Bray crest in the root cellar of a slave quarter some three decades after the last male Bray died are puzzling. Perhaps Burwell relatives eventually lived in the Bray house, although James III's sister Elizabeth and not his widow Francis, who married Lewis Burwell, owned Littletown after Thomas Bray's death in 1751. Explanation for the Bray crest at the slave quarter is harder to come by. It is possible that, if the Littletown slaves stayed with Thomas's sister Elizabeth when she acquired the property, it would not be beyond the realms of possibility that the former family servants of the Bray family would keep an attractive and perhaps nostalgic curio like the crest around for some years. The discovery of the anachronistic relic may also emphasize that slave labor forces were as much a permanent fixture on the landscape as the houses and livestock, regardless of how many times new families took over landownership.[36]

Symbolic too were the glass wine-bottle seals of the Kingsmill landowners (Figure 134). They clearly had a functional use, making sure that the order of wine from England was correctly filled, and perhaps the seals were there to discourage theft as well. There is no question that they were also a symbol announcing membership in the elite circle of plantation aristocrats. The laborers obviously could not afford such luxury but, perhaps like the Kingsmill Quarter slaves, that did not stop them from sharing the master's wealth on occasion (Figure 135).

The laborers at Kingsmill, of course, had no ostentatious symbols, but if they needed a symbol at all reflective of their station in life it would undoubtedly be the common iron plantation hoe (Figure 136). The cultivation of tobacco continually required its use in various forms, and it should not be surprising that a total of 90

Figure 134 Glass wine-bottle seals of Kingsmill landowners Lewis Burwell (upper left), Thomas Pettus (upper middle), Thomas Bray (lower left), and James Bray (lower right), and the seal of Nathaniel Burwell, Lewis Burwell III's uncle (upper right), all found at Kingsmill. (Virginia Historic Landmarks Commission.)

Figure 135 Mid–eighteenth-century wine bottles bearing the initialed seals of the private stock of Lewis Burwell, discarded in a root cellar beneath the house at Kingsmill Quarter, possibly to hide the evidence of theft; height, 9″. (Virginia Historic Landmarks Commission.)

hoes were recovered on the Kingsmill site (Figures 4 and 137). The Kingsmill hoes came in the two standard forms—the narrow, or hilling, hoe and the broad, or weeding, hoe—and for the production of tobacco these two tools were used as follows:

> The use of this [narrow] hoe is to break up the ground and throw it into shape; which is done by chopping the clods until they are sufficiently fine, and then drawing the earth round the foot until it forms a heap round the projected leg of the labourer like a mole hill, and nearly as high as the knee; he then draws out his foot, flattens the top of the hill by a dab with the flat part of the hoe, and advances forward to the next hill in the same manner, until the whole piece of ground is prepared.
>
> The more direct use of the weeding [broad] hoe commences with the first growth of the tobacco after transplantation, and never ceases until the plant is nearly ripe, and ready to be laid by, as they term the last weeding with the hoe; for he who would have a good crop of tobacco, or of maize, must not be sparing of his labour, but must keep the ground constantly stirring during the whole growth of the crop.[37]

Figure 136 Hoe gang, James Hopkinson's Plantation, Edisto Island, South Carolina, circa 1862. (New York Historical Society.)

The life of most of Kingsmill's colonial field workers was obviously a monotonous and exhausting experience.

But just as the nature of the labor force changed at Kingsmill from white tenants and servants to black slaves, so too did the size and form of the narrow and broad hoes change (Figure 135). Study of the 90 Kingsmill hoes, many from tightly datable contexts, and of others found on sites in the area shows changes in shape and a tendency to get heavier over time.[38] It may be that hoes for slaves were heavier while the earlier white servants and tenants made sure they had a lighter task. It could also be that American experience led to the rejection of the lighter English hoes of the seventeenth century in favor of the heavier and more durable eighteenth-century American-made types.

Other signs of industry were found at Kingsmill, emphasizing the variety of products that could come from a Tidewater Virginia plantation besides tobacco. Two pits with associated postholes were found in the northeast corner of the Bray's Littletown field (Figure 87), marking what appears to be the remains of a lumber-sawing operation, and leather scaps and a tool for attaching shoe soles were re-covered from the limited test excavations at the mill site (Figure 138). The postholes at the sawpits apparently held the booms needed to position the un-dressed timbers over the pits where one sawyer stood below (the "underdog") and another above (the "top dog"?) to work ripsaws. Shoe leather was found during the monitoring of modern construction at the mill dam, along with some frag-ments of late eighteenth-century pearlware, perhaps graphic evidence that the combined milling and shoemaking operation recorded in the Bray ledger endured for some years.[39]

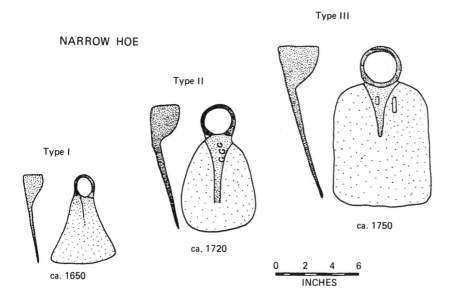

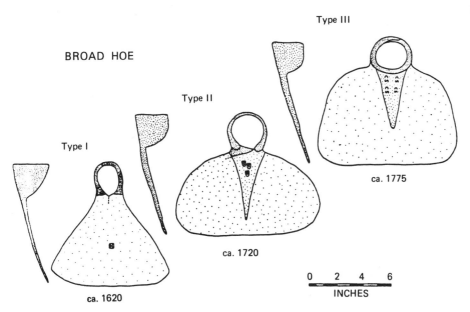

Figure 137 A typology of changing styles of hoe blades based on various archaeological contexts at Kingsmill. (Keith Egloff, Virginia Research Center for Archaeology.)

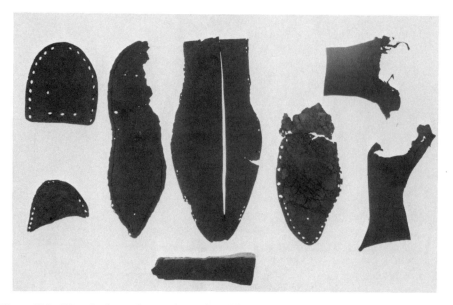

Figure 138 Waste leather and a wooden tool used for pegging soles, found at the mill dam site.

One other symbolic artifact deserves particular mention in that it crosses the fine line between artifactual and historical documents. The Landing Ordinary well produced parts of a musket and a brass buttplate engraved with the name "Col Verliac" (Figure 139). It was a common practice to mark military equipment with the name of the officer in charge, so the name does not necessarily mean that the gun belonged to the colonel himself. But its discovery does raise the question of the man's identity. Surely the French name and the records of the thousands of French troops landing along the James and fighting at Yorktown in 1781 have something to do with the butt plate in the well, but a search in the American and French records of the battle failed to produce any Colonel Verliac. It seems then that this object is the only historical record of that unit's role in the fighting, perhaps a new "fact" about the battle. But it may be that even if the colonel and his men fought at Yorktown, their presence had little effect on the outcome. Nonetheless, Colonel Verliac's musket certainly points out that the documentary record is, indeed, incomplete, that there can be sources of documentary evidence other than archives, and that objects can raise questions of the documents never asked before.

NOTES

[1]Duke De La Rochefoucault Liancourt, *Travels Through the United States of North America,* (London, 1800), Vol. III, pp. 37–38.
[2]*Virginia Magazine of History and Biography,* Vol. I, pp. 86–87.
[3]Burwell Papers, Ledger One, 1736–1746, James Bray Ledger, (mss. Colonial Williamsburg

Figure 139 Butt plate from a musket of probable German manufacture, with the name "Col. Verliac," perhaps the sole record of a French unit engaged eventually at Yorktown. (Virginia Historic Landmarks Commission.)

Foundation), n.p. in James P. McClure, "Littletown Plantation, 1700–1745," (Master's Thesis, College of William and Mary, Williamsburg, Virginia, 1977), p. 104. Liancourt, *Travels,* p. 143.

[4]Jefferson Papers, Massachusetts Historical Society, in E. M. Betts, *Thomas Jefferson's Garden Book,* (Philadelphia, 1944), p. 377.

[5]Maurice Beresford, Archaeologist, University of Leeds suggested that origin.

[6]Humphrey Harwood Ledgers, (mss. Colonial Williamsburg Foundation, Williamsburg, Virginia), Ledger B, Folio 67.

[7]James O. Breeden, ed., *Advice among Masters,* (Westport, Connecticut, 1980), pp. 155, 161.

[8]John Vince, *Wells and Water Supply,* (Aylesbury, England, 1978), and I. Noël Hume, *The Wells of Williamsburg: Colonial Time Capsules,* (Williamsburg, Va., 1969).

[9]Numerous hoes and other heavy iron tools were found at the bottom of colonial wells during excavations at the William Drummond site near Jamestown by the Virginia Research Center for Archaeology.

[10]Identical pipes found with a post-1688 lead cloth-bale seal are reported in: William M. Kelso, "Excavation of a Late Seventeenth Century Domestic Refuse Pit Near Lightfoot, James City County, Virginia, 1964–65," *The Archaeological Society of Virginia, Quarterly Bulletin,* Vol. 20, No. 4, 1966, and

"More Excavations at Lightfoot," *The Archaeological Society of Virginia, Quarterly Bulletin,* Vol. 22, No. 2, 1967.

[11]I. Noël Hume, *A Guide to the Artifacts of Colonial America,* (New York, 1970), pp. 297–302.

[12]Kelso, "Lightfoot" 1966 and 1967; see Note 10, this chapter.

[13]William Armstrong Crozier, *Virginia Heraldica,* (Baltimore, Maryland, 1953), p. 18, describes the Burwell family crest: "A lions gamb erect and erased or grasping three burr leaves vert."

[14]I. Noël Hume, *Guide to Artifacts,* p. 202.

[15]Mrs. Hattie Gillesppi of Williamsburg was still storing carrots and squash beneath straw in her suburban backyard during the winter in 1973, a practice she learned during the early twentieth century at her "homeplace" in the mountains of Southwest Virginia.

[16]To preserve the Revolutionary and Civil War earthworks at the landing, excavations were limited: only about 20% of the Burwell's Kingsmill site was excavated. Therefore, much more that dates to the seventeenth century may lie yet undiscovered at both sites.

[17]Burwell Papers, Ledger One, 1736–1746, (James Bray Ledger, mss. Colonial Williamsburg Foundation, Williamsburg, Virginia), n.p.

[18]Fraser D. Neiman, "Archaeology of Burwell's Kingsmill: The Storehouse," in William M. Kelso, "An Interim Report, Historical Archaeology at Kingsmill, the 1975 Season," (mss. Virginia Historic Landmarks Commission, Research Center for Archaeology, Yorktown, Virginia, 1977), pp. 46–58.

[19]I. Noël Hume, "Excavations at Tutter's Neck in James City County, Virginia, 1960–61," *Contributions From the Museum of History and Technology,* Paper 53, (Washington, D.C., 1966), pp. 46–49.

[20]Nicholas Luccketti, "North Quarter Salvage Excavation, Interim Report," (mss., Virginia Historic Landmarks Commission Research Center for Archaeology, Yorktown, Virginia, 1979), pp. 3–6. The Symap was produced by Douglas Sanford, Assistant Archaeologist, Thomas Jefferson Memorial Foundation.

[21]James O. Breeden, *Advice among Masters,* (Westport, Connecticut, 1980), p. 155, 161.

[22]For example see: Duke De La Rochefoucault Liancourt, *Travels Through the United States of North America,* (London, 1800), Vol. III, p. 173.

[23]Duke De La Rochefoucault Liancourt, *Travels Through the United States of North America,* (London, 1799), Vol. III, p. 231.

[24]John Solomon Otto, "Artifacts and Status Differences: A Comparison of Planter, Overseer, and Slave Sites from Cannon's Point Plantation (1794–1861), St. Simon's Island, Georgia, an Antebellum Plantation," in Stanely South, ed., *Research Strategies in Historical Archaeology,* (New York, 1977), and "Race and Class on Antebellum Plantations," in Robert L. Schuyler, ed., *Archaeological Perspectives on Ethnicity in America,* (Farmingdale, New York, 1980), pp. 10–11.

[25]Edmund S. Morgan, *American Slavery, American Freedom,* (New York, 1975), pp. 108–130.

[26]Merry A. Outlaw, Beverly A. Bogley, and Alain C. Outlaw, "Rich Man, Poor Man: Status Definition of Two Seventeenth Century Ceramic Assemblages from Kingsmill," (paper presented to the annual meeting of the Society for Historical Archaeology, Ottawa, Canada, 1977).

[27]Fraser Neiman's thesis that individual drinking vessels appear in the late seventeenth century–early eighteenth century in greater numbers as the result of a social shift from a corporate to a more individualistic society is not reflected in the numbers for the Kingsmill sites. Mr. Neiman's conclusions were based on total numbers of vessels, which may reflect an increased site population and not an increase in the common use of drinking containers. The Kingsmill figures are based on the percentages of drinking vessels compared to the total ceramic vessels found, which should filter out any distortion caused by a change in population density. See Fraser D. Neiman, *The Manner House Before Stratford,* (Stratford, Virginia, 1980), pp. 38–40.

[28]The author is indebted to Henry M. Miller, St. Mary's City Commission, for making his manuscript reports of his analysis of the Kingsmill faunal remains available for this publication, and I am equally grateful for Michael Barber's report on the Bray site faunal remains: Henry M. Miller, "Pettus,

Utopia, Bray, Kingsmill Tenement, and Kingsmill Plantation Faunal Analysis Preliminary Statements," (mss. Virginia Historic Landmarks Commission Research Center for Archaeology, Yorktown, Virginia), n.d.; Henry M. Miller, "Pettus and Utopia: A Comparison of the Faunal Remains from Two Late Seventeenth Century Virginia Households," (paper presented at the Conference on Historic Sites Archaeology, Winston–Salem, North Carolina, September, 1978); and Michael Barber, "The Vertebrate Fauna from a Late Eighteenth Century Well: The Bray Plantation, Kingsmill, Virginia," (mss. Virginia Historic Landmarks Commission Research Center for Archaeology, Yorktown, Virginia, 1976).

[29]The data for Kingsmill Quarter is based only on a small sample of the total collection and therefore should be taken with caution. I am grateful to Mr. Lawrence McKee for that analysis.

[30]Barber, "Vertebrate Fauna," p. 4.

[31]George Ewart Evans, *The Pattern under the Plow,* (London, 1966), pp. 197–203 in Miller, "Utopia Preliminary Statement," p. 6.

[32]Muriel and Malcolm Bell, Jr., *Drums and Shadows,* (Athens, Ga., 1940), *passim.*

[33]Edmund S. Morgan, *American Slavery, American Freedom,* (New York, 1975), pp. 108–130.

[34]Rodney Dennys, Somerset Herald of Arms, London, to William M. Kelso, February 14, 1974.

[35]Thomas Jefferson to Thomas Adams, February 20, 1771, Julian P. Boyd, ed., *The Papers of Thomas Jefferson,* (Princeton, New Jersey), Vol. I, p. 62.

[36]This assumes, perhaps erroneously, that the woman would drop a deceased husband's coat of arms after remarriage.

[37]William Tatum, *Essay of the Culture and Commerce of Tobacco,* (London, 1800), quoted in Keith Egloff, *Colonial Plantation Hoes of Tidewater, Virginia* (Williamsburg, Virginia, 1980), pp. 5–7.

[38] *Ibid.,* pp. 5–7.

[39]See Chapter 3, p. 40 above.

5

PATTERN

Certain reasonably clear patterns emerge from the comparison of the Kingsmill archaeological remains. The reasons for the similarities and their cultural meaning are not so easy to grasp. There are definite settlement patterns, certain architectural traditions, an evolving landscape architecture, and consistency in certain aspects of slave life and in the acquisition, use, and disposal of objects. What this has to say of significance about American culture both then and now is difficult to assess. In any case, the patterns do exist and deserve summary.

The two earliest sites, the Littletown and Kingsmill tenements, were both found several hundred yards from the river shore. Probably the choice of location as early as the 1620s was heavily influenced by defense. To be close enough to the river for transportation yet far enough to be invisible to Indian boats or foreign ships must have been a consideration so early in the century. Another factor must have been the availability of fresh water springs, as both of the early sites had no dug wells. After about 1635–1640, sites began to appear directly on the river shore where two of the landowners, Pettus and Higginson, built their houses and where the occupants of Utopia settled. Indians were little threat by then. It should not be surprising either that dug wells were found at all of these later seventeenth-century sites. Certainly wells represent some investment in time and money and a certain dedication to permanence. Conversely, it may be that the earlier tenants, cashing in on quick tobacco profits, did hop from virgin land to virgin land. Anything as unportable as a well was not a part of the temporary homestead program.

Wells must have been considered an unnecessary expense by the landlords, too, when constructing their fieldhand quarters. None of the five quarter sites had them. Indeed, the springs at Littletown and Kingsmill tenements were probably the reason why they were reoccupied with slave quarters, and the same holds true for the Tuttey's Neck site.

There can be no question that the two major eighteenth-century Kingsmill landlords chose the most dramatic and dominant location on their property to build their homes. The practical consideration of water and defense had long since passed; the native-born generation could afford wells, a vista, and a much more permanent architecture. But before Bray built at Littletown circa 1700, the more permanent brick construction was practically nonexistent, regardless of social and economic status. Why the seventeenth-century landlord Thomas Pettus chose to build in the more impermanent earthfast manner when he had the means to build otherwise is unclear. Perhaps it is true generally, as Carson contends, that the third-stage, more permanent house recommended by the homesteading literature was rarely built because of the high mortality rate.[1] The owners simply did not live long enough to get around to their dreamhouses. But although the Kingsmill sites seem to reflect the staging approach and the posthole patterns do show crude and small houses followed by larger and more substantially constructed earthfast housing through time, Pettus was content to stop with his original timber house even though he lived long enough in Virginia (1641–1669) and could well afford to have built something more permanent. Clearly, there were other reasons for staying with the earlier construction. Perhaps, as Carson's argument goes, the nature of the tobacco economy and its unstable market kept surplus capital, the means to build better houses, tied up. And the labor needed for permanent construction was equally occupied in cultivating and curing the tobacco plants and was not available for house construction.

Yet another and perhaps a more compelling reason for Pettus and his contemporary mid–seventeenth-century English immigrants to stay with their low investment earthfast houses could be that they never intended to stay long in Virginia. They perhaps planned to stay only long enough to accumulate enough of a fortune to return to England in style. Many of the Governor's Councillors had that attitude; there is a record that as many as 27 ultimately returned and finally died in England between 1607 and 1676.[2] It is reasonable to suppose that these men would look upon Virginia only as a means to an end, and built their houses accordingly. Although Pettus did not return to England as so many of his councillor colleagues did, the unfavorable economic climate of the 1660s may have delayed his decision until death overtook him in 1669.

If many of the immigrants in Virginia were transients, then it is reasonable to suppose that native-born Virginians might have looked upon the colony in a completely different light. After all, "home" to a native Virginian was Virginia. The Kingsmill Brays and Burwells were all natives of the colony. All chose to build Kingsmill's first substantial and well-planned houses and there is no doubt that they intended their estates to endure in the hands of their children and grandchildren. Of course, something available to the native sons and not to their forebears was gangs of slave laborers, in such numbers that major building programs could go on without disrupting the tobacco cultivation. But the contention that a switch to grain production produced a stable economic climate for house building does not seem to fit the Kingsmill evidence.[3] Although James Bray III turned some effort at Littletown to the production of corn and wheat, it was relatively insignificant compared to tobacco and it only began to happen some 40 years after the construction of the brick mansion. The figures are not available for Burwell's Kingsmill, but there is no reason to suppose there was any less domination of the tobacco culture there either.

The eighteenth-century floor plans of the Bray and Burwell houses were as radically unlike the seventeenth-century landowner Pettus's manor house design as the seventeenth-century earthfast construction was from the brick of the following century. It is easy to read into these changes James Deetz's concept that American society evolved from a corporate to an individualized "Anglo" society.[4] Indeed, the seventeenth-century, one-room-deep, hall–parlor scheme was no longer suitable for Bray, who along with Burwell planned his multiroom house accordingly. With so many rooms, both public and private domains could exist under a single roof.[5]

Dissimilar, too, was the approach to the landscape during the two colonial centuries. The seventeenth-century landowners and tenants accepted the natural environment as it was and consequently left relatively faint traces of their gardens and enclosures on the ground. The Burwells, on the other hand, literally reshaped the land into a very formal design, all in the mode of the French obsession with geometry. Yet, even with their pleasure garden appearance, the goal of plantation self-sufficiency kept the gardens practical. A description of a garden in Maryland to that effect fits the Kingsmill evidence and suggests that Burwell was rather typical:

> Saturday 19th. . . Mr. Pratts garden for beauty & elegance exceeds all that I ever saw—It is 20 rods long—and 18 wide An alley of 13 feet wide runs the length of the garden thro' the centre—Two others of 10 feet wide equally distant run parrallel with the main alley. These are intersected at right angles, by 4 other alleys of 8 feet wide—Another alley of 5 feet wide goes around the whole garden, leaving a border of 3 feet wide next to the pales—This lays the garden into 20 squares, each square has a border around it of 3 feet wide—Likewise the border of every square is decorated with pinks and a thousand other flowers, which is impossible for me to describe. The remaining part of each square, within the border, is planted with beans, pease, cabbage, onions, Betes, carrots, Parsnips, Lettuce, Radishes, Strawberries, cucumbers, Potatoes, and many other articles—Without the pales stand a row of trees upon three sides of the garden—These consist of Pear, Peach, apple, cherry, & mulberry trees. Within the pales, on the out border, are planted, Quince, snoball, Laylock, and various other small trees, producing the most beautiful flowers—The beauty, Taste, & elegance which attends it, is perfectly indescribable—It is an enchanting prospect, and carries the spectator, into an extacy, which he cannot describe—The effluvia arising from the various flowers—sweetens the air.[6]

On the laborers side, any pattern in the size and construction of the slave quarters does not seem to be obvious or reflective of any sweeping cultural changes or ethnic tradition. Slaves built English houses, which is not surprising: the master's overall plantation design ruled out much variation and by the mid- to late eighteenth century in Virginia many of the blacks were generations removed from their genetic and cultural African roots. "In Virginia mongrel negroes are found in greater number than in Carolina and Georgia who neither in point of colour nor features showed the least of their original descent. This superior number of people of colour is owing to the superior antiquity of the settlement of Virginia."[7]

But what slaves constructed later inside their houses, the many earthen or wood-lined root cellars, may be more Afro-American than English. Although the storage of roots in cellars was a long-standing English practice, the consistent appearance of cellars in great numbers in practically every Kingsmill dwelling suggests that they were built by the slaves themselves and probably without the knowledge of the master. Certainly the discovery of the numerous wine bottles bearing the seal of Burwell's private stock and the dozens of coins, usable tools, and ceramics found in the cellar fill at Kingsmill Quarter indicates that the earthen pits below the floorboards in the quarters played a vital role in a master–slave "sharing system," completely out of the master's field of vision. Even the discovery of the garbage bones in the cellar fill suggests that the root cellars were hiding places; a convenient and probably the only place for a slave to conceal the evidence of pilfered food. The exslave Charles Grandy explains the process:

> I got so hungry I stealed chickens off de roos'. Yessum, I did, checkens used roos' on de fense den, right out in de night. We would cook de chicken at night, eat him an' bu'n de feathers. Dat's what dey had dem ole paddyrollers fer. Dey come roun' an' search de qua'ters fer to see what you bin stealin'. We always had a trap in de floor fo' de do' to hide dese chickens in.[8]

Some of the masters did know of the cellar tradition, however. Landon Carter refers to them during his attempt to track down some contraband at Sabine Hall, Lancaster County, in 1770:

> This morning we had a complaint about a butter pot's being taken from the dairy door where it was put to sweeten last night . . . . Owen had gone over the River . . . . So he could not say whether the Servants that lay in house had done it or not. How[ever] I sent Billy Beale to search all their holes and boxes; And in their loft it was found, but both of them solemnly deniing they knew anything of it.[9]

But no object particularly Afro-American appears to have been found at the Kingsmill slave quarters. Of course, winning favor of the master must have been great incentive for the blacks to mimic the white culture and to suppress quickly any very visible African tradition.

One particularly Afro-American art form, however, has survived aboveground from slavery times: decorative slave-made quilts, the making of which may be reflected, in an indirect way, in the Kingsmill archaeological record. According to some ex-slave interviews, slaves were periodically given discarded clothing with which they fashioned quilts, items vital to survival during the cold, damp Virginia winters[10] (Figure 140). Apparently it was common for slave women to sit up all night in front of the hearth piecing together the rags. It is reasonable to suppose that the discarded clothing may still have had buttons attached that, because they were no longer useful, may have wound up on the floor and then fell through the floor boards and finally into the root cellars. That could account for the great

Figure 140 Afro-American quilts in front of black tenant farm quarters in Virginia, early 1900s. (Ogden Movement Collection, Valentine Museum, Richmond.)

number and variety of the buttons found so commonly in the cellar fill at all the Kingsmill quarters. But that does not necessarily explain the number of military buttons also commonly found in the cellars. On the other hand, Revolutionary War military activity of slaves might explain the military buttons. Many blacks accompanied their masters to battle and were generally camp followers, particularly when freed by invading British troops. Consequently, they acquired uniforms. They may well have acquired "surplus" uniforms after the surrender at Yorktown as well. In any case, the presence of the buttons in the Kingsmill slave cabin sites certainly paints a picture of slave life remarkably similar to that of the uniformed black tenant farmer and his cabin of a century later (Figure 141).

What wound up in the cellars could also have been strongly influenced by black superstition (Figure 142). Even today some people believe that if an enemy acquires some of their person effects, such as a lock of hair or perhaps a scrap of clothing, it could be used to cast spells and even cause death.[11] Such a belief, of course, might bring serious second thought to casually throwing personal trash out where it might possibly fall into the wrong hands. In that case, the secret root cellars may have seemed the best place for rubbish. But obviously the cellars could offer service for only so long. Perhaps that accounts for the great numbers of objects and cellars under some of the Kingsmill slave dwellings.

How much can be said about the quality of slave life at Kingsmill based on the archaeological remains of houses and artifacts is another matter. It is tempting to make certain generalizations rather quickly. For example, considering the great number of slaves known to have belonged to James Bray III, perhaps more than

Figure 141 Virginia black tenant farmer with "army surplus" clothing in front of a typical slave cabin. (Cook Collection, Valentine Museum, Richmond.)

80, the relatively few and small houses found archaeologically seem to suggest very crowded and spartan living conditions. By the same token, the sheer numbers of root cellars dug under the "barracks" at Kingsmill Quarter might suggest a crowded communal atmostphere rather than simply indicating any trash-disposal patterns for the fieldhands. On the other hand, if the house servants lived in the mansions and nearby kitchens and other more permanent outbuildings, as documents and archaeology suggest, then they were not housed any worse than the masters themselves, and were accommodated even better than the tenants and guests at the ordinary. And perhaps they did not give up as much of their private lives living in such close proximity to the master's house as some historical documents suggest. In fact, if the door-and-stair pattern in Burwell's dependencies do say anything about slave life on the second floor, it appears that house servants did have some life of their own even within the controlled atmosphere of the home plantation. If that is true, perhaps the good reputation of Lewis Burwell IV as a master is no exaggeration:

Figure 142   A Virginia black tenant family in front of cabin. (Library of Congress.)

> Lately died in the county of Mecklenburg, Lewis Burwell, Esq; formerly of Kingsmill, in
> an advanced age. It is not enough to say, that throughout the whole of his life, he was
> distinguished by a warm affection for his family and tenderness to his slaves; these being
> duties of the first necessity. But he was also known to be steady and sincere in his
> professions of friendship, unquestionable as to veracity, charitable to the distressed,
> sound in his understanding, and, in a word, upright in his public and private conduct.[12]

Still, the consistent discovery of decayed raw garbage in the root cellar backfill, material clearly thrown there when the houses were still occupied, plus the lack
of a ready supply of fresh water and an oversupply of stagnant water around does
not pose a very attractive picture of daily life at a fieldhand quarter. Conversely,
perhaps the absence of organic fill in the root cellars near the home "houses" and
the presence of wells suggest a far better atmosphere for those slaves closest to the
master.[13]

There appears to be some culturally meaningful pattern in the comparison of
the quantity of ceramic types and forms between the collections of landlord and
those of servant or tenant. This is particularly true for the vessels found at Pettus's
Littletown and Utopia, where the hollowware (bowls and drinking vessels) to

flatware (plates and dishes) ratios were so dramatically opposite, perhaps a reflection of the richer diet of the landowner (See Figure 121). But the recovery of so much Chinese porcelain, particularly overglazed patterns and matched sets at Burwell's fieldhand slave quarter (Kingsmill Quarter) (Figure 124), casts some doubt on the conclusion that slave pottery differed much from the master's. It would probably be safest to conclude that house servants and fieldhands were equipped with, or equipped themselves with, a good representative sampling of whatever the owner had on hand.

For the eighteenth-century sites, however, status is evidently not reflected in the form analysis, which again presumably reflects diet. Ratios of hollowwares to flatwares, unlike at the seventeenth-century sites, remain constant: about 2:1 for the slaves and master (Figure 121). Why the two centuries were so unlike is curious, but as far as the eighteenth century is concerned, historical records suggest an answer. A survey of estate settlement inventories of one Virginia county, Albemarle, 1770–1800, shows what people ate off and out of, and it is clear that more than half of the flatware listed was made of pewter.[14] A combination of that with the ceramics listed shows that the actual inventory ratio of flat to hollow is exactly opposite to the archaeological record (2:1) for rich and poor alike. Also, practically all hollowware listed was made of pottery. Obviously that is why there were so many hollowware vessels in the ground; there were simply more ceramic hollowwares to break, and, conversely, pewter plates do not break and nobody would intentionally throw away pewter anyway, because it had intrinsic value.

One is tempted from the inventory evidence, then, to agree with curators that "most people in America until about 1820, ate with pewter spoons, off pewter plates, from tables filled with pewter dishes."[15] Yet if that is true, the presence of the thousands of ceramic sherds found on every colonial site deserves explanation. Perhaps the real answer lies both in the inventories *and* in the ground: what went unrecorded in the one shows up in the other. For example, for the Bray site, combining the entries in two Bray inventories spanning the years 1725 to 1744— the years of the deaths of both James Bray II and III—with all of the ceramic vessels from the three major trash deposits from the archaeological site dating to the same period produces twice as many flatwares to hollowwares, a ratio that does seem to reflect, in terms of meat, a richer diet (see Appendix A, Tables 1 and 2). Of course, that cannot be done for the Littletown slave quarter because there is no inventory, but perhaps the archaeological ceramic figures alone are more realistic there; the slaves may have had little or no pewter. Obviously there are some uncontrollable variables at work here. James Bray III's inventory may be including the same pewter plates that he inherited from his grandfather, for example, and perhaps some of the pewter listed had been used in the quarter. Nonetheless, such integrated studies do deserve more than passing consideration in historical archaeological analysis generally, and the results could prove quite enlightening.

As for other artifact patterns, matched sets of ceramics, monogrammed wine bottles, book clasps, jewelry, and coats of arms are indisputably all items that indicate wealth and high status far more strongly than whatever one can tentatively conjecture from masses of numbers of mugs or cups or bowls that happened to have been broken and thrown away. But showing the growth and disappearance over time of certain material objects, particularly ceramics, by counting does seem significant. Changes in the percentages of vessel forms, types, and places of manufacture, and even how people fashion their iron tools does seem to have cultural explanation and reflects the way people do things differently as time passes.

So it is that these things from the earth and the documents from above it reconstruct the setting within which landlords and laborers went about their lives within Virginia's tobacco empire. That life was grand for the men who held the land and that life was something less for those who worked the soil, cannot be denied. And certainly, the interplay of history and archaeology at Kingsmill more clearly defines what the "grand" and the "something less" meant for what must be a representative cross-section of Virginia's colonial rural society.

NOTES

[1]Cary Carson *et al.,* "Impermanent Architecture in the Southern American Colonies," *Winterthur Portfolio,* (Chicago, Illinois, 1981), Vol. 16, nos. 2/3, p. 169.

[2]W. M. Stanard, *The Colonial Virginia Register,* (Baltimore, Maryland, 1965), *passim.* Martha McCartney to William M. Kelso, March 31, 1983.

[3]Carson, "Impermanent Architecture," p. 171.

[4]James Deetz, *In Small Things Forgotten,* (New York, 1977), pp. 28–43.

[5]Dell Upton, "Vernacular Domestic Architecture in Eighteenth Century Virginia," *Winterthur Portfolio,* (Chicago, Illinois, 1982), Vol. 17, pp. 102–106.

[6]Lewis Beebe, Ms Journal, 1776–1801, (Historical Society of Pennsylvania), Vol. III, p. 108.

[7]Duke De La Rochefoucault Liancourt, *Travels Through the United States of North America,* (London, 1800), pp. 161–162; and Gerald W. Mullin, *Flight and Rebellion,* (London, Oxford, New York, 1972), pp. 34–82.

[8]Charles Perdue, Jr. *et al., Weevils in the Wheat; Interviews with Virginia Ex-Slaves,* (Charlottesville, Virginia, 1976), p. 116, quoted in Martin C. Purdue, "Nineteenth Century and Late Eighteenth Century Slave Dwellings," (mss. Thomas Jefferson Memorial Foundation, Monticello, Virginia, Fall, 1981), p. 5.

[9]Jack P. Greene, ed., *The Diary of Colonel Landon Carter of Sabine Hall, 1752–1778,* (Charlottesville, Virginia, 1966), Vol. I, p. 495.

[10]George W. McDaniel, *Hearth and Home,* (Philadelphia, Pennsylvania, 1982), pp. 108–109.

[11]Muriel and Malcolm Bell, Jr., *Drums and Shadows,* (Athens, Georgia, 1940), pp. 195–218.

[12]*Virginia Gazette,* Nicholson and Prentis, October 30, 1784.

[13]There is no description of the Kingsmill Quarters except for a post–Civil War reference to "old frame houses which were formerly used as 'Quarters'" and the great suffering by the blacks still living there in 1867, Margaret Newbold Harper, "Life in Virginia by a Yankee Teacher," *Virginia Magazine of History and Biography,* (Richmond, Virginia, April, 1956), Vol. 64, No. 2, p. 191.

[14]Ann Morgan Smart, "The Role of Pewter as "Missing Artifact": Evidence from Late Eighteenth Century Probate Inventories, Albemarle County, Virginia," (paper presented at the annual meeting of the Society for Historical Archaeology, Williamsburg, Virginia, January 7, 1984).

[15]Charles F. Montgomery, *A History of American Pewter,* (New York, 1973), p. 15.

INVENTORIES

TABLE 1
Inventory of the Estate of James Bray II, 1725[a]

Furnishings/Accessories

5	feather beds			brass fenders
4	dozen leather chairs		2	silver candlesticks
6	silk camlet chairs		1	pair silver snuffers
1	clock		2	brass candlesticks
	several pictures		1	pair brass snuffers
2	bureaus		2	silver candle cups
4	walnut tables		1	pair money scales
3	pairs of andirons		5	looking glasses
2	pairs of tongs			

Linens/Textiles

3	quilts		2	large tablecloths
2	rugs		2	small tablecloths
5	blankets		1	dozen diaper napkins
3	pair household sheets		1	dozen coarse napkins
3	pair coarse sheets			

Table/Kitchen

1	dozen pewter plates		1	copper kettle
1	dozen deep pewter plates		12	60-gal. cider casks
6	small dishes		1	large still
6	large dishes		2	quart silver tankards
3	gross "& odd" quart bottles		2	dozen silver spoons
	other bottles		2	silver salvers
12	gallon stone[ware] jugs		2	bell metal skillets
3	iron pots		1	dozen maple handled knives
			1	dozen maple handled forks
			1	chocolate pot
			1	coffee pot

(continued)

TABLE 1 (*Continued*)

Personal
    1 saddle and bridle
    1 pair silver spurs
    1 pair silver shoe buckles
    1 silver headed cane
    1 amber headed cane
    1 silver hilted sword and belt
    2 razors with case
    2 coats of arms

Livestock
  "Little Town"

25	cows	4	draft oxen
6	3 and 4-year old steers	3	cart horses
8	cow yearlings	2	saddle horses
2	bulls	1	young horse
		1	young mare

  Debb's Quarter
    10 cows "young and old"
    10 steers "about 7 years old"
    12 hogs, sows, barrows
    16 young pigs
  Jacko's Quarter

18	steers "about 14 years old" (?)	24	shoats, "about 1 year old"
2	"old" bulls	5	"breeding sows"
13	cows and 2-year olds	2	boars
45	sheep "young and old"	5	barrows "about 2 years old"
			"30-odd pigs"

  "Chickahominy"
    Rogers' Quarter

5	"large" steers	2	"Yearling colts"
15	cows and heifers	5	barrows
5	2-year olds	2	sows
7	calves	10	"pigs"
2	mares	4	shoats

    Bridges Quarter

5	"large" steers	10	barrows
9	cows and heifers	7	sows
3	"small" steers	7	shoats
1	bull	[15?]	pigs

    Dubblerum's Quarter

3	"young" steers	1	mare
9	cows and heifers	1	colt
6	calves	5	barrows
5	2-year olds	2	"Sows from shoats"(?)
1	bull stagg [a gelded bull]	5	pigs

    Nero's Quarter
      2 sows

TABLE 1 (*Continued*)

     3 barrows
     6 pigs
   New Kent Quarter
     4 "large" steers   2   sows
     6 cows   4   shoats
     5 2-year olds   6   pigs
     4 yearlings   1   mare
     6 barrows
   Rockahock Quarter
    25 cattle "young and old"
    30 hogs "young and old"
  TOTALS
   227 Cattle
    14 Horses
   225 Swine (approx.)
    45 Sheep
   511 (approx.)

*a*Source: Will of James Bray, Nov. 18, 1725, inventory taken Jan. 3, 1725/26.

TABLE 2

Inventory of the Estate of James Bray III, 1744–1746*a*

Furnishings/Accessories
  1   desk and bookcase   1   iron back band
  1   trunk   1   pair brass candlesticks
  3   chests   1   old candlestick
 14   leather chairs   1   old sundial
  1   old spinning wheel   3   looking glasses
 14   walnut chairs   1   tea chest with pot and pail
  1   walnut tea table   1   old tea table with tea kettle
  2   field beds   3   iron trivets & heaters
  6   maple chairs   1   pair andirons
  2   old oval tables   2   candlesticks
  4   old broken chairs   1   old box iron and heaters
  3   beds "& furniture"   1   old warming pan
  1   large table
  1   old brass fender

Linens/Textiles
  1   new bed tick, bolster, and pillows
  1   port manteau
  9   pairs sheets
  1   pair fine sheets
  9   table cloths
  3   diaper table cloths napkins
 10   towels

(*continued*)

TABLE 2 (*Continued*)

Table/Kitchen

1	marble mortar		1	gridiron
2	dozen "hard-mottle" plates		6	candle molds
2	stout jugs		3	pair bellows
2	chafing dishes		1	brass kettle
5	piggins		1	water pot
30	milk pans		1	dozen pewter plates
1	cold still		4	small wine glasses
1	plate stand		16	wine glasses
			2	decanters
6	earthen plates		1	parcel of old china
2	earthen dishes		1	butter boat
1	gallon pot		1	butter dish and salt
1	large funnel		1	counterpin
1	China tea pot		1	large iron mortar and pestle
5	China cups		2	old chocolate pots
1	spice mortar and pestle		1	watering can
	cruets and stand		1	frying pan
4	stone[ware] chamberpots		1	old grindstone
5	pewter dishes		1	old pot
6	pewter plates		1	quart pot
4	iron pots		1	pot rack
5	tin cannisters		1	pair tongs and shovel
1	leaden milk stand		1	bell metal skillet
6	tin dish covers		1	hand mill

Other

1	pair garden shears			other books
8	books		1½	gross of pipes
	Bradley's Book on Gardening		80	oz. silver
	Gordon's Geographical Grammar		2	old wigs
1	new *Common Prayer Book*		1	powdering tub

Livestock

Cattle

128	cows
73	steers
29	calves
10	bulls
7	heifers
44	yearlings
16	oxen and draft steers
9	"young cattle"
41	2-year olds
8	3-year olds
7	4-year olds
372	

372	Cattle

TABLE 2 (*Continued*)

Swine			
29+	hogs and boars		
1	shoat		
8	sows		
18+	pigs		
1	"barren sow"		
57+		57+	Swine
Sheep			
192	unspecified sheep		
9	"Muttons before Appraisement"		
201		201	Sheep
Horses			
8	mares		
3	colts		
4	stallions and geldings		
2	unspecified or other		
17		17	Horses
		Total:	647+

*a*Source: Bray Ledger, fol. 100–123.

TABLE 3

An Inventory of the Estate of Mr. Thos. Pettus, Deceas'd, Belonging to His Orphand [1692–]

Servants
    1 English Boy named Tho. Taylor about 5 years to serve
    1 Negro man named Briby aged about 25
    1 Negro man named Sylliman aged about 50
    1 Negro boy named Webb aged about 12
    1 Negro woman named Nan aged about 30
    1 Negro woman named Moll aged about 32
The Plate
    1 large salt
    2 candle cups and covers
    1 small tankard
    1 small porringer
    1 sack cup
    1 pr. broad snuffers
    1 wraugh sugar dish
    4 plates
    5 new spoons
    1 old spoon with a fork
    5 old spoons
    weighing in all sixteen pounds and fourteen ounces

(*continued*)

TABLE 3 (*Continued*)

Chattle att Utopia
    4 stears
    8 cows
    3 old cows
    3 yearlings
    2 bulls
    2 two year olds
Chattle att Little Town
    6 stears
    8 cows
    2 bulls
    2 two year olds
    62 sheep
Horses and mares
    6 mairs of Levevalle Cullers (?)
    1 young coalt
    1 two year old horse coult
    2 maires, ditto a colt
    ------------, broak horse

All the hoggs belonging to the plantation sold to Mr. James Bray	2300
1 Negro man rec'd from aboard Capt. Jacob Green itt being the produce of Indian Corne sent by Mrs. Bray in the time of her widowhood and sold to Will Beck for	5000
Chest of goods and a cask of nails rec'd from aboard Capt. Norrington sent by Alderman Jeffrey as invoice will appear	45:0:00

"And as for the household goods when we went to inventory them; the time agreed on Mr. James Bray told us that we came too late for he had carried them away."

signed Nathaniel Bacon

*a*Source: Henrico County, Miscellaneous Court Records, Vol. I (1650–1717), pp. 73–74.

KINGSMILL CERAMIC VESSELS: TYPE AND FORM

TABLE 4
Minimum Number of Kingsmill Ceramic Vessels by Type

Site	Chinese porcelain	Delft	American
Kingsmill Tenement	5	33	63
Pettus	2	111	152
Utopia	—	15	35
Bray	14	77	20
Littletown Quarter	3	15	1
Kingsmill Quarter	39	37	4
North Quarter	9	17	2

TABLE 5
Minimum Number of Kingsmill Ceramic Vessels by Form

	Kingsmill Tenement	Pettus	Utopia	Bray	Littletown Quarter	Kingsmill Quarter	North Quarter
Plates	11	51	6	15	16	29	19
Dishes	12	8	—	1	—	9	4
Bowls	7	59	8	26	10	26	13
Mugs	7	20	9	15	16	18	13
Jugs	5	12	1	5	5	—	3
Cups	3	3	2	13	5	20	26
Bottles	5	44	2	2	—	1	1
Pitchers	21	—	—	—	1	—	—
Jars	15	90	17	8	3	9	16

(continued)

TABLE 5 (*Continued*)

	Kingsmill Tenement	Pettus	Utopia	Bray	Littletown Quarter	Kingsmill Quarter	North Quarter
Pots	2	—	4	—	8	—	—
Butter pots	1	4	1	—	—	—	—
Porringers	2	1	1	1	—	3	1
Pans	20	31	7	12	4	8	10
Chafing dishes	2	—	—	—	—	—	—
Pipkins	4	6	—	—	—	5	2
Cooking vessels	3	—	—	1	—	1	—
salts	1	2	—	—	—	—	—
Chamber pots	1	—	—	6	1	11	5
Collanders	1	1	—	—	—	—	—
Watering cans	1	—	—	—	—	—	—
Sugar bowls	—	—	—	—	—	1	—
Platters	—	—	—	—	3	2	—
Tureens	—	—	—	—	2	—	1
Tea caddies	—	—	—	—	—	1	—
Bowls/saucers	—	—	—	—	1	10	13
Tea pots	—	—	—	—	—	5	3
Punch bowls	—	—	—	—	—	5	—
Jardiniere	—	—	—	—	—	1	—
Sauce boats	—	—	—	—	—	1	—
Patty pans	—	—	—	5	—	1	—
Ointment pots	—	11	—	—	—	9	5
Posset pots	—	1	—	—	—	—	—
Basins	—	—	1	—	—	1	—
Salt castors	—	—	—	—	—	1	—
Candy dishes	—	—	—	—	—	—	—
Candlesticks	—	—	—	—	1	—	1
Misc. hollow	5	—	—	5	—	8	1
Misc. flat	5	—	1	1	—	—	—
Misc.	—	8	—	3	—	—	—
	134	352	60	119	76	186	137

FAUNAL ANALYSES

TABLE 6
Species Identified at the Kingsmill Tenement Site

Species	Number of elements	%	Minimum number of individuals	Estimated pounds of meat	%
Cattle	262	29.3	8	2700.0	47.6
Swine	236	26.1	22	2050.0	36.2
Sheep/goat	46	5.1	3	90.0	1.6
Chicken	12	1.3	3	7.5	.1
Deer	54	6.1	4	400.0	7.1
Beaver	15	1.6	3	60.0	1.0
Raccoon	26	2.9	5	75.0	1.3
Opossum	12	1.3	3	24.0	.4
Cottontail rabbit	2	.2	1	1.5	.02
Gray squirrel	3	.3	1	.8	.01
Turkey	4	.4	1	7.5	.13
Canada goose	2	.2	2	12.0	.21
Hawk (red shouldered)	12	1.3	2	—	—
Duck (*Aras* sp.)	4	.4	2	4.0	.07
Duck (*Aythya* sp.)	1	.1	1	2.0	.03
Double crested cormorant	6	.6	1	5.0	.08
Eastern box turtle	31	3.5	5	2.0	.03
Snapping turtle	20	2.2	3	30.0	.5
Cooter turtle	3	.3	1	5.0	.08
Musk turtle	11	1.2	1	.3	.00
Painted turtle	1	.1	1	.4	.00
Sturgeon	5	.5	1	100.0	1.7
Gar	35[a]	3.8	1	4.0	.07
White perch	16	1.7	5	4.0	.07
Catfish (bullhead)	14	1.5	4	8.0	.14

(*continued*)

TABLE 6 (*Continued*)

Species	Number of elements	%	Minimum number of individuals	Estimated pounds of meat	%
Catfish (sp.)	7	.7	1	2.0	.03
Striped bass(?)	36		2	40.0	.7
Black drum	5	4.5	1		.35
Sea trout	1	.1	1	3.0	.05
Blue crab	24	2.6	6	1.2	.02
	906	99.9	94	5663.2	99.8

[a]Not including 2048 scales.

TABLE 7

Species Identified from Well Fill,[a] Utopia, circa 1680–1710

Species	Number of elements	%	Minimum number of individuals	Estimated pounds of meat	%
Cattle	462	54.23	14	5352	69.09
Swine	207	24.30	20	1750	22.60
Sheep/goat	38	4.46	5	130	1.68
Dog	4	.47	1	—	—
Domestic cat	39	4.57	2	—	—
Chicken	8	.93	2	4	.05
Turkey	7	.82	1	7.5	.09
Goose	1	.11	1	7	.09
Horse	21	2.46	3	—	—
Deer	20	2.34	3	300	3.87
Raccoon	9	1.05	2	30	.39
Opossum	3	.35	1	8	.10
Squirrel	3	.35	1	1	.01
Duck	1	.11	1	2	.02
Sturgeon	4	.47	1	100	1.29
Gar	5	.58	2	8	.10
Striped bass	9	1.05	1	20	.26
Red drum	5	.59	2	20	.26
Eastern box turtle	5	.59	2	.8	.01
Cooter turtle	1	.11	1	5	.06
	852	99.96	66	7745.3	99.97

[a]KM 312 A–N.

TABLE 8

Species Identified from Cellar Fill, Utopia, circa 1680–1710

Species	Number of elements	%	Minimum number of individuals	Estimated pounds of meat	%
Cattle	63	63.00	3	1200	75.00
Swine	21	21.00	3	300	18.75
Horse	14	14.00	2	—	—
Deer	2	2.00	1	100	6.25
	100	100.00	9	1600	100.00

TABLE 9

Species Identified in Lower Well Fill,[a] Pettus, circa 1680–1700

Species	Number of elements	%	Minimum number of individuals	Estimated pounds of meat	%
Cattle	94	4.46	4	1100	25.89
Swine	1591	75.51	32	3000	70.56
Sheep/goat	126	5.98	5	100	2.35
Horse	2	.09	1	—	—
Domestic cat	56	2.66	4	—	—
Dog	1	.04	1	—	—
Chicken	107	5.08	7	15.5	.36
Turkey	14	.66	1	7.5	.17
Goose(?)	1	.04	1	6	.14
Rabbit	108	5.12	6	7.5	.17
Raccoon	1	.04	1	15	.35
Rat	6	.28	2	—	—
	2107	99.96	65	4251.5	99.9

[a] ER 64, AA–AD.

TABLE 10

Species Identified from Units in the Smokehouse Area, Pettus, circa 1680–1710

Species	Number of elements	%	Minimum number of individuals	Estimated pounds of meat	%
Cattle	55	40.15	3	1200	61.22
Swine	51	37.24	4	400	20.41
Sheep/goat	9	6.56	1	30	1.53
Deer	19	13.87	3	300	15.31
Raccoon	1	.72	1	15	.76
Snapping turtle	1	.72	1	10	.51
Cooter turtle	1	.72	1	5	.25
	137	99.98	14	1960	99.99

TABLE 11

Species Identified from the Pettus Trash Pit,[a] circa 1680–1700

Species	Number of elements	%	Minimum number of individuals	Estimated pounds of meat	%
Cattle	80	44.19	4	1350	63.35
Swine	71	9.23	6	600	28.15
Sheep/goat	16	8.84	2	70	3.28
Horse	2	1.10	1	—	—
Turkey	2	1.10	1	7.5	.35
Deer	3	1.66	1	109	4.69
Rabbit	6	3.31	1	1.5	.07
Catfish	1	.55	1	3	.09
	181	99.98	17	2132.0	99.98

[a] KM 55 A–F.

TABLE 12

Species Identified from the Pettus Cellar Fill,[a] circa 1685–1710

Species	Number of elements	%	Minimum number of individuals	Estimated pounds of meat	%
Cattle	270	69.05	8	3200	72.23
Swine	104	26.60	13	1200	27.08
Horse	2	.51	1	—	—
Domestic cat	2	.51	1	—	—
Chicken	2	.51	1	—	—
Raccoon	5	1.28	1	10	.22
Opossum	3	.76	1	8	.18
Falcon (probably wild)	1	.25	1	—	—
Cooter turtle	2	.51	2	10	.26
	391	99.98	29	4460	99.97

[a] KM 54 B–J.

TABLE 13

Species Identified from Trash Pit,[a] Bray, circa 1730–1740

Species	Number of elements	%	Minimum number of individuals	Estimated pounds of meat	%
Cattle	104	40.46	3	1200	57.72
Swine	96	37.35	6	550	26.45
Sheep	22	8.56	3	90	4.33
Horse	1	.39	1	—	—

TABLE 13 (*Continued*)

Species	Number of elements	%	Minimum number of individuals	Estimated pounds of meat	%
Domestic cat	1	.39	1	—	—
Chicken	6	2.33	2	5	.24
Turkey	1	.39	1	7.5	.36
Goose (domestic)	6	2.33	2	14	.67
Pigeon/dove(?)	1	.39	1	.4	.02
Deer	6	2.33	2	200	9.62
Gray fox	1	.39	1	—	—
Gray squirrel	3	1.16	2	1.6	.07
Eastern box turtle	4	1.56	1	.4	.02
Snapping turtle	3	1.16	1	10	.48
Falcon (wild?)	1	.39	1	—	—
Shark tooth (fossil)	1	.39	1	—	—
	257	99.97	29	2079.0	99.98

[a]KM 9–10.

TABLE 14

Species Identified in Well Fill,[a] Pettus, circa 1735–1745 (Bray Ownership)

Species	Number of elements	%	Minimum number of individuals	Estimated pounds of meat	%
Cattle	131	5.15	7	1800	60.96
Swine	209	8.23	6	550	18.63
Sheep/goat	789	31.06	18	460	15.58
Dog	134	5.27	4	—	—
Chicken	4	.16	2	5	.17
Turkey	1	.03	1	7.5	.26
Goose (domestic)	2	.08	1	7	.24
Deer	1	.04	1	100	3.28
Cottontail rabbit	1202	47.33	45	—	—
Mink	6	.23	1	1	.03
Mouse(?)	1	.03	1	—	—
Canada goose	10	.39	2	12	.40
Whistling swan	14	.55	1	10	.34
Mud turtle	3	.12	1	—	—
Black racer snake	33	1.30	1	—	—
	2540	99.97	92	2952.5	99.99

[a]KM G4 V–W.

TABLE 15

Species Identified from Well,[a] Bray, 1770–1790

Species	Elements	%	Minimum number	%	Pounds of usable meat	%
Mammals						
Horse	2	.10	1	.74	—	—
Cow	282	14.34	7	5.19	2800	59.70
Swine	391	19.89	11	8.15	600	12.79
Sheep	278	14.13	15	11.11	550	11.73
Goat	20	1.02	2	1.48	50	1.07
Dog	10	.51	2	1.48	—	—
House cat	192	9.76	13	9.63	—	—
Norway rat	1	.05	1	.74	—	—
Black bear	3	.15	1	.74	350	7.46
Striped skunk	1	.05	1	.74	5	.11
Eastern cottontail	70	3.56	7	5.19	10.5	.22
Muskrat	2	.10	1	.74	2	.04
Mink	3	.15	1	.74	—	—
White-footed mouse	5	.25	1	.74	—	—
	1260	64.06	64	47.41	4367.5	93.12
Birds						
Turkey	71	3.61	6	4.44	45	.96
Canada goose	25	1.27	7	5.19	42	.89
Goose	18	.92	2	1.48	12	.26
Chicken	175	8.90	14	10.37	42	.89
Black duck/Mallard duck	23	1.17	2	1.48	6	.13
Blue-winged teal	1	.05	1	.74	1.5	.03
Wood duck	4	.20	1	.74	2	.04
Crow	5	.25	1	.74	0.3	.01
Black vulture	3	.15	1	.74	—	—
Passenger pigeon	3	.15	2	1.48	.25	.01
Song birds	31	1.58	7	5.19	—	—
Duck	16	.82	2	1.48	6	.13
	375	19.07	46	34.07	157.05	3.35
Reptiles						
Snapping turtle	18	.92	1	.74	10	.21
Slider	12	.61	1	.74	1	.02
Painted turtle	5	.25	1	.74	.25	.01
Eastern box turtle	1	.05	1	.74	.25	.01
Water snake	104	5.29	3	2.23	—	—
	140	7.12	7	5.19	11.50	.25
Amphibians						
Southern toad	12	.61	3	2.22		
Spadefoot toad	5	.25	1	.74		
Leopard frog	3	.15	1	.74		
Bullfrog	2	.10	1	.74		
	22	1.11	6	4.44		

TABLE 15 (*Continued*)

Species	Elements	%	Minimum number	%	Pounds of usable meat	%
Fish						
Channel catfish	1	.05	1	.74	3	.06
Shortnose gar	1	.05	1	.74	—	—
Alligator gar	19	.97	2	1.48	—	—
Longnose gar	4	.20	1	.74	—	—
Gar	41	2.08	4	2.96	—	—
Sucker	1	.05	1	.74	1	.02
Sturgeon	103	5.24	2	1.48	150	3.20
	170	8.64	12	8.88	154	3.28
All species	1967	100.00	135	99.99	4690.05	100.00

[a]KM 18.

TABLE 16

Species Identified from Kitchen Well,[a] Kingsmill Plantation, circa 1760

Species	Number of elements	%	Minimum number of individuals	Estimated pounds of meat	%
Cattle	660	42.12	15	5000	68.19
Swine	316	20.16	18	1600	21.83
Sheep	294	18.76	17	405	5.52
Domestic cat	23	1.46	3		
Chicken	37	2.36	4	9	.12
Turkey	13	.83	3	21.5	.30
Goose	11	.70	2	14	.19
Duck (domestic?)	5	.32	2	4	.05
Duck (ringneck)	1	.06	1	1.5	.02
Canvasback duck	2	.12	1	2	.02
Deer	1	.06	1	100	1.37
Raccoon	12	.76	2	30	.40
Opossum	1	.06	1	8	.11
Beaver	1	.06	1 ? (intrusive?)		
Cottontail rabbit	1	.06	1	1.5	.02
Gray squirrel	5	.32	1	.8	.01
Rat (Black)	13	.83	4		
Sturgeon	119	7.59	1	100	1.37
Striped bass	5	.32	1	5	.07
White perch	4	.25	2	1.8	.02
Catfish (bullhead)	5	.32	1	2	.02
Sheepshead	2	.12	1	5	.06
Gar	2	.12	1 (intrusive?)	4	.05
Fish? (Drum?)	1	.06	1	5	.07

(continued)

TABLE 16 (*Continued*)

Species	Number of elements	%	Minimum number of individuals	Estimated pounds of meat	%
Crab	1	.06	1	.2	.00
Eastern box turtle	1	.06	1	.4	.00
Snapping turtle	7	.44	1	10	.13
Cooter turtle	6	.38	1	5	.07
Musk turtle	17	1.08	1		
	1567	99.9	91	7335.7	99.9

[a]KM 720 AA–BA.

BIBLIOGRAPHY

Abbott, H. I. "Campaign Maps, Army of the Potomac, Yorktown to Williamsburg, Map 1.", September, 1862.

Bailyn, Bernard, "Politics and Social Structure in Virginia," in James M. Smith, ed., *Seventeenth Century America,* University of North Carolina Press, Chapel Hill, North Carolina, 1959.

Barka, Norman F., "The Kiln and Ceramics of the Poor Potter of Yorktown: A Preliminary Report," in Ian M. G. Quimby, ed., *Ceramics in America,* University Press of Virginia, Charlottesville, Virginia, 1973.

Barber, Michael, "The Vertebrate Fauna from a Late Eighteenth Century Well: The Bray Plantation, Kingsmill, Virginia," ms. Virginia Historic Landmarks Commission, Research Center for Archaeology, Yorktown, Virginia, 1976.

Beebe, Lewis, *Ms Journal, 1776–1801.* Historical Society of Pennsylvania, Philadelphia, n.d.

Bell, Muriel and Malcolm Bell, Jr., *Drums and Shadows,* University of Georgia Press, Athens, Georgia, 1940.

Betts, E. M., *Thomas Jefferson's Garden Book,* The American Philosophical Society, Philadelphia, 1944.

Beverly, Robert, *The History and Present State of Virginia,* Louis B. Wright, ed., University of North Carolina Press, Chapel Hill, North Carolina, 1947.

Billings, Warren W., *The Old Dominion in the Seventeenth Century,* University of North Carolina Press, Chapel Hill, North Carolina, 1975.

Boyd, Julian P., ed., *The Papers of Thomas Jefferson,* Vol. I, Princeton University Press, Princeton, New Jersey, 1950.

Breeden, James O., ed., *Advice among Masters,* Greenwood Press, Westport, Connecticut, 1980.

Byrd, William, *The Secret Diary of William Byrd of Westover,* Louis B. Wright and Marion Tinling, eds., The Dietz Press, Richmond, Virginia, 1941.

Calver, William Louis and Reginald Pelham Bolton, *History Written with Pick and Shovel,* New York Historical Society, New York, 1950.

Carr, Lois Green and Lorena S. Walsh, "Inventories and Analysis of Wealth and Consumption Patterns in St. Mary's County, Maryland, 1658–1777." Paper presented at the Newberry Library Conference on Quantitative and Social Science Approaches in Early American History, n.d.

Carson, Barbara and Gary Carson, "Styles and Standards of Living in Southern Maryland, 1670–1752." Paper presented to the annual meeting of the Southern Historical Association, Atlanta, Georgia, 1976.

Carson, Cary, *et al.*, "Impermanent Architecture in the Southern American Colonies," *Winterthur Portfolio,* Vol. 16, nos. 2/3, The University of Chicago, Chicago, Illinois, 1981.

Chappell, Edward, "Slave Housing," *The Interpreter,* Colonial Williamsburg Foundation, Williamsburg, Virginia, 1982.

Clemens, Paul G. E., *The Atlantic Economy and Maryland's Eastern Shore,* Cornell University Press, Ithaca and London, 1980.

Crozier, William Armstrong, *Virginia Heraldica,* Southern Book Co., Baltimore, Maryland, 1953.

Davis, Richard Beale, ed., *William Fitzhugh and his Chesapeake World, 1676–1701,* University of North Carolina Press, Chapel Hill, North Carolina, 1963.

Deetz, James, *In Small Things Forgotten,* Anchor Press, New York, 1977.

Egloff, Keith, *Colonial Plantation Hoes of Tidewater, Virginia,* Virginia Historic Landmarks Commission, Williamsburg, Virginia, 1980.

Evans, George Ewart, *The Pattern Under the Plow,* Faber & Faber, London, 1966.

Genovese, Eugene D., *Roll Jordan Roll,* Pantheon Books, New York, 1974.

Glassie, Henry, *Folk Housing in Middle Virginia,* The University of Tennessee Press, Knoxville, Tennessee, 1975.

Goodwin, Mary R. M., "Kingsmill Plantation, James City County," ms. Colonial Williamsburg Foundation, Williamsburg, Virginia, 1958.

Greene, Jack P., ed., *The Diary of Colonel Landon Carter of Sabine Hall, 1752–1778,* University Press of Virginia, Charlottesville, Virginia, 1966.

Harper, Margaret Newbold, "Life in Virginia by a Yankee Teacher," *Virginia Magazine of History and Biography,* Vol. 64, No. 2, Richmond, Virginia, 1956.

Harwood, Humphrey, "Ledger B. Folio 67," ms. Colonial Williamsburg Foundation, Williamsburg, Virginia, n.d.

Hening, William Walter, *Statutes at Large,* Samuel Shepherd, Richmond, Virginia, 1820.

Henrico County Miscellaneous Court Records, Vol. I.

Hiden, Martha W., *Adventurers in Purse and Person,* Princeton University Press, Princeton, New Jersey, 1956.

Hudgins, Carter L., "The King's Realm: An Archaeological and Historical Study of Plantation Life at Robert Carter's Corotoman," Master's Thesis, Wake Forest University, Winston–Salem, North Carolina, 1981.

Isaac, Rhys, *The Transformation of Virginia, 1740–1790,* University of North Carolina Press, Chapel Hill, North Carolina, 1982.

James City County Tax Lists, 1768–1769.

Jefferson, Thomas, *Notes on the State of Virginia,* John Stockdale, London, 1787.

Kelso, William M., "An Interim Report on the Historical Archaeology at Kingsmill, 1972, 1973, 1974, 1975," ms. Virginia Historic Landmarks Commission, Research Center for Archaeology, Yorktown, Virginia.

Kelso, William M., "A Report on the Archaeological Excavations at Monticello, Charlottesville, Virginia, 1979–1983," ms. Thomas Jefferson Memorial Foundation, Charlottesville, Virginia, 1984.

Kelso, William M., "Archaeological Survey of the Log Slave Quarter at Bremo Recess," ms. Thomas Jefferson Memorial Foundation, Charlottesville, Virginia, 1982.

Kelso, William M., "Excavation of a Late Seventeenth Century Domestic Refuse Pit Near Lightfoot, James City County, Virginia, 1964–65," *The Archaeological Society of Virginia Quarterly Bulletin,* Vol. 20, No. 4, 1966.

Kelso, William M., "More Excavations at Lightfoot," *The Archaeological Society of Virginia, Quarterly Bulletin,* Vol. 22, No. 2, 1967.

Kelso, William M., "Rescue Archaeology on the James," *Archaeology,* September/October, 1979.

Kingsbury, Susan M., ed., *Records of the Virginia Company of London,* Government Printing Office, Washington, 1935.

Kukla, Jon, "Political Institutions in Virginia, 1619–1660," Master's Thesis, University of Toronto, 1979.

Liancourt, Duke De La Rochfoucault, *Travels Through the United States of North America,* London, 1800.

Luccketti, Nicholas, "North Quarter Salvage Excavation, Interim Report," ms. Virginia Historical Landmarks Commission, Research Center for Archaeology, Yorktown, Virginia, 1979.

McClure, James P., "Littletown Plantation, 1700–1745," Master's Thesis, College of William and Mary, Williamsburg, Virginia, 1977.

McDaniel, George W., *Hearth and Home,* Temple University Press, Philadelphia, Pennsylvania, 1982.

McIlwaine, H. R., ed., *Minutes of the Council and General Court of Colonial Virginia,* The Colonial Press, Richmond, Virginia, 1924.

Mercer, Eric, *The English Vernacular House,* H. M. Stationery Office, London, 1975.

Miller, Henry M., "Pettus and Utopia: A Comparison of the Faunal Remains from Two Late Seventeenth Century Virginia Households," ms. St. Mary's City Commission, St. Mary's City, Maryland, 1978.

Miller, Henry M., "Pettus, Utopia, Bray, Kingsmill Tenement, and Kingsmill Plantation Faunal Analysis Preliminary Statements," Virginia Historic Landmarks Commission, Research Center for Archaeology, Yorktown, Virginia, n.d.

Miller, Randall M., *Dear Master, Letters of a Slave Family,* Cornell University Press, Ithaca and London, 1978.

Montgomery, Charles F., *A History of American Pewter,* Praeger, New York, 1973.

Morgan, Edmund S. *American Slavery, American Freedom,* Norton, New York, 1975.

Mullin, Gerald W., *Flight and Rebellion,* Oxford University Press, London, New York, 1972.

Neiman, Fraser D., *The Manner House Before Stratford,* Robert E. Lee Memorial Association, Stratford, Virginia, 1980.

Newman, Eric P., "Coinage for Colonial Virginia," *Numismatic Notes and Monographs,* (The American Numismatic Society, 1956), p. 36.

Noël Hume, Ivor, *A Guide to the Artifacts of Colonial America,* Knopf, New York, 1970.

Noël Hume, Ivor, "Excavations at Tutter's Neck in James City County, Virginia, 1960–61," *Contributions from the Museum of History and Technology,* Washington, D.C., 1966.

Noël Hume, Ivor, *The Wells of Williamsburg: Colonial Time Capsules,* Colonial Williamsburg Foundation, Williamsburg, Virginia, 1969.

Nugent, Nell, *Cavaliers and Pioneers, Abstracts of the Virginia Land Patents, 1623–1666,* Dietz Printing Co., Richmond, 1929–1931.

Otto, John Solomon, "Artifacts and Status Differences: A Comparison of Planter, Overseer and Slave Sites from Cannon's Point Plantation (1794–1861), St. Simon's Island, Georgia, an Antebellum Plantation," in Stanley South, ed., *Research Strategies in Historical Archaeology,* Academic Press, New York, 1977.

Otto, John Solomon, "Race and Class on Antebellum Plantations," Robert L. Schuyler, ed., *Archaeological Perspectives on Ethnicity in America,* Baywood Publishing Company, New York, 1980.

Outlaw, Alain C., "Excavations at the Maine Site, James City County, Virginia," ms. Virginia Historic Landmarks Commission, Research for Archaeology, Yorktown, Virginia, 1979.

Outlaw, Merry A., Beverly A. Bogley, and Alain C. Outlaw, "Rich Man, Poor Man: Status Definition of Two Seventeenth Century Ceramic Assemblages from Kingsmill," ms. Virginia Historic Landmarks Commission, Research Center for Archaeology, Yorktown, Virginia, 1977.

Percy, George, "Observations Gathered Out of a Discourse of the Plantation of the Southern Colony in Virginia by the English, 1606," David B. Quinn, ed., University Press of Virginia, Charlottesville, Virginia, 1967.

Perdue, Charles, Jr., *et al., Weevils in the Wheat: Interviews with Virginia Ex-Slaves,* University Press of Virginia, Charlottesville, Virginia, 1976.

Perdue, Martin C., "Nineteenth Century and Late Eighteenth Century Slave Dwellings," ms. Thomas Jefferson Memorial Foundation, Charlottesville, Virginia, 1981.

Simcoe, Lt. Colonel, *A Journal of the Operation of the Queen's Rangers from the End of the Year 1777 to the Conclusion of the Late American War,* Exeter, 1787.

Smart, Ann Morgan, "The Role of Pewter as "Missing Artifact": Evidence from Late Eighteenth Century Probate Inventories, Albemarle County, Virginia," ms. Thomas Jefferson Memorial Foundation, Charlottesville, Virginia, 1984.

Smith, James M., *Archaeology of Yorke Village and the First and Second Parish Churches, Yorktown, Va.,* College of William and Mary, Williamsburg, Virginia, 1978.

Smyth, J. F. D., *Tour in the United States of America,* London, 1794.

South, Stanley, *Method and Theory in Historical Archaeology,* Academic Press, New York, 1977.

Stacey, Pocahontas H., *The Pettus Family,* Washington, D.C., N.P. 1957.

Stanard, W. G., *The Colonial Virginia Register,* Geneological Publishing Co., Baltimore, Maryland, 1965.

Stephenson, Mary A., "A Record of the Bray Family, 1658–ca. 1800," ms. Colonial Williamsburg Foundation, Williamsburg, Virginia, 1963.

Swem, Earl Gregg, "Brothers of the Spade," *Proceedings of the American Antiquarian Society,* Philadelphia, April, 1948.

Tate, Thad W., *The Negro in Eighteenth Century Williamsburg,* Colonial Williamsburg Foundation, Williamsburg, Virginia, 1965.

Tatum, William, *Essay of the Culture and Commerce of Tobacco,* London, 1800.

Upton, Dell, "Slave Housing in Eighteeneth Century Virginia," ms. Report to the Department of Social and Cultural History, National Museum of American History, Smithsonian Institution, Washington, D.C., 1982.

Upton, Dell, "Venacular Domestic Architecture in Eighteenth Century Virginia," *Winterthur Portfolio,* Vol. 17, No. 1, University of Chicago Press, 1982.

Vince, John, *Wells and Water Supply,* Aylesbury, England, 1978.

The Virginia Gazette.

The Virginia Magazine of History and Biography, Vol. III, Richmond, Virginia, 1895–1896.

Vlach, John Michael, *The Afro-American Tradition in Decorative Arts,* The Cleveland Museum of Art, Cleveland, Ohio, 1978.

Waterman, Thomas Tileston, *The Mansions of Virginia, 1706–1776,* University of North Carolina Press, Chapel Hill, North Carolina, 1946.

Wells, Ann Camille, "Kingsmill Plantation, A Cultural Analysis," Master's Thesis, University of Virginia, Charlottesville, Virginia, 1976.

Whiffen, Marcus, *The Eighteenth Century Houses of Williamsburg,* Colonial Williamsburg Foundation, Williamsburg, 1960.

York County Will Book Number 14.

INDEX